Mozzarella di Bufala Campana DOP
History and How It Is Made

History
An Ancient Process

Milking
Curdling
Kneading
Manual Shaping
Tasting

History

Mozzarella di bufala Campana DOP (Denominazione di Origine Protetta, or protected designation of origin) is a fresh *pasta filata* (stretched curd) cheese that was first mentioned in a Longobard document from the eleventh century attesting that a *mozza* was given to the monks of an abbey located just outside Aversa.

Cited in a 1570 treatise on cooking by Bartolomeo Scappi, the pope's chef, it became famous in the late eighteenth century in part owing to the Bourbon Reggia di Carditello estate, where the buffaloes were bred for their delicious milk. The name of the cheese comes from the verb *mozzare*, to lop off.

The Bourbon estate in Carditello (eighteenth century).
From *"Mozzarella di Bufala Campana. Storia, tradizioni e immagini di un formaggio nato all'ombra del mito della Magna Grecia"*
Published by the Consorzio per la Tutela del Formaggio Mozzarella di Bufala Campana, 2004

Buffaloes grazing along the Asa stream near the Salerno-Battipaglia railway bridge, Pontecagnano, 1920.
Archivio Azienda Agricola Morese

No one is sure how the first buffaloes arrived in Italy. Some sources theorize that they are an indigenous breed, while others suggest they were brought to Italy by the Normans or the Goths.

Made only with the fresh milk of an Italian Mediterranean breed of buffalo, the mozzarella served in our restaurants comes mostly from the Campania region, especially Piana del Sele and Piana del Volturno, though some is from southern Lazio and the Puglia region. All of the cheese is produced by select certified dairies located within the area of origin established by the guidelines of the Consorzio di Tutela della Mozzarella di Bufala Campana DOP.

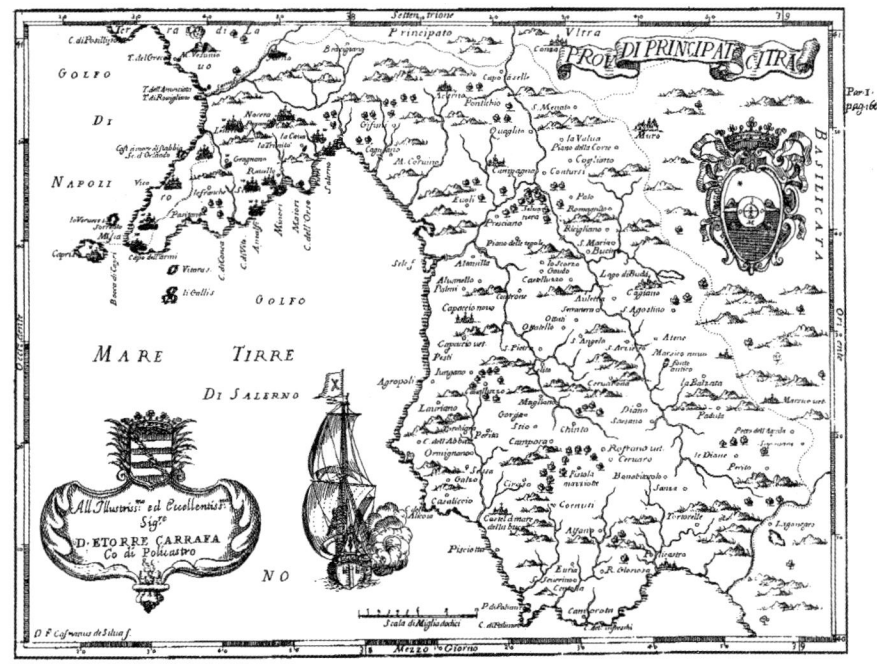

Detail of a map of Terra di Lavoro.
From Gio. Battista Pacichelli
"Il Regno di Napoli in Prospettiva,"
Naples, 1703

OPPOSITE:

Map of the Principality of Citra.
From Gio. Battista Pacichelli
"Il Regno di Napoli in Prospettiva,"
Naples, 1703

An Ancient Process

The mozzarella di bufala Campana DOP that is served in our restaurants is still produced artisanally. The *mozzatura* (cutting) is done by hand to preserve the taste of the cheese as well as it nutritional properties, and the timing and various phases of the process are closely monitored.

Milking

Made from delicious buffalo milk, obtained with care by dairy workers who have handed down the trade through generations, mozzarella di bufala Campana DOP is the result of the art of using an age-old ritual and an ancient recipe to work with milk today.

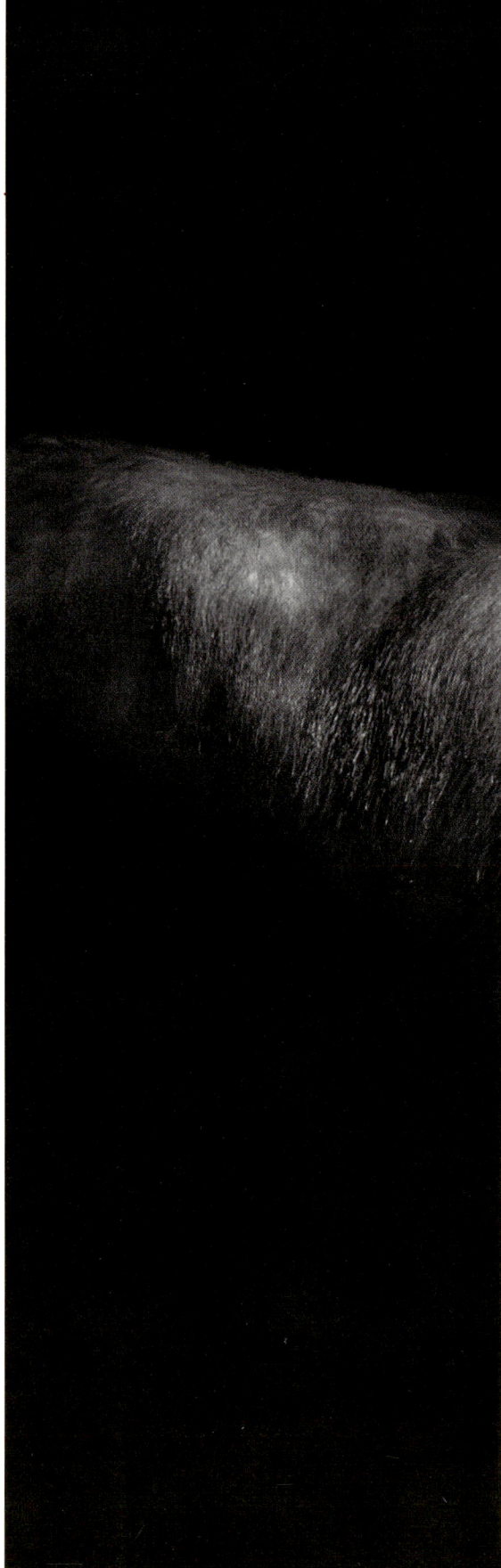

© Fabrizio Ferri

Curdling

Ancient and skillful movements are used to curdle the milk, which is inoculated with a starter culture of whey from the previous day's cheese making and salt, and later drained to eliminate the whey. The soft curd is then broken up into pieces and immersed in boiling water and stirred until it is just the right texture.

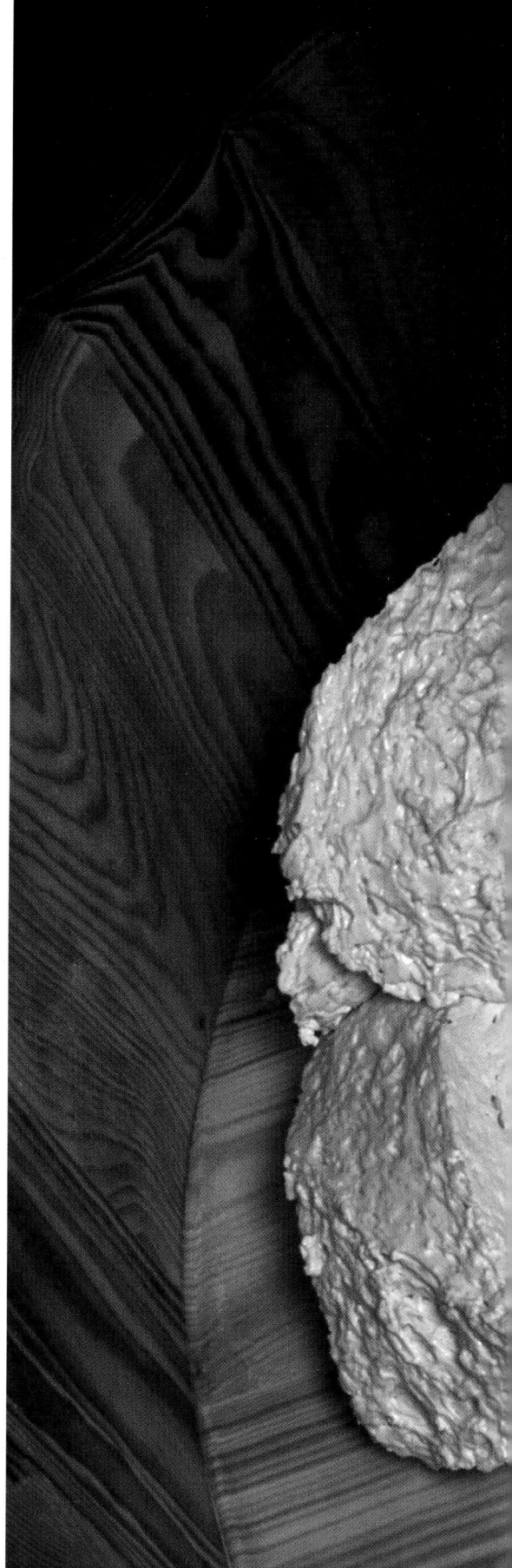

Kneading

Master cheesemakers knead the curds in large wooden vats until the surface of the paste is smooth and shiny. A wooden stick is used to spin or stretch the paste to achieve just the right elasticity, so that the mozzarella will have the soft yet compact texture that's typical of mozzarella di bufala Campana DOP.

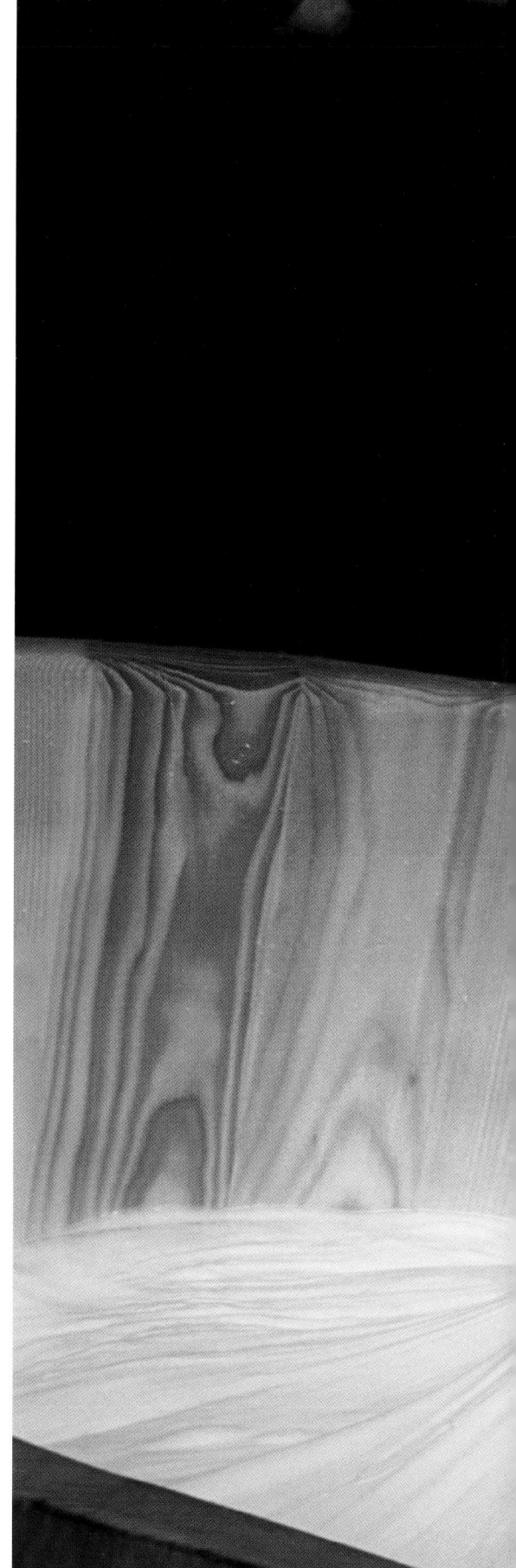

© Fabrizio Ferri

Manual Shaping

A cheesemaker quickly and deftly cuts off a section of the paste by squeezing it between the thumb and index finger, creating a single round form with the two characteristic "little ears" on one side that distinguish all handmade mozzarella. The mozzarella is then delicately placed to rest in the same milky liquid used for the curdling and kneading.

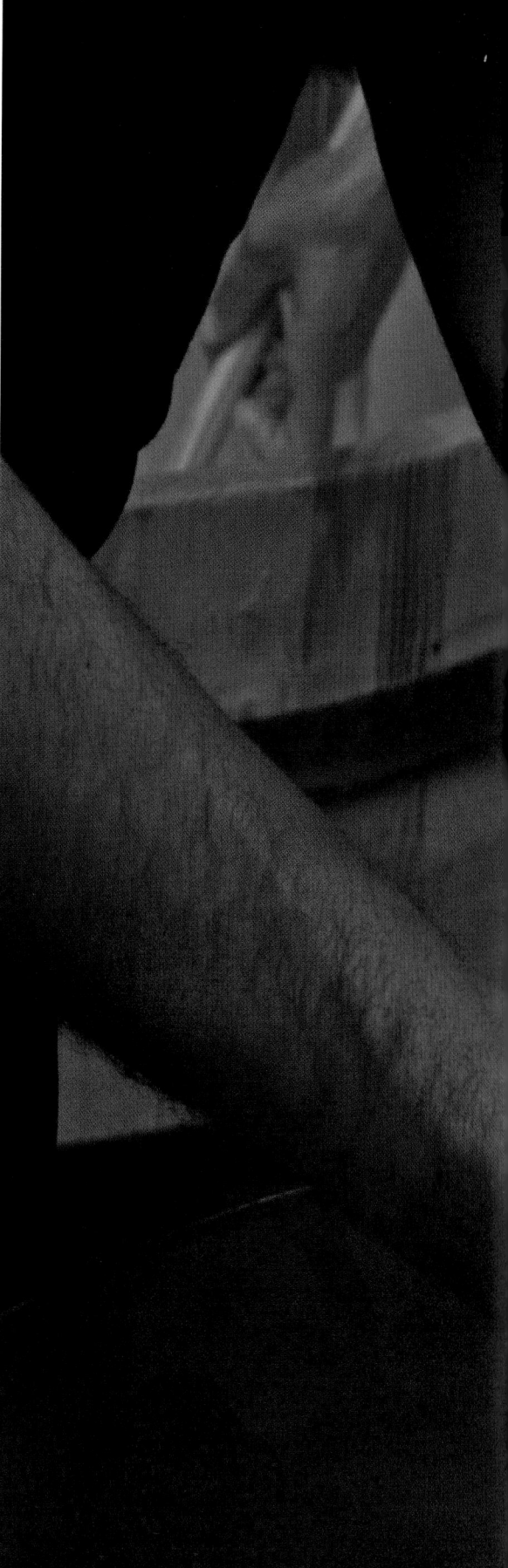

© Fabrizio Ferri

Tasting

Here's how to tell whether a mozzarella di bufala Campana DOP is fresh: it should be a pure white color that resembles shiny porcelain and have a natural elasticity. When cut, it should be compact or just slightly loose, and the white liquid it releases should have the intense aroma of lactic cultures and the slightly acidic and musky scent of cream. Each bite of mozzarella should leave a pleasant aftertaste of butter and hazelnut.

© Fabrizio Ferri

> "All around that meets the eye is cool and fresh."
>
> Matsuo Bashō
> (1644-1694)

Mozzarella di Bufala Campana DOP
History and How It Is Made

History
An Ancient Process

Milking
Curdling
Kneading
Manual Shaping
Tasting

History

Mozzarella di bufala Campana DOP (Denominazione di Origine Protetta, or protected designation of origin) is a fresh *pasta filata* (stretched curd) cheese that was first mentioned in a Longobard document from the eleventh century attesting that a *mozza* was given to the monks of an abbey located just outside Aversa.

Cited in a 1570 treatise on cooking by Bartolomeo Scappi, the pope's chef, it became famous in the late eighteenth century in part owing to the Bourbon Reggia di Carditello estate, where the buffaloes were bred for their delicious milk. The name of the cheese comes from the verb *mozzare,* to lop off.

The Bourbon estate in Carditello (eighteenth century).
From *"Mozzarella di Bufala Campana. Storia, tradizioni e immagini di un formaggio nato all'ombra del mito della Magna Grecia"*
Published by the Consorzio per la Tutela del Formaggio Mozzarella di Bufala Campana, 2004

Buffaloes grazing along the Asa stream near the Salerno-Battipaglia railway bridge, Pontecagnano, 1920.
Archivio Azienda Agricola Morese

No one is sure how the first buffaloes arrived in Italy. Some sources theorize that they are an indigenous breed, while others suggest they were brought to Italy by the Normans or the Goths.

Made only with the fresh milk of an Italian Mediterranean breed of buffalo, the mozzarella served in our restaurants comes mostly from the Campania region, especially Piana del Sele and Piana del Volturno, though some is from southern Lazio and the Puglia region. All of the cheese is produced by select certified dairies located within the area of origin established by the guidelines of the Consorzio di Tutela della Mozzarella di Bufala Campana DOP.

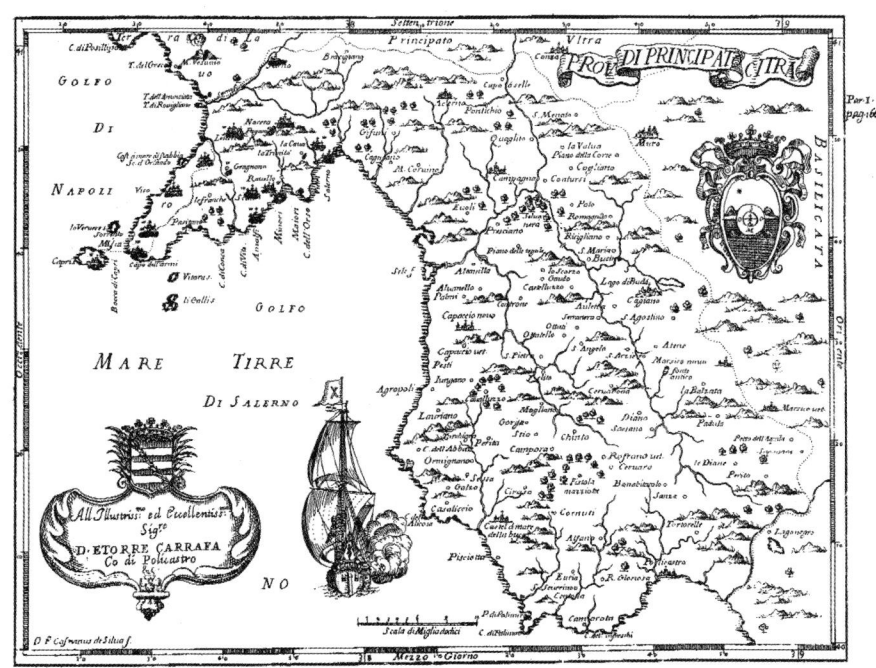

Detail of a map of Terra di Lavoro.
From Gio. Battista Pacichelli
"Il Regno di Napoli in Prospettiva,"
Naples, 1703

OPPOSITE:
Map of the Principality of Citra.
From Gio. Battista Pacichelli
"Il Regno di Napoli in Prospettiva,"
Naples, 1703

An Ancient Process

The mozzarella di bufala Campana DOP that is served in our restaurants is still produced artisanally. The *mozzatura* (cutting) is done by hand to preserve the taste of the cheese as well as it nutritional properties, and the timing and various phases of the process are closely monitored.

Milking

Made from delicious buffalo milk, obtained with care by dairy workers who have handed down the trade through generations, mozzarella di bufala Campana DOP is the result of the art of using an age-old ritual and an ancient recipe to work with milk today.

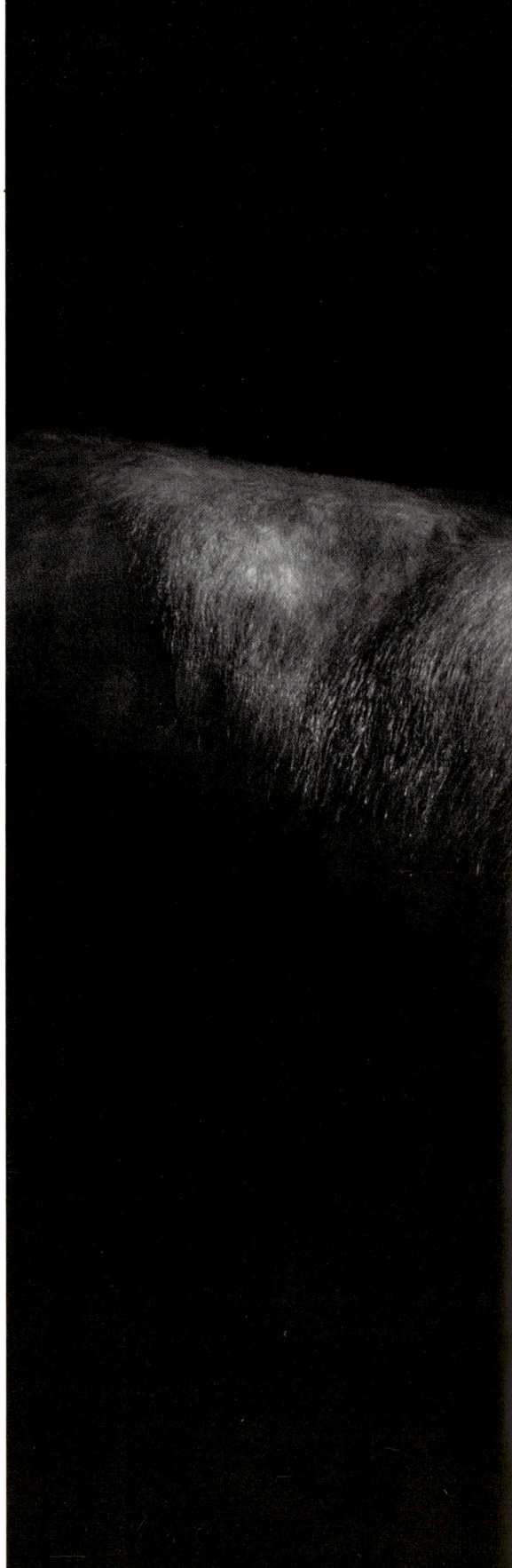

Curdling

Ancient and skillful movements are used to curdle the milk, which is inoculated with a starter culture of whey from the previous day's cheese making and salt, and later drained to eliminate the whey. The soft curd is then broken up into pieces and immersed in boiling water and stirred until it is just the right texture.

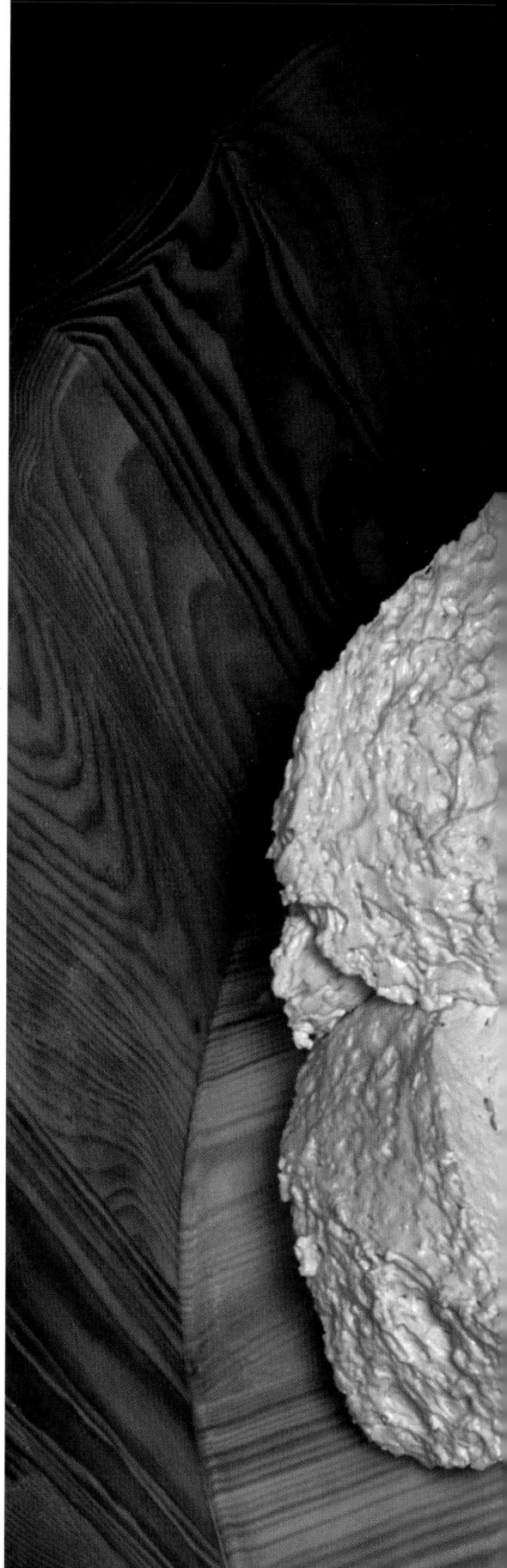

Kneading

Master cheesemakers knead the curds in large wooden vats until the surface of the paste is smooth and shiny. A wooden stick is used to spin or stretch the paste to achieve just the right elasticity, so that the mozzarella will have the soft yet compact texture that's typical of mozzarella di bufala Campana DOP.

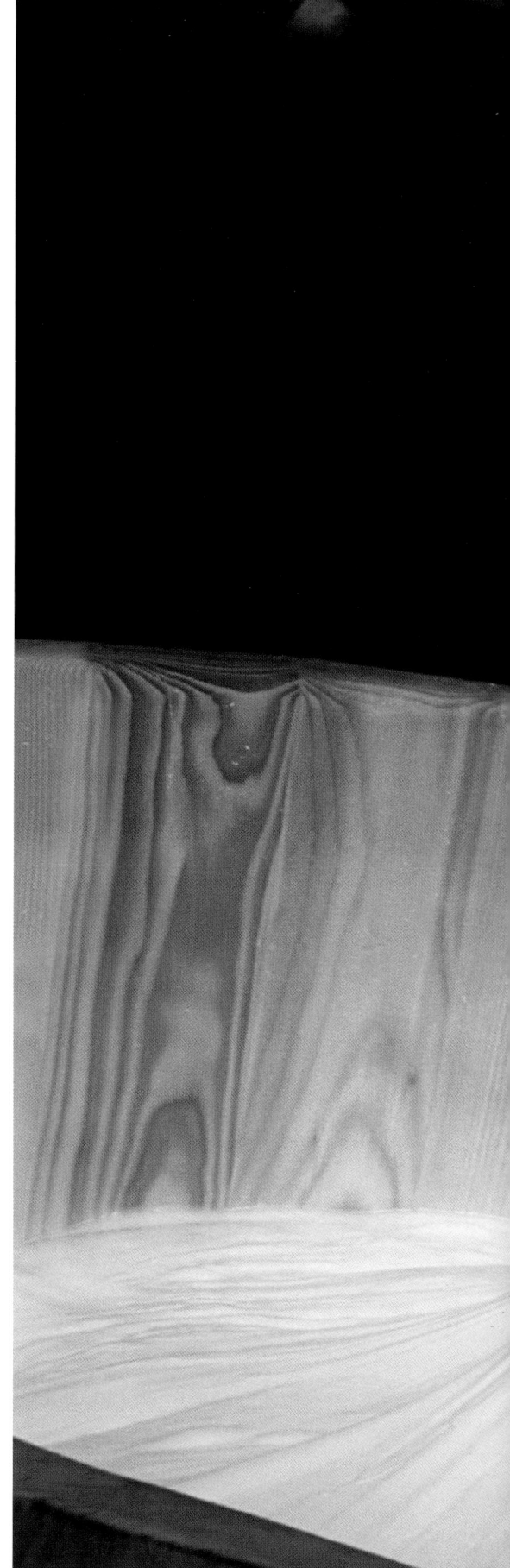

Manual Shaping

A cheesemaker quickly and deftly cuts off a section of the paste by squeezing it between the thumb and index finger, creating a single round form with the two characteristic "little ears" on one side that distinguish all handmade mozzarella. The mozzarella is then delicately placed to rest in the same milky liquid used for the curdling and kneading.

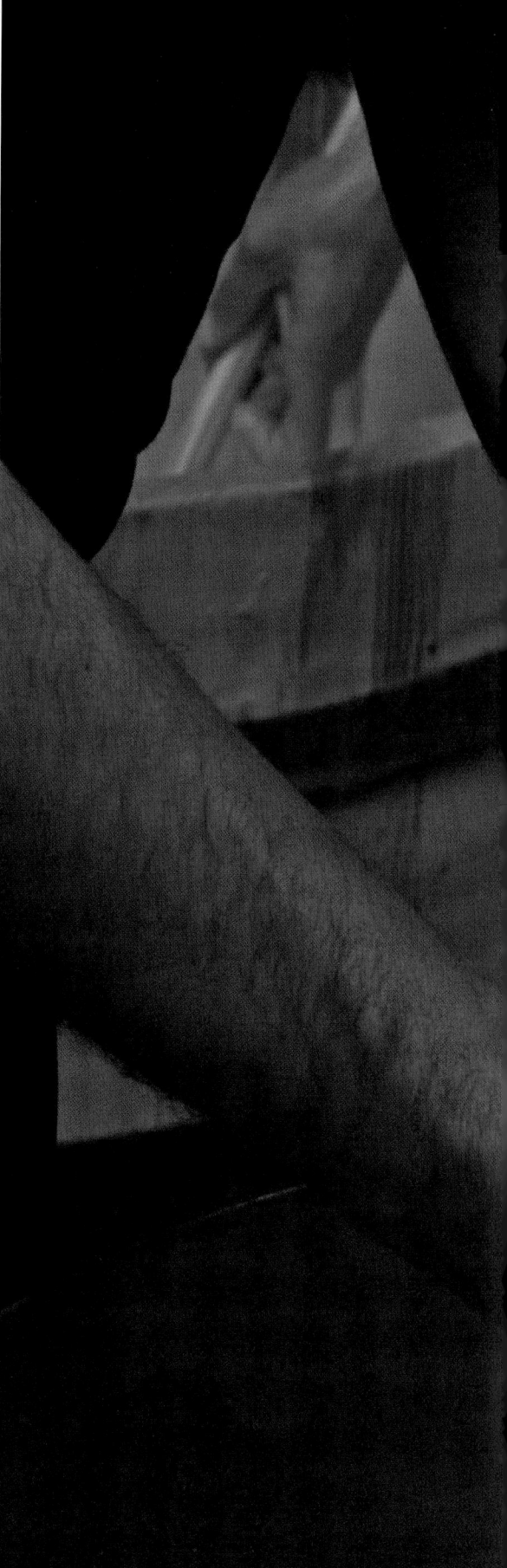

© Fabrizio Ferri

Tasting

Here's how to tell whether a mozzarella di bufala Campana DOP is fresh: it should be a pure white color that resembles shiny porcelain and have a natural elasticity. When cut, it should be compact or just slightly loose, and the white liquid it releases should have the intense aroma of lactic cultures and the slightly acidic and musky scent of cream. Each bite of mozzarella should leave a pleasant aftertaste of butter and hazelnut.

Mozzarella Bar
Some Obvious Pairings and Some Less Obvious Ones

Fresh Tomatoes with Basil Pesto

La Motticella Peeled Tomatoes and Andria Mozzarella Braid

Piennolo del Vesuvio Tomatoes

Neapolitan Papaccella

Castellammare Purple Artichokes

Speck di Trota with Herbs

Cetara Anchovies and Dried Tomatoes

Bottarga di Cabras

Capocollo di Martina Franca

Culatello di Zibello, Aged 18 Months

Prosciutto Crudo di Parma DOP, Aged 20 Months

Prosciutto Nero dei Nebrodi

Mortadella di Prato

Bresaola di Fassona

Soppressata di Gioi

Ciauscolo di Visso

Speck di Sauris

Violino di Capra della Valchiavenna

Presidio Slow Food

Fresh Tomatoes with Basil Pesto

Sicilia

Serves 1

¾ cup grape tomatoes
3 to 4 baby spinach leaves
4½ ounces mozzarella di bufala Campana DOP, drained
3 tablespoons basil pesto (see page 124)

Halve the tomatoes lengthwise. Place them in a colander to drain for a few minutes. On a plate, arrange the sliced tomatoes and make a bed of spinach. Set the mozzarella on top of the spinach. Serve the basil pesto in a small bowl.

Suggested Wine Pairing

Falanghina
Producer:
Feudi di San Gregorio
Grape:
Falanghina
Region:
Campania

Raw tomatoes have always been the most popular accompaniment for buffalo milk mozzarella. The pure white of the mozzarella next to the bright red of the tomato and the dark green of the basil, all of which glisten when a touch of olive oil is added, are an irresistible temptation for every palate: just one forkful of this heavenly combination and you'll feel as though you've just tasted a morsel of summertime. Known as an *insalata caprese*, or Capri salad—perhaps because the island of Capri represents the archetype of the Mediterranean environment—this dish, however disarmingly simple it may be, is actually quite a challenge. That challenge lies in the quest to locate the finest ingredients in order to re-create Italy's aromas and flavors even when far away. So we've had to grapple with the problem of tracking down the right tomato in every country where we've opened. A tomato has to meet a high standard indeed, and in the process we've discovered some truly excellent local products.

In the United States, we use a type of heirloom tomato, a variety of the Marmande cultivar with a sweet, powerful, juicy taste, as well as a firm, crisp, and compact texture.

In Japan, we use delicious Nagano tomatoes, which are medium-sized, dark red in color, and sweet.

In Italy, we rely upon two varieties: Albenga's Cuore di Bue, or Oxheart tomato, which has firm pulp, a sweet but also slightly sour flavor, and a very pointy heart shape, and Sicilian *datterini*, or grape tomatoes. These are small vine tomatoes with an elongated shape. Their higher sugar content makes them especially tasty.

Every place has its tomato.

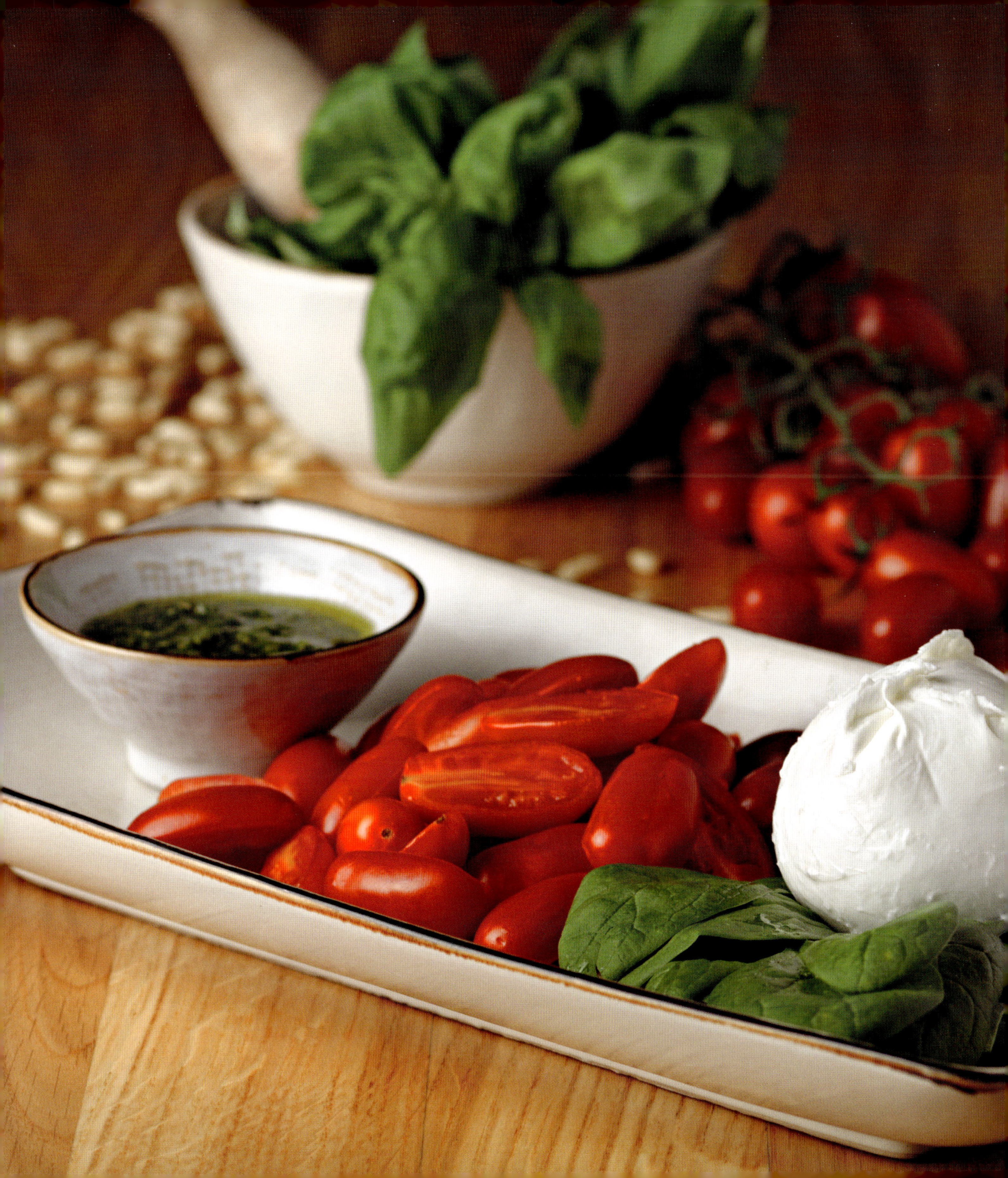

La Motticella Peeled Tomatoes and Andria Mozzarella Braid

Puglia

Serves 1

4½ ounces Andria mozzarella braid, drained
3 to 4 baby spinach leaves
¾ cup (5½ ounces) La Motticella peeled tomatoes, drained
Extra-virgin olive oil to taste

On a plate, arrange the cheese on a bed of baby spinach. Slice the tomatoes into thin strips, arrange on the same plate, and drizzle with oil.

Suggested Wine Pairing

Ryocello
Producer:
Tormaresca
Grape:
Fiano
Region:
Puglia

In this dish we combine the specialties from two provinces in the Puglia region: from the province of Barletta-Andria-Trani, the delicacy known as *treccina di latte vaccino d'Andria* (cow's milk mozzarella braid), and from Lucera, in the province of Foggia, *La Motticella* organic peeled tomatoes. The braid gets its delicate nature from the mild Mediterranean climate of the Murge area. It has a smooth, compact, and fairly firm surface, and it's ivory white. It's savory with a mild, milky aroma, and it's braided to produce those delightful twirls that add texture to a mozzarella. The firm pulp and the highly concentrated flavor of the organic peeled tomatoes from Paolo Petrilli's La Motticella farms originate with the warm sun of the Tavoliere delle Puglie, about sixty miles to the north. The tomatoes are bright red. This ancient variety is cultivated by very few farmers. They are grown on only seventy-five acres of rocky terrain. The soil's natural fertility is exploited so that no acidifiers need to be added. Picked and peeled by hand, the tomatoes preserve all their original flavor and natural goodness.

The harvest runs from late February to April or May; the middle period coincides with Easter festivities.

POMODORI PELATI

PAOLO PETRILLI
LUCERA

La Motticella

At La Motticella, they still pick and peel tomatoes by hand. Then the tomatoes are washed and preserved in glass containers.

The tomato seeds for this heirloom variety, true San Marzano tomatoes, are planted by very few farmers. The tomatoes have a low yield and an intense flavor. This tomato variety was lost at one time because factory farms were unable to grow it properly, as each tomato has its own specific ripening cycle. La Motticella rescued these authentic San Marzano tomatoes.

The label states that the contents are tomatoes and basil with no artificial coloring or preservatives, proof of the high quality of this product.

OPPOSITE:
Paolo Petrilli, owner of La Motticella, with Silvio Ursini in Lucera.

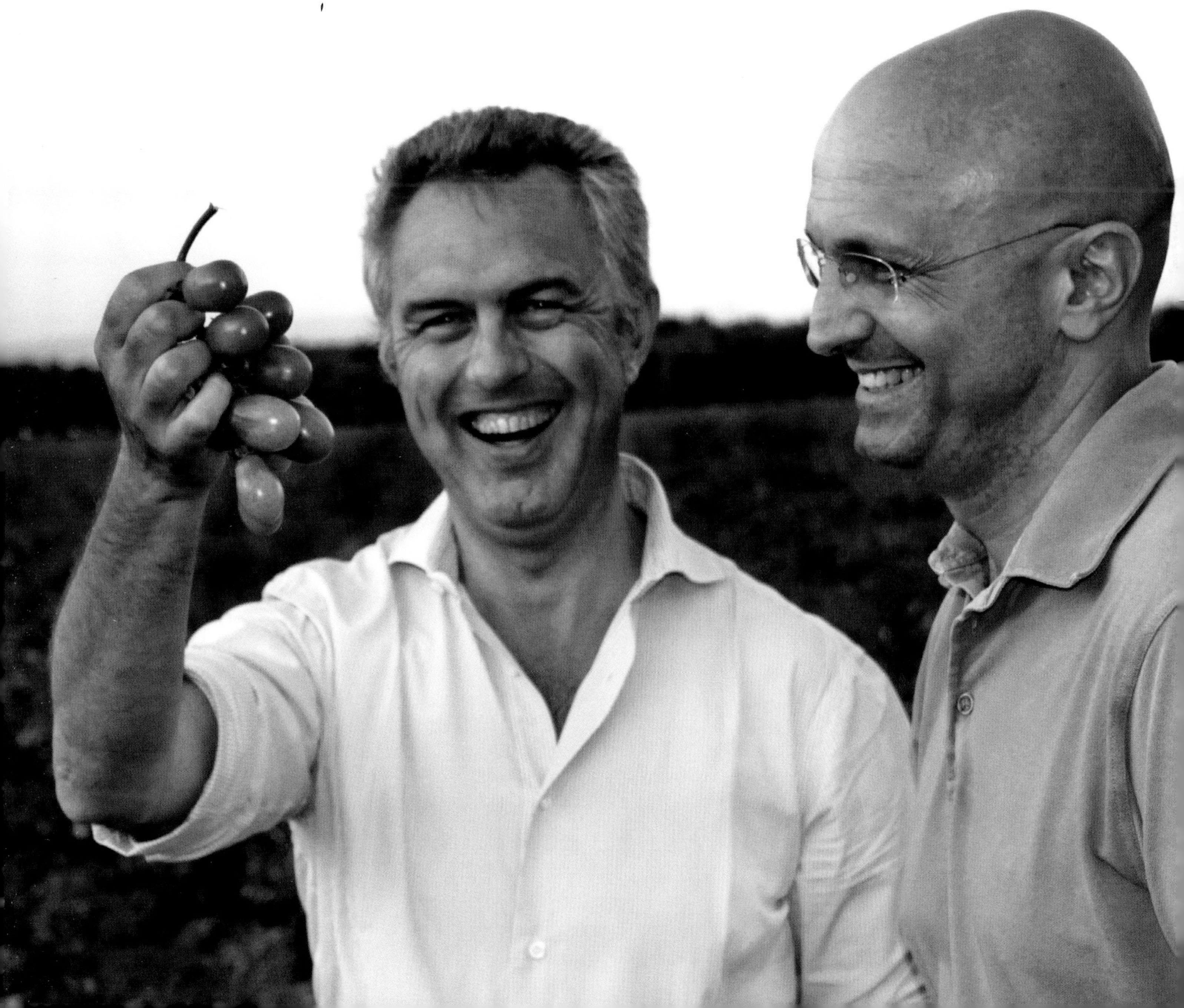

Piénnolo del Vesuvio Tomatoes

A signature of the Vesuvius area, these tomatoes are known as *pomodori da serbo col pizzo* (preserved tomatoes with a peak) and also as *piénnoli* (hangers) due to the custom of hanging them from the walls or ceiling in bunches tied together with hemp strings. These are small (less than one ounce) cherry-shaped tomatoes that can be distinguished from Pachino tomatoes by a pair of ribs, which start at the stalk end and give the tomato its square shape and sharp peak. Their skin is thick and hardy, the flesh firm and compact. These tomatoes aren't especially juicy, as they are dried by the sun that shines on the volcano's dry soil. They're planted in March and April and ripen in July and August. However, the age-old preserving process dictates that they be picked in bunches at the start of the summer so that they can be hung in a dry, cool, well-aerated place until winter or even the following spring. They then can be used for months to make Campania's famous and outstanding tomato sauce, which appears in fish recipes, pizza, and pastas.

These tomatoes have thick red skin, firm flesh, and a sweet and sour taste. Both their flavor and fragrance grow in intensity as times goes by: as they dry out they become more concentrated. They are a traditional mid-morning snack for farmers working the fields: a tomato is flattened onto a piece of bread, then flavored with a drizzle of oil, a pinch of salt, and basil leaves. In the kitchen, they're used to make quick dishes, such as vermicelli with clam sauce, or fish in acquapazza.

Campania

Serves 1

¾ cup Piénnolo del Vesuvio tomatoes
Extra-virgin olive oil to taste
Salt to taste
5 fresh basil leaves
2 slices country-style bread
4½ ounces stracciatella di burrata
3 to 4 baby spinach leaves

Slice the tomatoes in half, drain the excess water, and toss with oil and salt. Tear the basil leaves and toss with the tomatoes. Grill the slices of bread and then spread the tomatoes on top. Arrange the bread on a plate. Place the cheese in a small bowl and arrange the spinach on the plate. Set the bowl on top of the bed of spinach.

Suggested Wine Pairing

Pino & Toi
Producer:
Maculan
Grapes:
Friulano, Pinot Grigio
Region:
Veneto

Presidio Slow Food

Producer: Az. Agr. Casabarone, *Massa di Somma*
(Province of Naples)

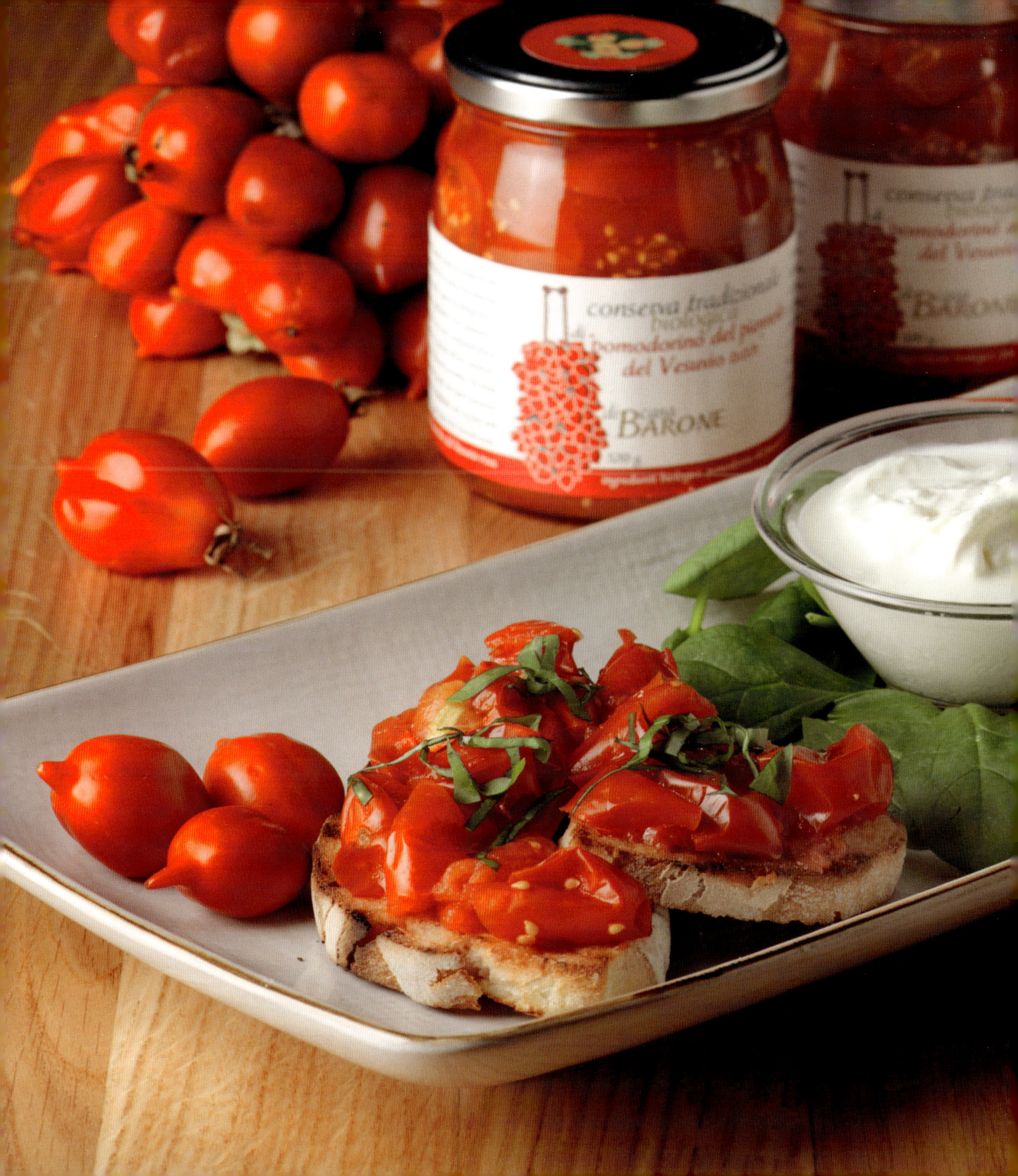
BARONE

Neapolitan Papaccella

Campania

Serves 1

2 slices country-style bread
Extra-virgin olive oil to taste
½ cup grilled papaccella peppers
4½ ounces smoked mozzarella di bufala Campana DOP
3 to 4 baby spinach leaves
2 tablespoons baked black olives, pitted
2 grape tomatoes

Grill the bread and drizzle with the oil. Cut the peppers in strips and arrange them on the slices of bread. Drain the mozzarella and arrange it on a bed of baby spinach. Place the bread alongside. Garnish with the olives and tomatoes.

Suggested Beer Pairing

Lurisia 8
Producer:
Lurisia
Description:
Pure malt barley beer
Region:
Piedmont

The Neapolitan *papaccella* is a small, meaty, and very tasty pepper that's slightly flat and ribbed. From July until the start of the first cold weather, Neapolitan market stands overflow with colorful peppers, but only a real Neapolitan can quickly pick out a genuine papaccella. Actually, it isn't hard to identify them: real papaccella peppers are small, 3 to 4 inches across at the very most.

The bright color of this small vegetable ranges from dark green to sunny yellow (generally, the yellow ones are larger) to green streaked with wine red.

Sweetness distinguishes the papaccella from other hybrid varieties of similar appearance, but it also has a decidedly peppery taste. Its scent is particularly intense, with fresh, herbaceous notes. The seeds are planted from mid-March through the first ten days in July, and the vegetables are hand-picked from mid-June to early November.

Papaccella peppers can be eaten raw, roasted, sautéed in a skillet, or oven-baked, and traditionally they are stuffed with tuna or salted anchovies, olives, breadcrumbs, raisins, pine nuts, tomatoes, and capers. The smallest ones are preserved in red wine vinegar and are the main ingredient in *insalata di rinforzo*, a sumptuous salad typically served during the Christmas season in Naples. The name comes from the tradition of adding new ingredients daily to the leftover salad to "reinforce" it.

Presidio Slow Food

Producer: Az. Agr. Bruno Sodano, *Pomigliano d'Arco (Province of Naples)*

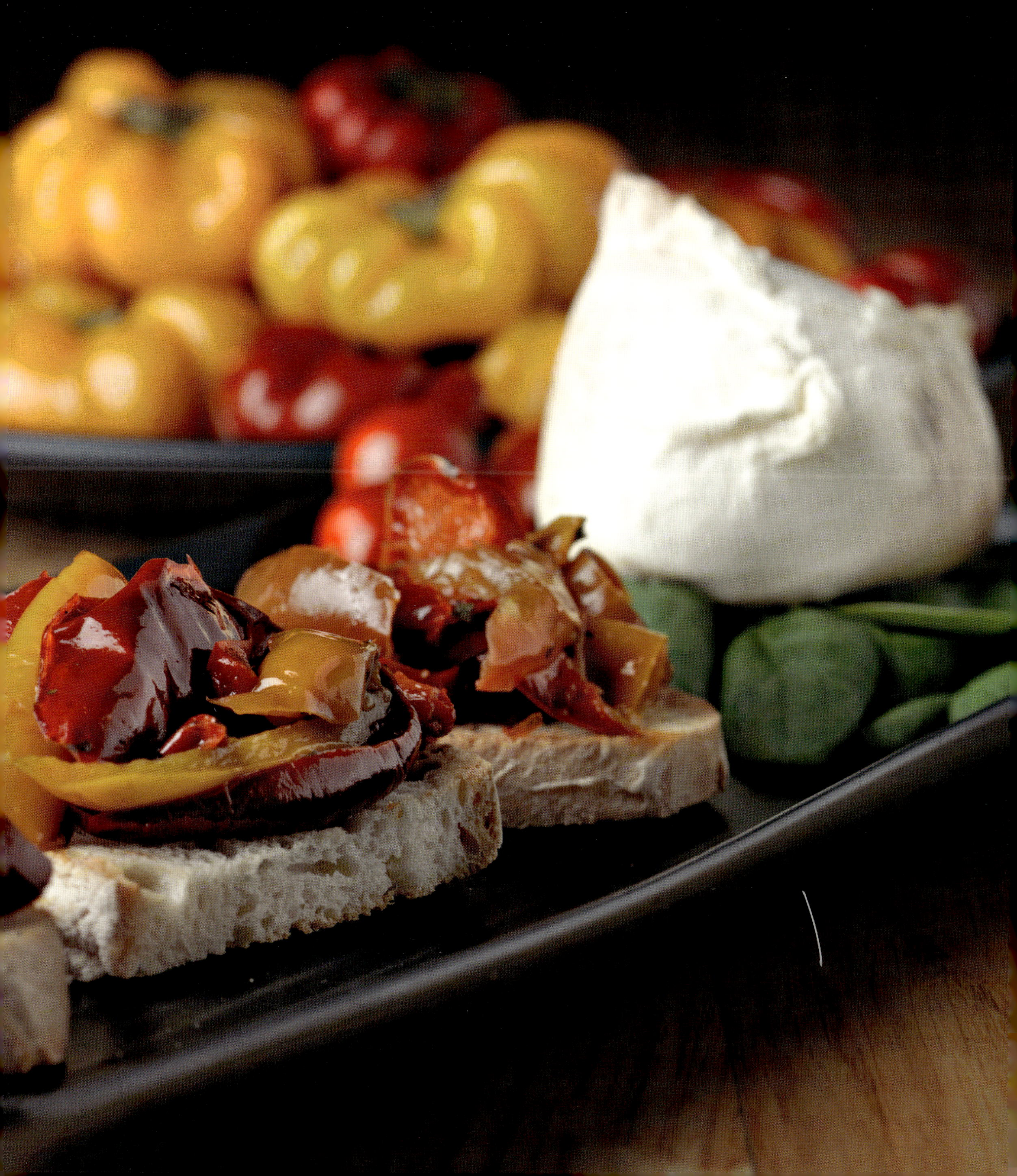

Castellammare Purple Artichokes

Campania

Serves 1

4½ ounces smoked mozzarella di bufala Campana DOP
½ cup roasted Castellammare artichokes preserved in oil
3 to 4 baby spinach leaves
2 tablespoons baked black olives, pitted
2 grape tomatoes

Drain the mozzarella. Cut the artichokes in half and arrange both ingredients on a bed of spinach. Garnish with the olives and tomatoes.

Suggested Water Pairing

Stille
Producer:
Lurisia
Description:
Still water
Region:
Piedmont

This artichoke is also known as a Schito artichoke, after the name of a part of Castellammare di Stabia held to be particularly suited to horticulture as far back as the Roman era.

The Castellammare artichoke is a sub-variety of the Roman artichoke, from which it is distinguished by the period during which it's produced, from February to May, and by the color of its bracts (as an artichoke's leaves are called), which are green with shades of purple.

The fact that this vegetable ripens early is due to the particularly mild climate and the custom of regenerating the plants each year. Another traditional method for growing this type of artichoke is to place a terracotta cap called a *pignatella* (handcrafted by local artisans) on the mamma, i.e. the first and largest bloom. As the artichoke grows, the *pignatella* shelters it from the sun's rays so that it will be especially tender and light colored. Each plant has not only a mamma, which is generally grilled, but six slightly smaller "children," which can be used in all sorts of dishes, and two "grandchildren," which are preserved in oil.

Neapolitans traditionally roast these artichokes on Easter Monday. They place them directly on the embers of a fire, then remove any burnt leaves and season the artichokes with salt, black pepper, parsley, garlic, and oil. We serve these slightly smoky roasted artichokes with mozzarella di bufala Campana DOP, which has a sweetness they magically accentuate.

Presidio Slow Food

Producer: Imp. Agricola Sabato Abagnale, *Sant'Antonio Abate (Province of Naples)*

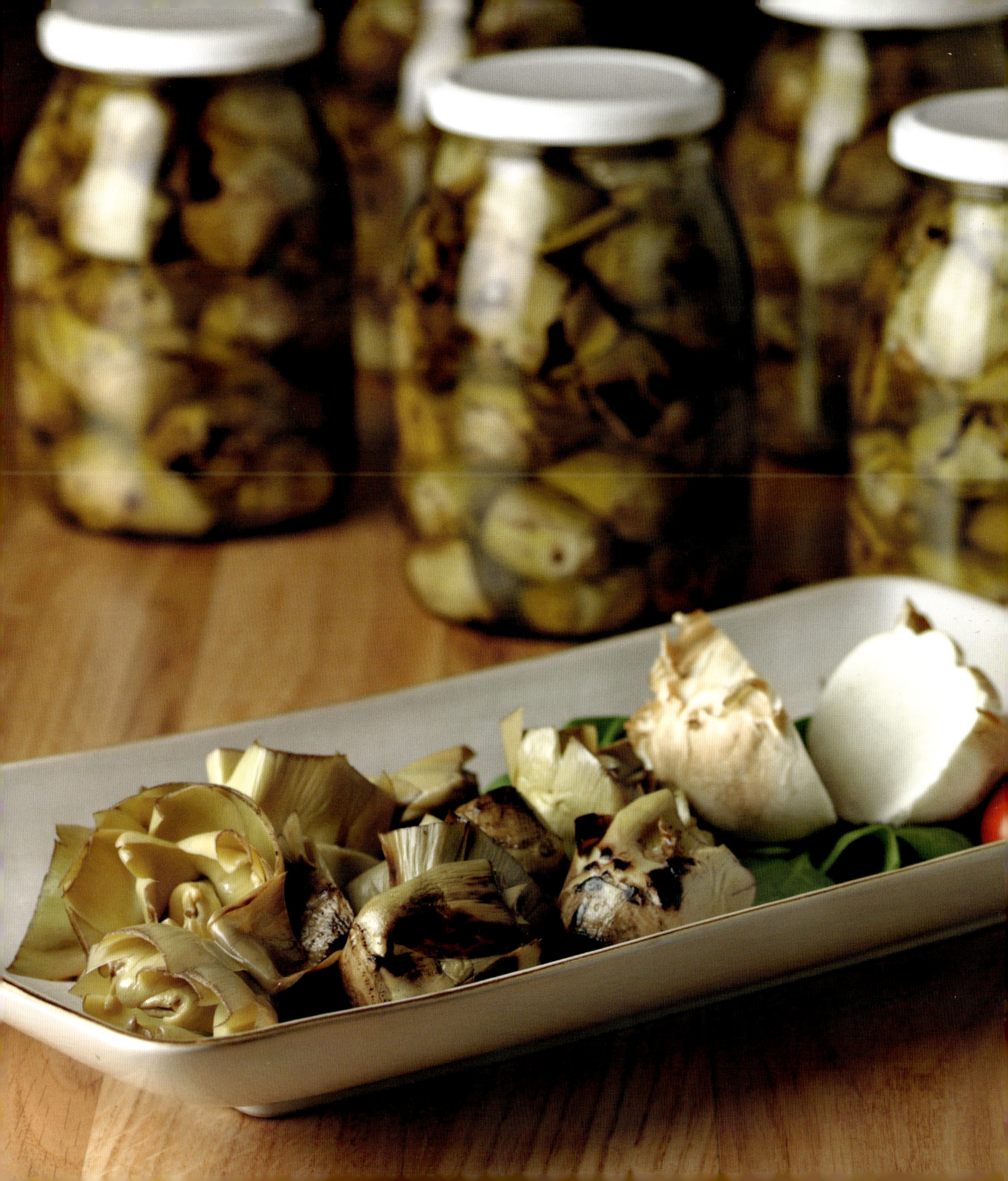

Speck di Trota with Herbs

Trentino Alto Adige

Serves 1

2½ ounces trout speck
Extra-virgin olive oil to taste
4½ ounces smoked mozzarella di bufala Campana DOP
3 to 4 baby spinach leaves
2 grape tomatoes

Cut the speck into ¼- to ½-inch-wide strips, arrange them in a row on a serving platter, and drizzle with oil. Drain the mozzarella and arrange it on a bed of baby spinach. Garnish with the tomatoes.

Suggested Wine Pairing

Pinot Nero Rosé Cruasé
Producer:
Tenuta Mazzolino
Grape:
Pinot Nero
Region:
Lombardy

The Trentino region is home to some of the greatest and most renowned trout farms in Italy. Trout farming in these mountains started in the mid-nineteenth century, when Emperor Franz Joseph would go hunting there. The emperor especially enjoyed eating Trentino trout. Nowadays this region produces about 15 percent of the entire national output of trout meat, and 90 percent of the eggs and material required for reproduction.

Trout speck was conceived by the Armanini company in Storo on the occasion of its fiftieth birthday. Chef Claudio Pregl had the idea for this exclusive recipe, which is available in a limited edition. The finest species of rainbow trout are bred in fresh, pure water until they are six years old and weigh about ten pounds. The meat is then rubbed with a mixture of aromatic herbs, after which it is aged, smoked, and aged again.

The skillful combination of herbs (all of which are rigorously organic) and their fresh, pungent aroma completes and lightens the mellow, full flavor of the smoked trout. In our kitchen, this delicious treasure is served alongside mozzarella di bufala Campana DOP. In this unique dish, trout speck takes the place of traditional speck—made with pork—and satisfies even the most refined palates.

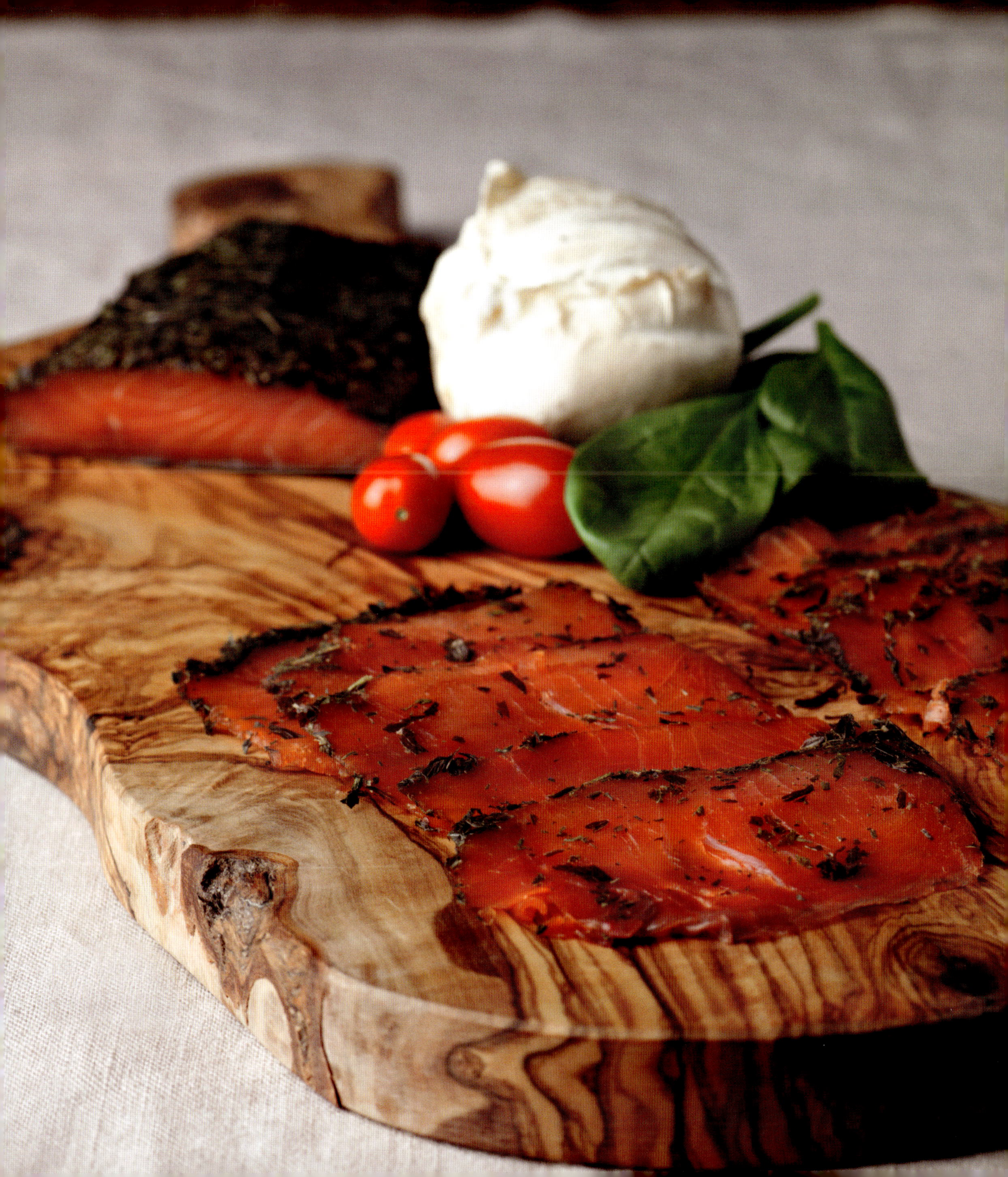

Cetara Anchovies and Dried Tomatoes

Campania

Serves 1

5 Cetara anchovy fillets
¼ cup sun-dried tomatoes preserved in oil
4½ ounces mozzarella di bufala Campana DOP
3 to 4 baby spinach leaves
2 cherry tomatoes

Drain the oil from the anchovy fillets and dried tomatoes. Cut the tomatoes in half. Cut the mozzarella into five slices and arrange in a circle on a round serving platter (preferably one that is a dark color to accentuate the pure whiteness of the mozzarella). Curl a drained anchovy fillet on each slice of mozzarella. Arrange the spinach in the center of the plate and top with the dried tomatoes.

Suggested Wine Pairing

SP 68
Producer:
Occhipinti
Grapes:
Nero d'Avola, Frappato
Region:
Sicily

Cetara is a charming village by the sea on the Amalfi coast that's famous for its anchovies, which are preserved in salt. In the spring, the Gulf of Salerno is filled with fleets of boats with fishermen fishing by lamplight, because in that season, owing to the particular conditions of the gulf's waters and the life cycle of these fish, the anchovies have a low fat content that makes them especially suited to the salt pickling process.

As soon as the anchovies are caught, they're gutted and filleted by hand and placed in a special oak container in layers alternating with layers of salt. Then the container is covered and pressure is exerted on its contents.

As the anchovies age under pressure, liquid is formed that rises to the surface. This liquid is discarded when it is given off by standard preserved anchovies, but the liquid that is created by aging Cetara anchovies, known as *colatura*, is collected and then exposed to the sun for the whole summer, and the concentrate is then poured back into the wooden barrels with the anchovies to enhance their taste and flavor.

For our recipe we pair these anchovies with another intensely flavored ingredient: dried tomatoes preserved in oil from Calabria. These tomatoes are traditionally dried in the sun and seasoned with extra-virgin olive oil, salt, vinegar, and oregano. They are ideal for appetizers and bruschetta.

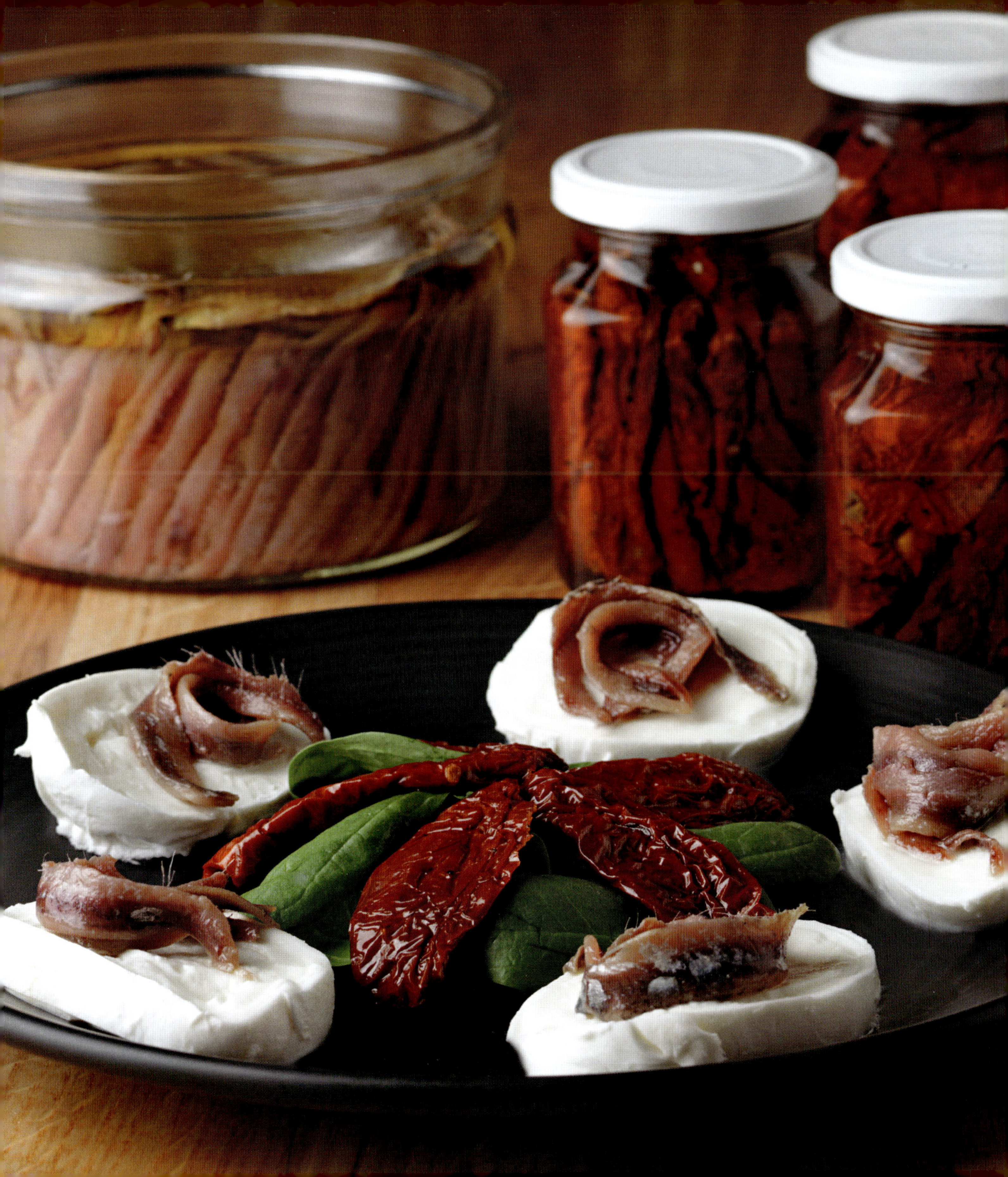

Bottarga di Cabras

Sardegna

Serves 1

2 slices country-style bread
1 Oxheart tomato
Amalfi lemon to taste
¾ ounce bottarga di Cabras
Extra-virgin olive oil to taste
4 basil leaves
3 to 4 arugula leaves
4½ ounces stracciatella di burrata
2 tablespoons baked black olives, pitted
¼ cup grape tomatoes

Toast the bread. Slice the tomato and arrange them on the bread. Slice the lemon paper thin and arrange them on top of the tomato slices. Shave the bottarga and place on top of the lemon. Drizzle with oil and add the basil leaves. Serve with arugula, stracciatella, olives, and grape tomatoes.

Suggested Wine Pairing

Capichera
Producer: Capichera
Grape: Vermentino di Gallura
Region: Sardinia

The word *bottarga*, or salted fish roe, comes from the Arabic *bottarikh*, and this delicacy has a very long history. It is said to have been appreciated by the ancient Phoenicians, Egyptians, and Romans. In time, the custom of eating mullet roe spread to several parts of Italy, especially to the Sardinian coast near Cabras, in the province of Oristano. Bottarga was ideal for fishermen who spent lots of time on the open sea, and it was easily stored for long periods. To make bottarga, fish eggs are salted, pressed, and dried into a block. Tuna and mullet have tough egg sacs, so their roe is best suited to the technique. Mullet roe is amber colored and has an aromatic flavor that is more delicate and less bitter than tuna roe. Though bottarga was once produced and consumed mostly by fishermen, it eventually became a specialty. In Cabras it was offered to rulers and heads of state, and sometimes used for trade, almost like a currency.

Oro di Cabras, or Cabras gold, is mellow, artisanally produced fish roe with almond notes and amber gold tones. We like to present it simply on slices of bread, the way it used to be eaten by fishermen, and pair it with creamy stracciatella di burrata, tasty Oxheart tomatoes, and sweet Amalfi lemons.

The dish is finished with extra-virgin olive oil and basil.

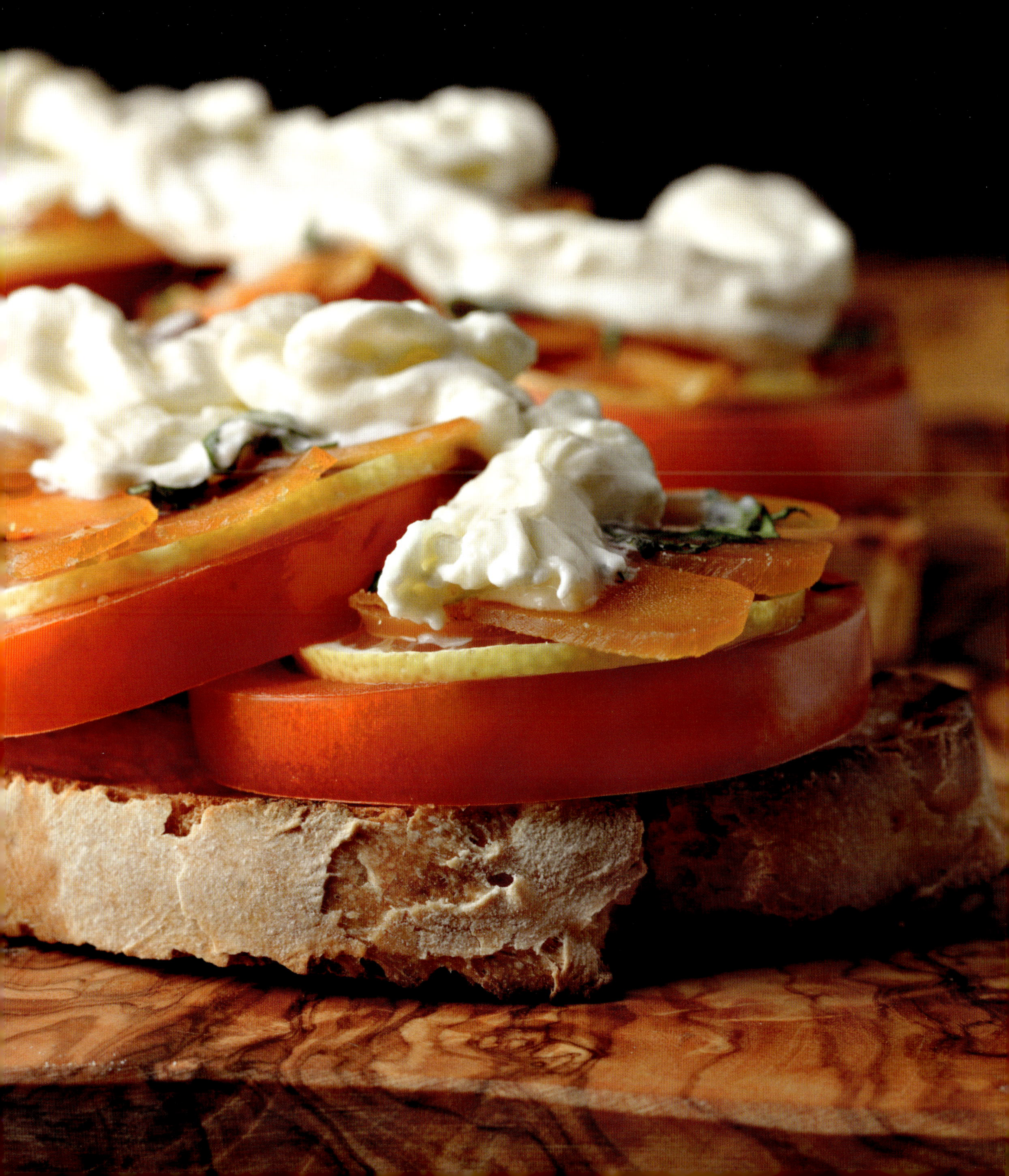

Capocollo di Martina Franca

Puglia

Serves 1

2½ ounces capocollo di Martina Franca
4½ ounces smoked mozzarella di bufala Campana DOP
3 to 4 baby spinach leaves
2 tablespoons baked black olives, pitted
2 grape tomatoes

Slice the capocollo ¼- to ½-inch thick and then arrange it on a plate. Drain the mozzarella and place it on a bed of spinach. Garnish with the olives and tomatoes.

Suggested Wine Pairing

Neprica
Producer:
Tormaresca
Grapes:
Negroamaro, Primitivo, Cabernet Sauvignon
Region:
Puglia

Everyone knows that the best cured meat products in Puglia have always come from Martina Franca. Proof of this is that in the past, in the Tarantino or Salento areas, when the time came to butcher a pig, skilled workers from Martina Franca were summoned for the task. In this lovely city in the Itria Valley, many traditional pork-butchering techniques are still used to make local specialties. Among these, the most famous is unquestionably capocollo or capicollo, the name in Southern Italy for coppa or lonza, that is, cured meat made from the part of the pig between the neck and ribs.

Once capocollo has been cleaned and shaped, it is aged in salt for fifteen to twenty days, then rinsed with a solution made from cooked grape must and spices. The capocollo is then stuffed into casing made from pig intestine and dried, first wrapped in cloths and then arranged on boards and left to rest for about ten days. Once the capocollo is perfectly dry, it's smoked. At one time, this was done by covering the floor with sprigs of thyme, myrtle, bay leaves (plants that grow abundantly in the almost forty acres of woods and Mediterranean brush in the area) and lighting them so that they smoldered. Today, these plants, along with the bark of Macedonian oak trees, are burned in fireplaces instead. While some of the signature fragrance has been lost, the results are easier to control. After smoking, the meat is aged for up to ninety days.

Presidio Slow Food

Producer: Salumificio Santoro, *Cisternino*
(Province of Brindisi)

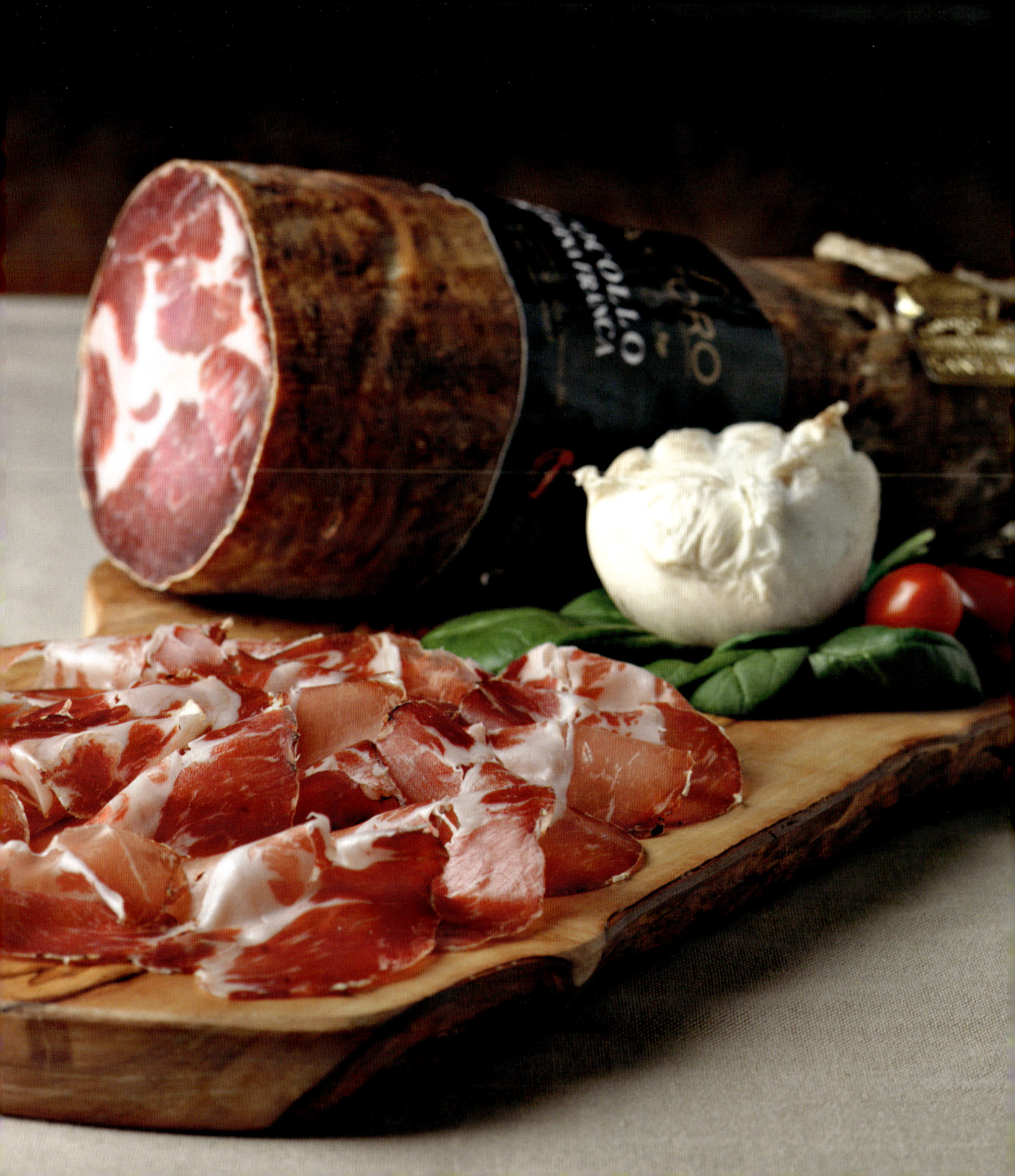

Culatello di Zibello, Aged 18 Months

Emilia Romagna

Serves 1

2½ ounces culatello di Zibello
4½ ounces mozzarella di bufala Campana DOP
3 to 4 baby spinach leaves
2 tablespoons baked black olives, pitted
2 grape tomatoes

Slice the culatello about ¼ inch thick and then arrange it on a plate. Pair it with drained mozzarella served on a bed of spinach. Garnish with the olives and tomatoes.

Suggested Wine Pairing

Otello Nero
Producer:
Ceci
Grape:
Lambrusco Maestri
Region:
Emilia Romagna

Culatello di Zibello is an exquisite cured meat with DOP status produced in the province of Parma, mainly in the town of Zibello and the surrounding area. Only the meat of pigs born, bred, and butchered in Lombardy and Emilia Romagna is used. Production is limited to about 60,000 pieces annually.

Italian writer Gabriele D'Annunzio described culatello di Zibello as "solid salted pork," and it is one of the standout cured meat products in this pork-loving region, due to the mist and fog around the Po River that dampens the meat as it ages in ancient cellars. Tradition dictates that culatello be made with the highest quality part of the pig—the rear haunch—and that countless bottles of the local Fortana wine be sacrificed, as they are poured out onto the floor of the aging area to lend a special aroma to this celebrated pear-shaped cured meat.

The culatello di Zibello that we serve is produced by Antica Ardenga, a small company that, together with twelve other producers, is part of the Consorzio del Culatello di Zibello. The meat is aged for eighteen months and is protected by a Slow Food presidium. Its aromatic, slightly musky flavor goes very well with the sweet delicate flavor of mozzarella di bufala Campana DOP, the undisputed star of our table.

Presidio Slow Food

Producer: Antica Ardenga di Massimo Pezzani, *Diolo di Soragna (Province of Parma)*

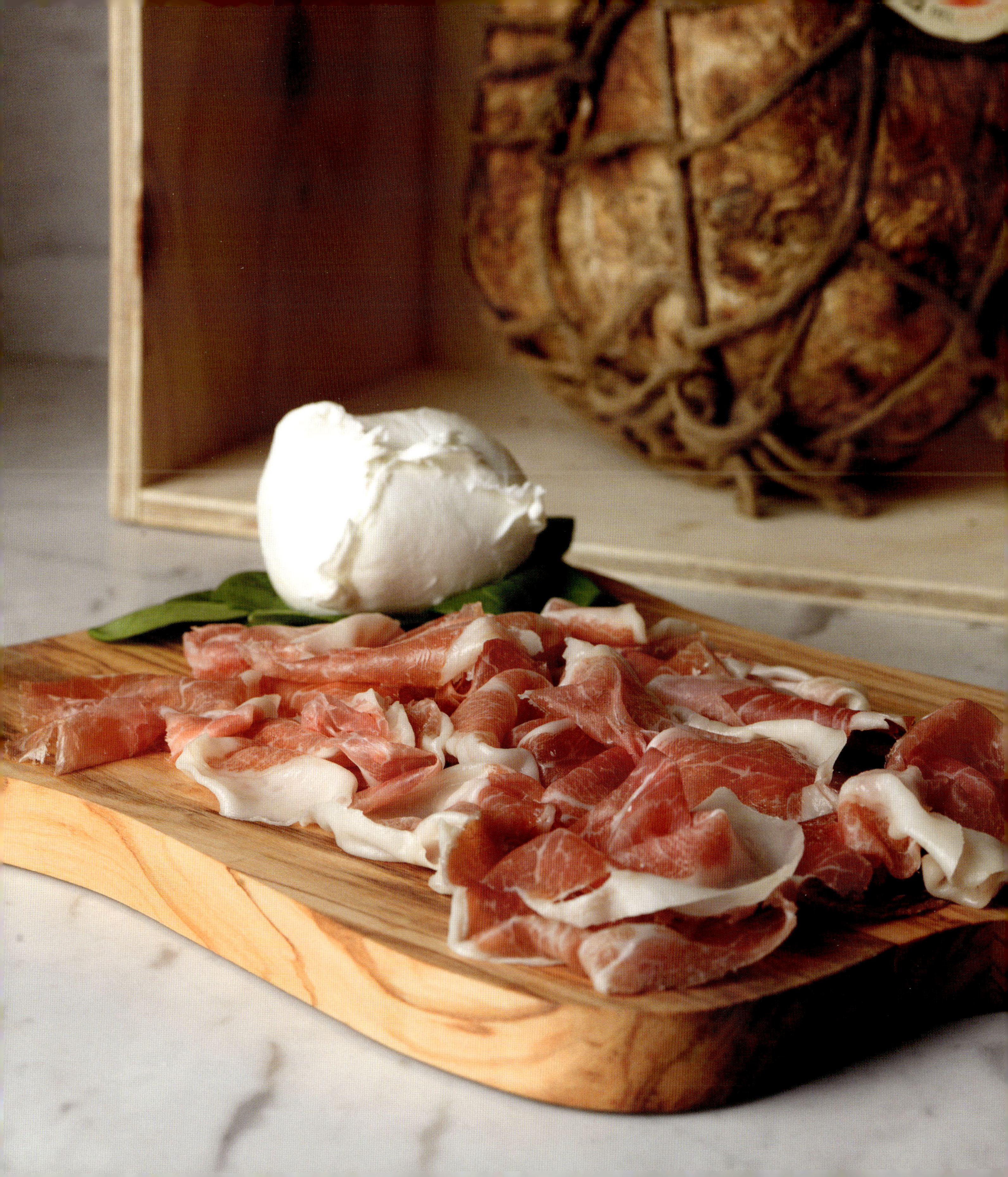

Prosciutto Crudo di Parma DOP, Aged 20 Months

Emilia Romagna

Serves 1

2½ ounces prosciutto di Parma DOP
4½ ounces mozzarella di bufala Campana DOP
3 to 4 baby spinach leaves
2 tablespoons baked black olives, pitted
2 grape tomatoes

Slice the prosciutto ¼- to ½-inch thick. Trim and discard the rind, but leave the precious fat that's so sweet and melts in your mouth. Arrange the slices of prosciutto on a plate and serve with drained mozzarella on a bed of spinach. Garnish with the olives and tomatoes.

Suggested Wine Pairing

Primedizione Cuvée 13 S.A.
Producer:
Fattorie Vallona
Grapes:
Pignoletto and others
Region:
Emilia Romagna

Attention to detail during the aging process; passion for a task that involves ancient traditions handed down from generation to generation; balanced aromas and tastes from a rich and generous land; quality and care in selecting raw materials: these are the elements that make prosciutto crudo di Parma DOP one of the most beloved Italian foods in the world.

Prosciutto di Parma (the word "prosciutto" comes from the Latin *perex-suctum*, literally meaning "dried out") is a completely natural product that has neither preservatives nor additives, the result of the work of the skilled hands of master curers, and of the dry and delicate breeze of the fragrant Parma hills. The production process follows strict guidelines that the consortium has imposed on all the companies that make this product, thereby regulating all the phases in the process—isolation, cooling, trimming, salting, rest, washing, drying, pre-aging, grooming, covering with lard, aging, testing, and branding—according to a specific methodology, with complete respect for tradition.

When twelve months have passed and the inspectors from the Istituto Parma Qualità have examined the prosciutto, the product is branded with a five-pointed crown symbol. This legal recognition from the Consorzio del Prosciutto di Parma is also a government seal, and it guarantees that the marked product will be sweet, high quality, and absolutely compliant with traditional methods.

For this recipe we chose a very fine prosciutto di Parma aged up to twenty months.

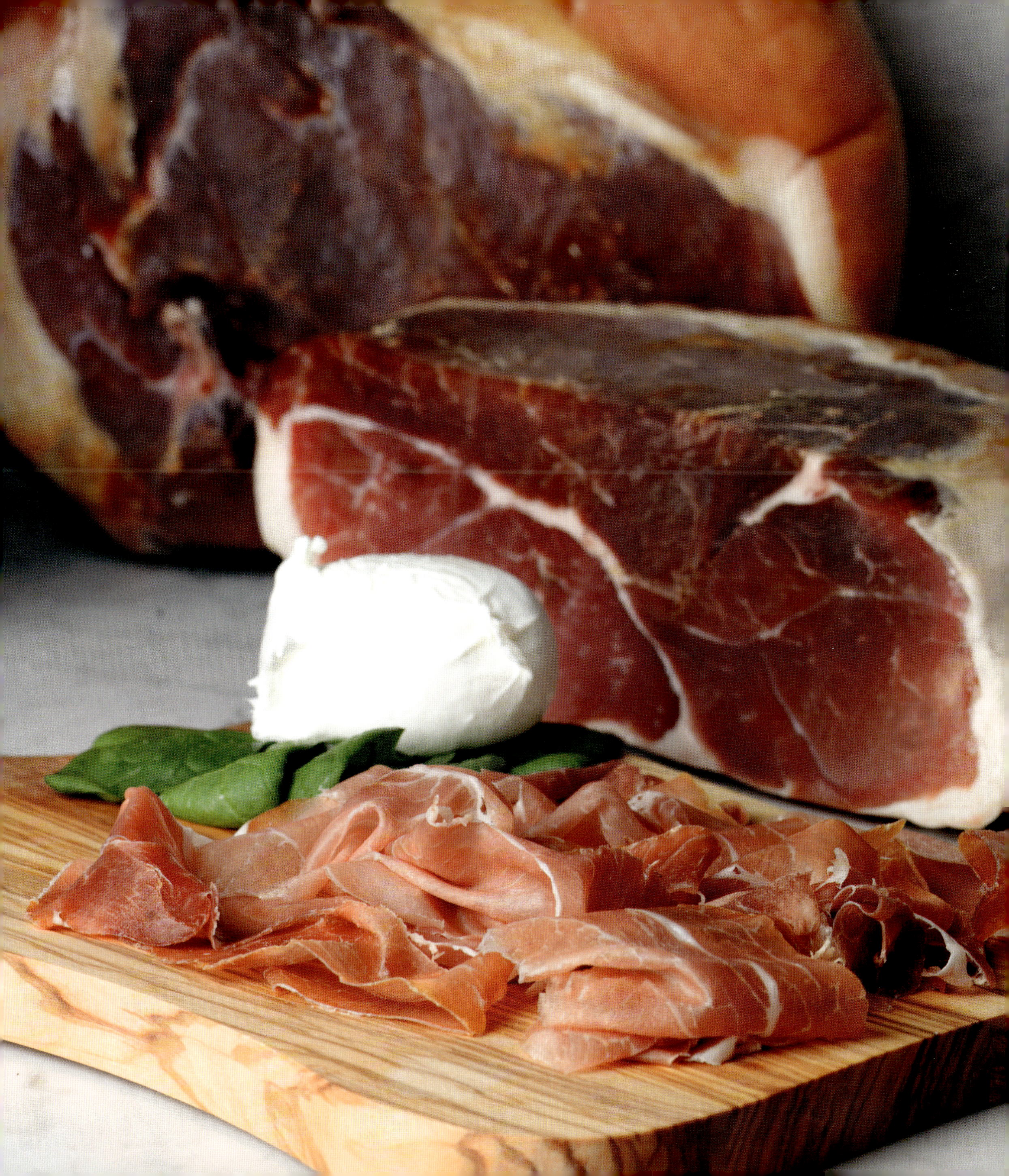

Prosciutto Nero dei Nebrodi

Sicilia

Serves 1
2 ounces prosciutto nero dei Nebrodi
3 fresh figs
4½ ounces stracciatella di burrata
3 to 4 baby spinach leaves

Slice the prosciutto ¼ to ½ inch thick, trimming and discarding the rind but not the fat, which is a delicacy and exquisitely sweet. Arrange the prosciutto on a plate next to the figs. Place the stracciatella di burrata in a glass bowl and serve on a bed of spinach arranged next to the prosciutto and figs.

Suggested Wine Pairing

Cerasuolo di Vittoria
Producer:
Gulfi
Grape:
Nero d'Avola, Frappato
Region:
Sicily

The traditional pairing of prosciutto and figs with mozzarella di bufala Campana DOP is a must on our summer menu, because the delicate flavor of the cheese contrasts beautifully with that of delicious fresh figs available in early summer, as well as with the fine flavor of prosciutto nero dei Nebrodi, which is protected by Slow Food. Only a few have had the pleasure of tasting this special prosciutto because it is produced in small amounts and is really only eaten locally and by the family members of those who make it. We're so pleased that we can serve this prosciutto, which is made using pigs from an heirloom breed long famous in Sicily. These pigs were bred by the ancient Greeks and yield particularly flavorful and nutritious meat that's low in fat. Bred in a wild or semi-wild state, the pigs feed on acorns and beech tree berries. One month before they're slaughtered they're fed broad beans and grains, which inject the meat with particular aromas and flavors. Haunches are initially salted for a few days, then dried and preserved under salt and spices in a wooden cupboard for twenty to forty more days. During this period, the meat is turned frequently. Finally, it's covered with finely ground black pepper, red pepper, oregano, and garlic and dried further. No additives are used. The prosciutto is cured in brine from fifteen to forty days and then is aged in a special building with a tile roof for another few months.

Presidio Slow Food

Producer: Salumificio Agostino Sebastiano, *Mirto*
(Province of Messina)

Mozzarella Bar · Some Obvious Pairings and Some Less Obvious Ones

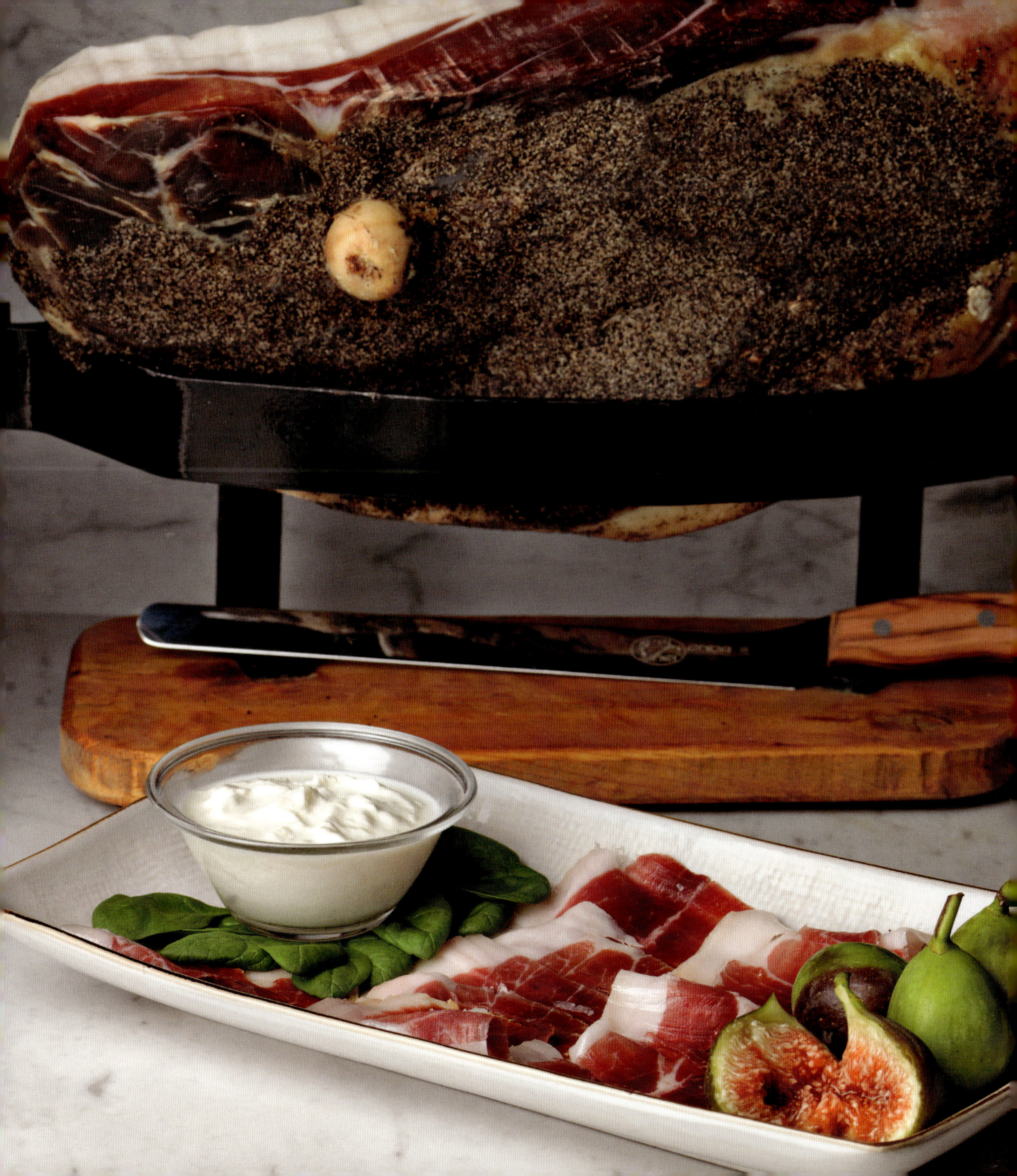

Mortadella di Prato

Toscana

Serves 1

2½ ounces mortadella di Prato kept at room temperature
4½ ounces mozzarella di bufala Campana DOP
2 tablespoons baked black olives, pitted
2 grape tomatoes

Slice the mortadella di Prato ¼ to ½ inch thick and arrange it on a plate. Drain the mozzarella and arrange it on a bed of spinach. Garnish with the olives and tomatoes.

Suggested Wine Pairing

Mongrana IGT
Producer:
Querciabella
Grapes:
Sangiovese, Cabernet Sauvignon, Merlot
Region:
Tuscany

In Tuscany, mortadella was invented to make good use of all the parts of a butchered pig. Rather than simply discarding what remained after the choice cuts of meat had been obtained and top-shelf local salami had been created, in the early twentieth century, people in Prato and some other areas in the province of Pistoia started stuffing the meat into casings, curing it with spices and liquors, and then boiling it in water. During the postwar period, this local product all but disappeared, but about thirty years ago a *salumeria* in Prato began making it again.

Today, mortadella di Prato is a cooked, refined pork product, typically dark pink in color—due to the alchermes liquor used to make it—with delightfully exotic spicy aromas.

A Slow Food Presidium created guidelines for those who currently produce mortadella so that they use certain standard techniques while each maintains its own special character. Among other things, the guidelines dictate that the pigs used must be bred in Italy and may not be raised on genetically modified feed; they also restrict the use of preservatives, provide the acceptable ingredients for the curing mixture (garlic, mace, pepper, coriander, cinnamon, clove, alchermes), and require that natural intestines be used as casings.

Like all cooked pork products, mortadella di Prato is delicious straight out of the pot, but reheating it later mutes its flavor, so if you're not fortunate enough to buy mortadella so fresh that it is still warm from being cooked, you're better off eating it at room temperature.

Mortadella di Prato goes perfectly with figs, preferably the Dottato variety (from Carmignano), and the bread from Prato known as *bozza*.

Presidio Slow Food

Producer: Salumificio Fratelli Conti, *Prato*
(Province of Prato)

Mozzarella Bar · Some Obvious Pairings and Some Less Obvious Ones

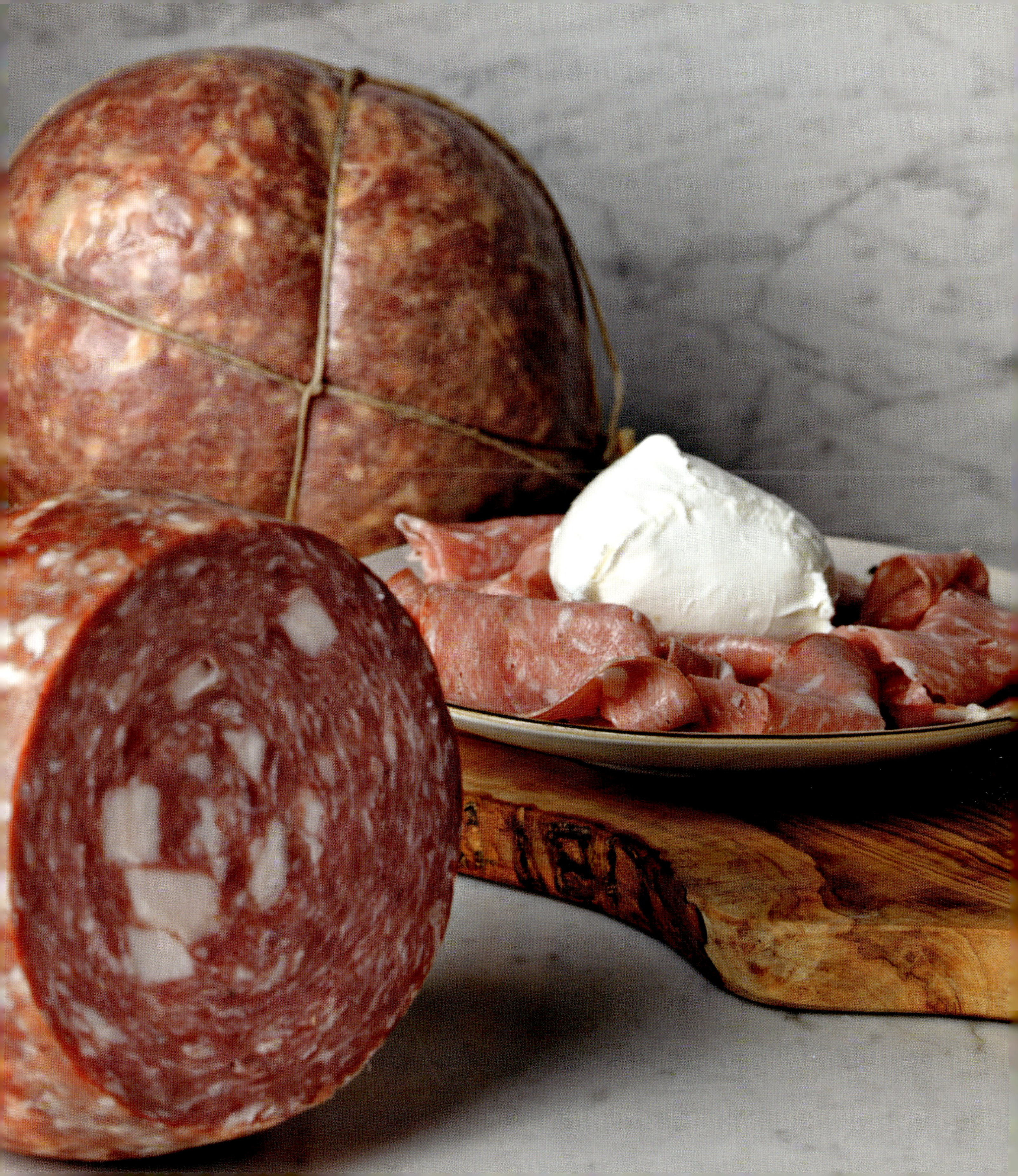

Bresaola di Fassona

Piemonte

Serves 1

2½ ounces bresaola di Fassona
4½ ounces mozzarella di bufala Campana DOP
3 to 4 baby spinach leaves
Extra-virgin olive oil to taste
Juice of ½ lemon

Slice the bresaola di Fassona ¼ to ½ inch thick and arrange it on a plate. Drain the mozzarella and serve on a bed of spinach. Whisk the oil and lemon juice in a small bowl and serve on the side.

Suggested Beer Pairing

Chiara
Producer:
L'Orso Verde
Description:
Malt beer made from wheat, barley, and hops
Region:
Lombardy

Bresaola is cured beef from the Valtellina area. We serve bresaola made from the meat of very fine Piedmontese Fassona breed cattle. This cattle comes from the cross-breeding with the zebu cattle of Pakistan, though how and why these animals got to Italy remains a mystery. Genetic mutation has made this breed uniquely muscular. Indeed, its name is a reference to muscle fasciae and is a word taken from the French and altered by Piedmontese dialect.

Bresaola di Fassona is tender, lean, and tasty. It is made with salt, ground pepper, and natural aromatics, then dried and aged from four to eight weeks. During the aging process it loses much of its weight as liquid evaporates, making the flavor more concentrated. Each producer has its own special recipe, but all comply with the requirements that allow the product to be granted IGP status, meaning that it is a product of protected geographical indication.

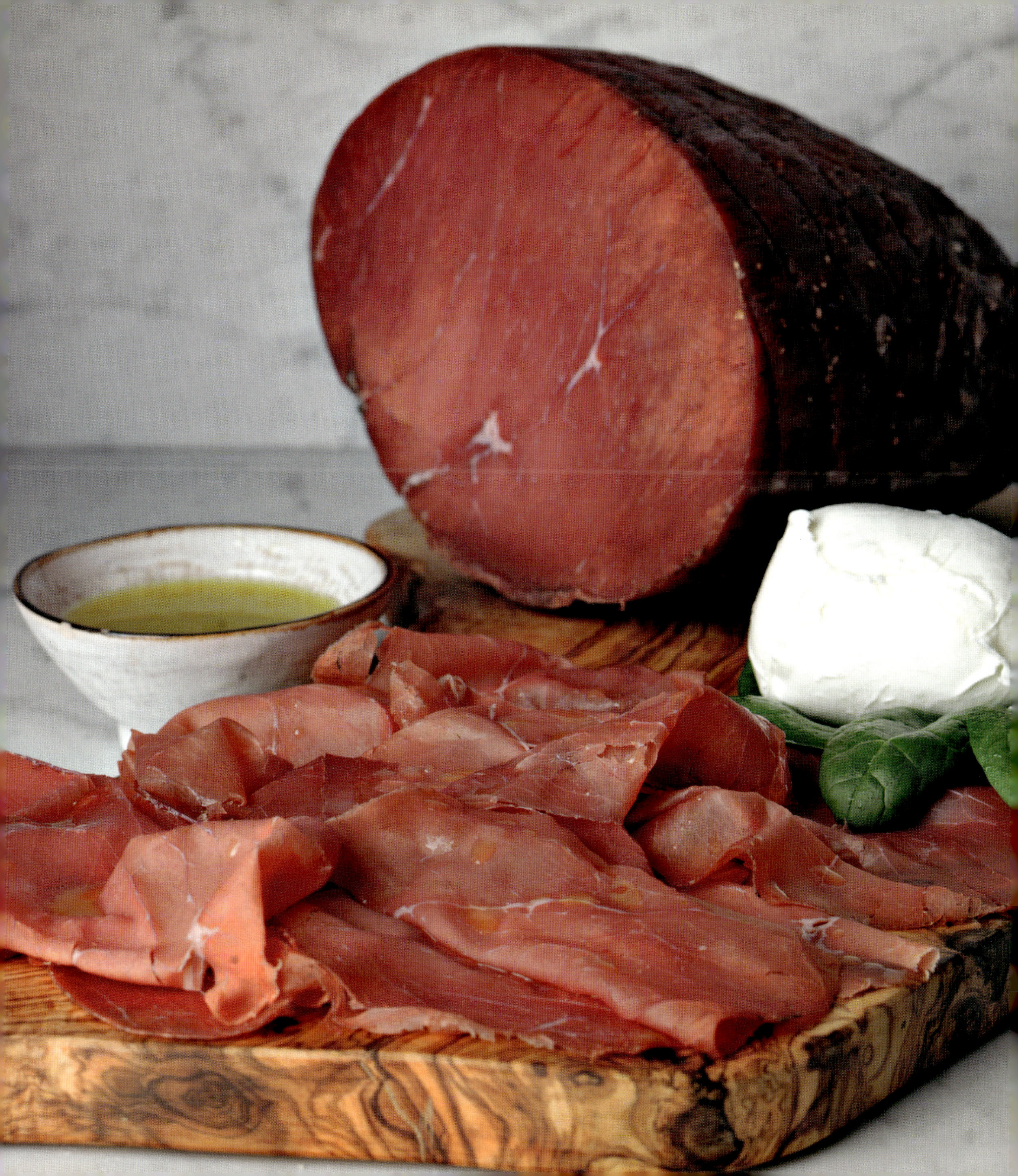

Soppressata di Gioi

Campania

Serves 1

2 ounces soppressata di Gioi
4½ ounces mozzarella di bufala Campana DOP
3 to 4 baby spinach leaves
2 tablespoons baked black olives, pitted
2 grape tomatoes

Peel the casing off of the soppressata and discard, then slice ¼ to ½ inch thick. Arrange the slices of salami on a plate and serve with the mozzarella on a bed of spinach. Garnish with the olives and tomatoes.

Suggested Wine Pairing

Aglianico del Vulture
Producer:
D'Angelo
Grape:
Aglianico
Region:
Basilicata

The Compendio di Agricoltura Pratical (Compendium of Practical Agriculture) published in 1835 frequently references soppressata di Gioi and discusses its long history and the unique technique employed, namely larding, which is used to soften meat with little or no fat of its own.

Choice pork cuts—chops, thighs, loins, and shoulders—are used to make soppressata di Gioi, a raw-pressed salami. Red pepper and fennel seed are used as well.

The carefully blended mixture rests for about ten hours and is then stuffed into natural intestine casings. A strip of fat the length of the casing is placed in the center. This not only looks striking, but helps keep the mixture moist during the aging process, which tends to dry out meat. The aging phase, which may be preceded by mild smoking, takes place in a natural environment and lasts forty to forty-five days.

For longer preservation, the salami is soaked in olive oil or lard. Soppressata di Gioi is shaped like a loaf. Its red-brown color is accentuated by the contrast with the marblelike white lard in its interior. This soppressata has an intense and aromatic fragrance, but the mineral and smoked notes are tempered enough that spicy, musky nuances can also be detected. It has a rich and long-lasting flavor with a chestnut aftertaste.

Presidio Slow Food

Producer: Piccolo Salumificio Gioi, *Gioi (Province of Salerno)*

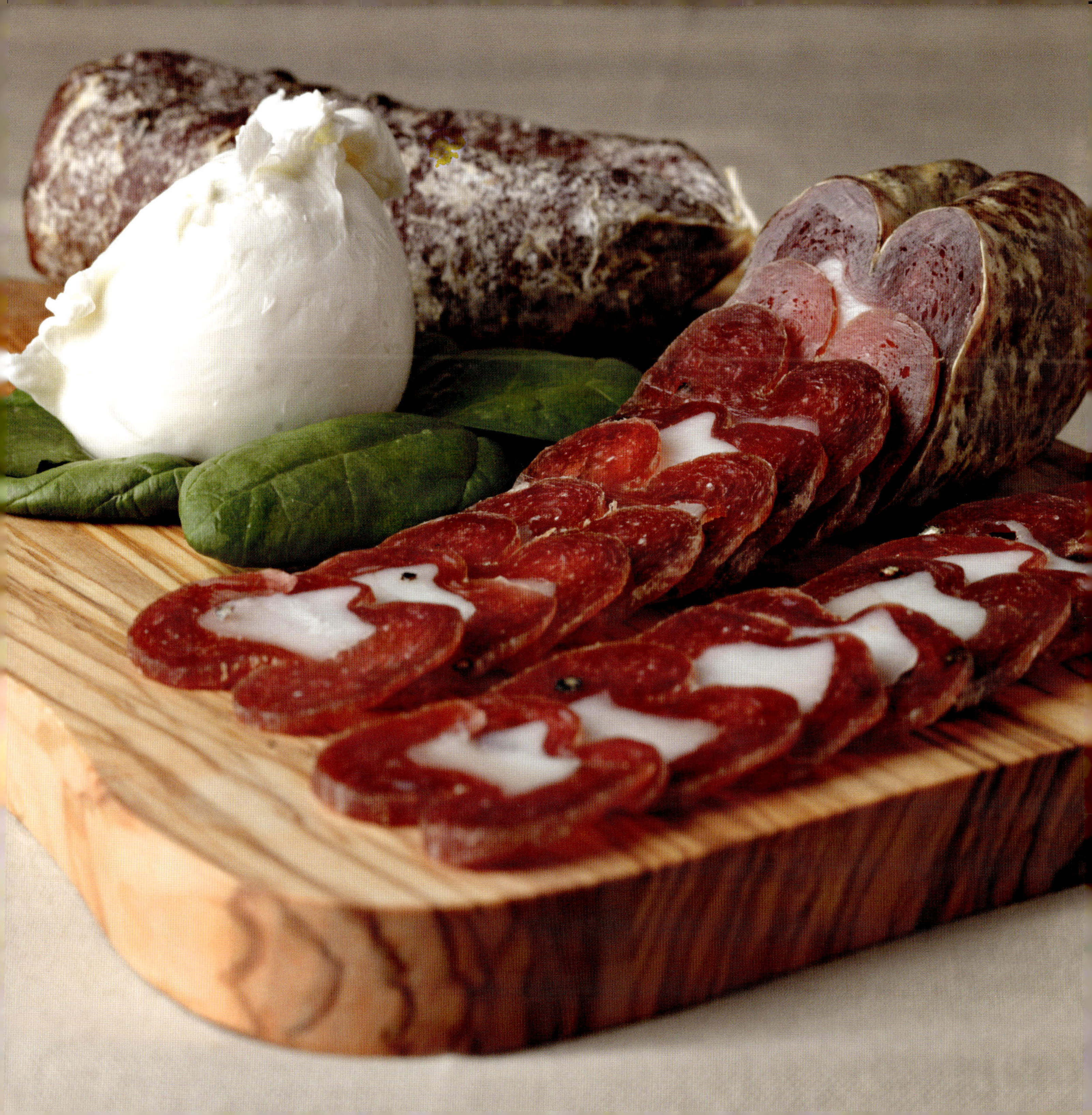

Ciauscolo di Visso

Marche

Serves 1

1 large or 2 small tigelle flatbreads
2 ounces ciauscolo di Visso
4½ ounces smoked mozzarella di bufala Campana DOP
3 to 4 baby spinach leaves
2 tablespoons Leccine olives, pitted
2 cherry tomatoes

Heat the tigelle in a nonstick pan, turning once (alternatively, use a toaster), and then spread with the ciauscolo. Arrange the tigelle and ciauscolo on a plate. Serve with the mozzarella on a bed of baby spinach, garnished with the olives and tomatoes.

Suggested Wine Pairing

Chardonnay
Producer:
Planeta
Grape:
Chardonnay
Region:
Sicily

Ciauscolo di Visso is an Italian product with IGP status, which means that it's a product of protected geographical indication. But ciauscolo di Visso bears another label: it is an official *prodotto della montagna*, meaning that it comes from areas geographically defined as mountainous, such as Pievetorina, Visso, Camerino, and Matelica. This salami's most notable feature is that it is spreadable. It is made according to a recipe and a technique handed down from generation to generation during the period when pigs are slaughtered and sausages are crafted—a celebratory time in a farming culture, as were the threshing and harvesting periods. The mixture is finely ground three times until it reaches a creamy consistency; then salt, black pepper, cooked grape must (a frequent ingredient in the Marche region), and ground garlic are added. The mixture is stuffed into a natural intestine casing and then smoked for about three weeks over a wood and juniper berry fire kept at a moderate temperature. This process mimics the process used in earlier days, when the ciauscolo was smoked by being buried in the embers in a fireplace while farmers were out working in the fields. After smoking, the meat is aged two to three months in a well-ventilated space.

The interior of ciauscolo is pink and white, and it gives off an intense, aromatic fragrance. We serve it with fragrant *tigelle*, flatbreads from Modena made with milk and flour, and our ever-present mozzarella di bufala Campana DOP.

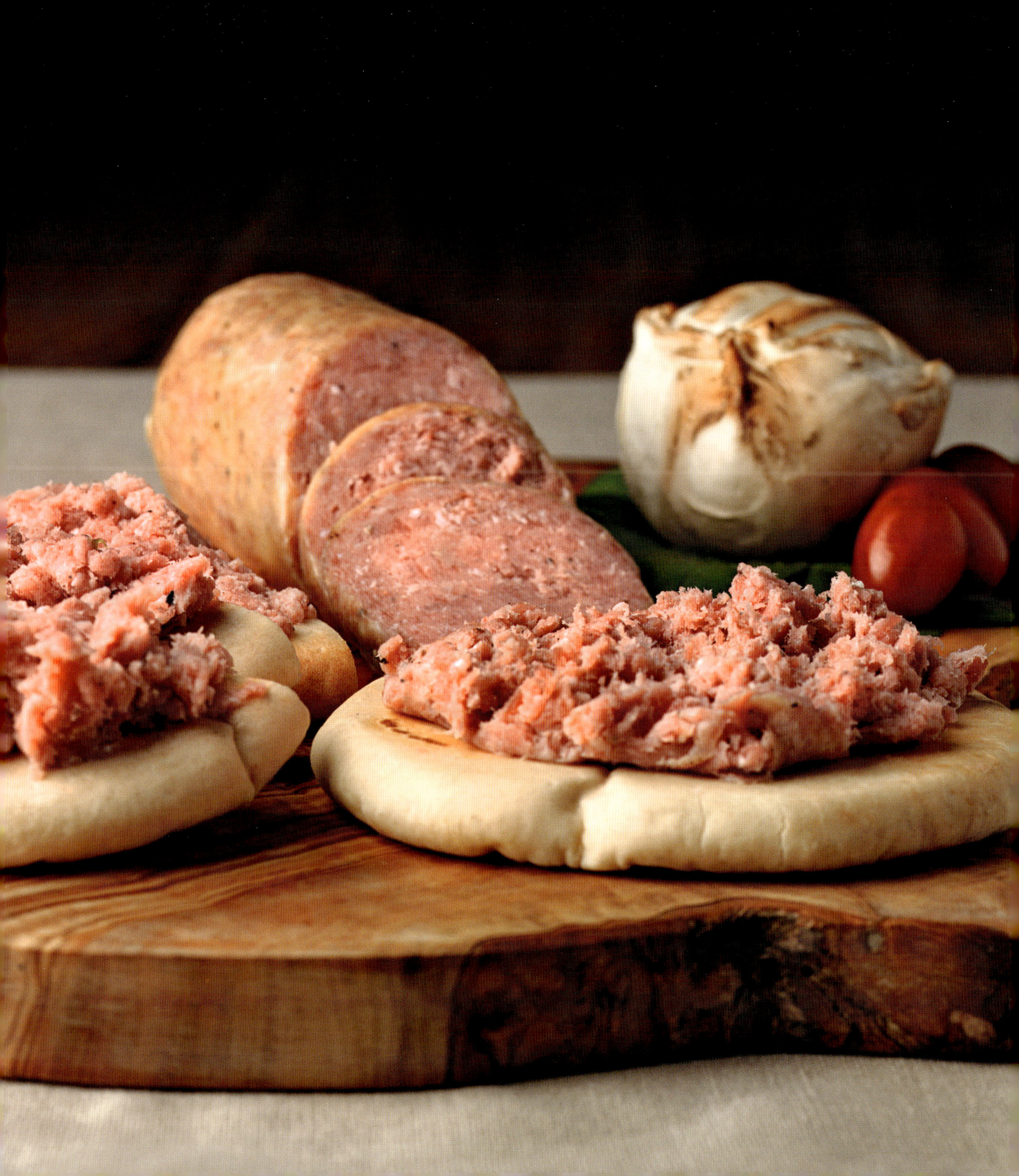

Speck di Sauris

Friuli V.G.

Serves 1

2½ ounces speck di Sauris
4½ ounces stracciatella di burrata
3 to 4 baby spinach leaves

After removing and discarding the rind from the speck, cut it into thin slices, about ¼ inch thick. Arrange the slices on a plate and serve with the stracciatella di burrata in a bowl on a bed of baby spinach.

Suggested Wine Pairing

Vinnae
Producer:
Jermann
Grapes:
Ribolla Gialla, Friulano, Riesling
Region:
Friuli

In the province of Udine we discovered an Italian specialty: speck di Sauris, a rare smoked pork product from the mountains that is the perfect accompaniment to mozzarella di bufala Campana DOP. The microclimate in Sauris, a small town in Carnia 4,000 feet above sea level, gives this traditional speck from Friuli its mild flavor and pleasantly spicy fragrance.

Speck di Sauris is made from the deboned thigh of a locally bred pig with all of the rump removed. After salting, the thigh is smoked in special rooms where aromatic shrubs such as juniper branches, along with wood and oils from beech, pine, and other resinous trees are burned to accentuate the smoky taste. The smoking phase lasts a few days, after which the slow aging phase begins. Sauris offers ideal aging conditions because of its dry climate. The speck ages for four to six months, during which it turns unusually soft and sweet.

This dense, dry speck releases its full flavor when contrasted with the mild taste of mozzarella di bufala Campana DOP.

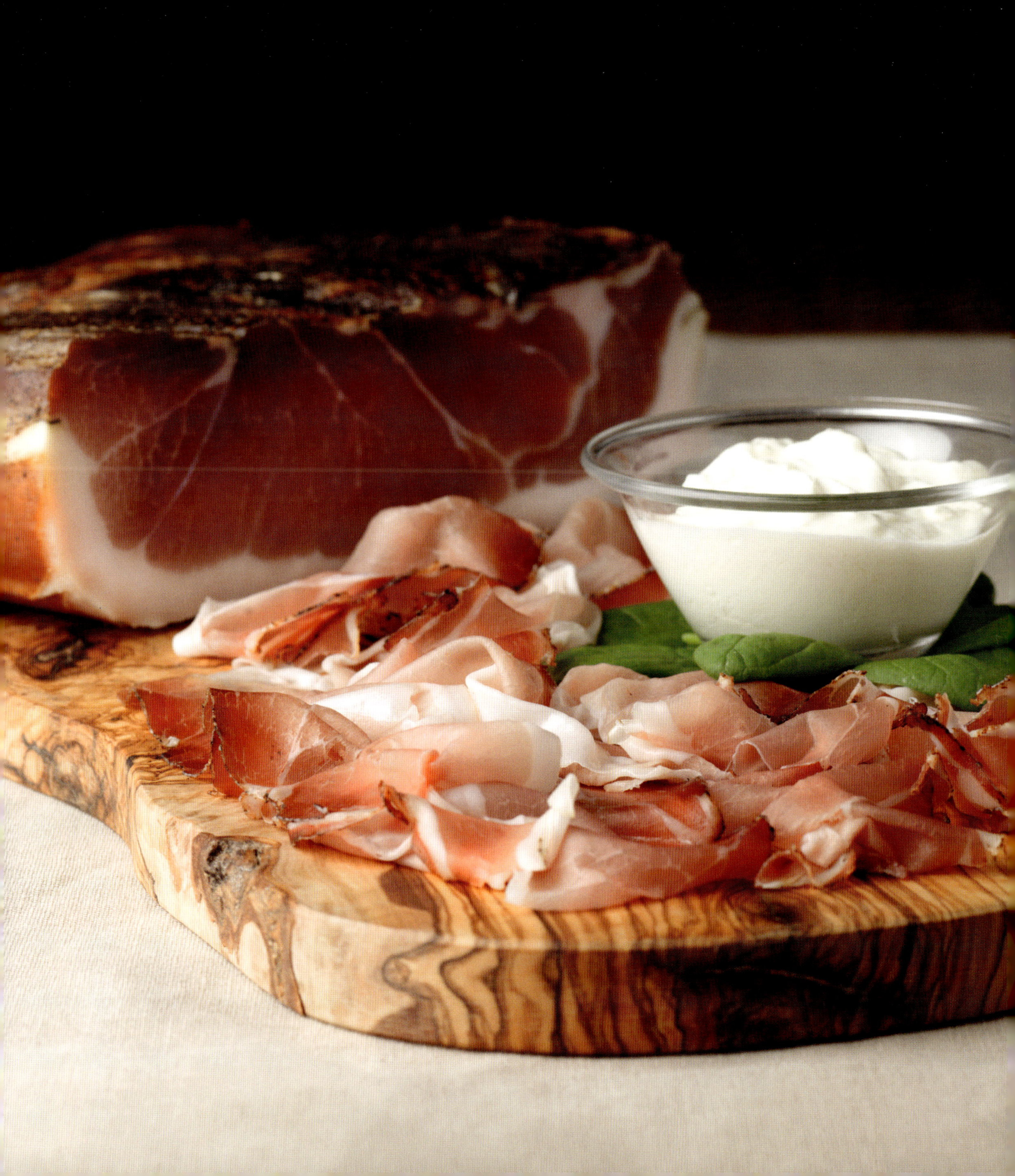

Violino di Capra della Valchiavenna

Lombardia

Serves 1

2½ ounces violino di capra della Valchiavenna
4½ ounces mozzarella di bufala Campana DOP
3 to 4 baby spinach leaves
½ teaspoon fresh lemon juice
1½ tablespoons mustard seeds
1 tablespoon honey
1½ tablespoons extra-virgin olive oil

By hand, slice the meat into ½-inch slices and arrange them on a plate. Drain the mozzarella and serve on a bed of baby spinach. In a small bowl, whisk the lemon juice and mustard seeds, then whisk in the honey and finally the oil. Serve this dressing on the side.

Suggested Wine Pairing

Quadrio Valtellina Superiore
Producer:
Nino Negri
Grape:
Nebbiolo
Region:
Piedmont

This unique cured meat made from goat thigh and shoulder really is shaped like a violin—hence its name—with the leg as the neck of the instrument and the muscular mass as its bout. Traditionally, it is passed around at the table so that each diner can slice off his or her own portion.

A typical product of the Valchiavenna area, it is protected by Slow Food, which regulates its manufacture. Traditional techniques are used to make it, and the animals used (Frisa, also known as Fontalasca, or Orobica breed goats, hybrid goats, or mountain goats) must be raised in a semi-wild state in the province of Sondrio. The animals are fed herbs and wild plants from the mountain pastures, supplemented solely with ground corn and bran. The meat is aged slowly and naturally at a constant temperature of 54°F from three months to one year. Violino was at one time aged in what were known as *crotti*, spaces dug out of rock that were used as cellars for aging meat and cheese, but which also served as a place for friends to gather and perhaps share a meal.

Violino di capra della Valchiavenna is firm but not dry. The color is so dark that it verges on burgundy, and the flavor is spicy and harks back to an earlier era, with a smoked aroma of oak, juniper, and sometimes beech wood, bay leaves, or rosemary. Each producer has his own closely guarded recipe and aging technique, so each violino has its own special taste.

Presidio Slow Food

Producer: Stefano Masanti, *Madesimo*
(Province of Sondrio)

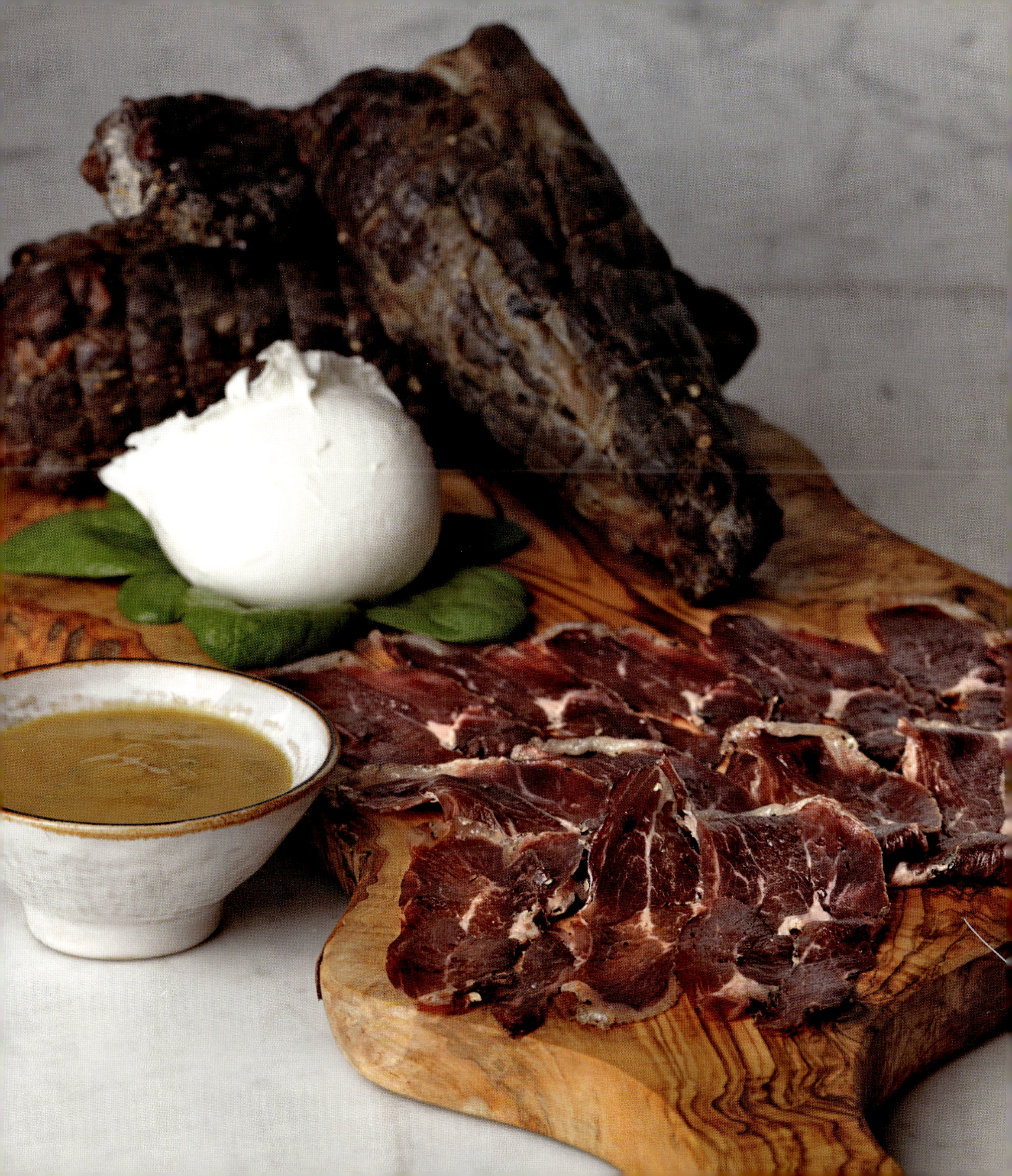

ROME,
Piazza Firenze

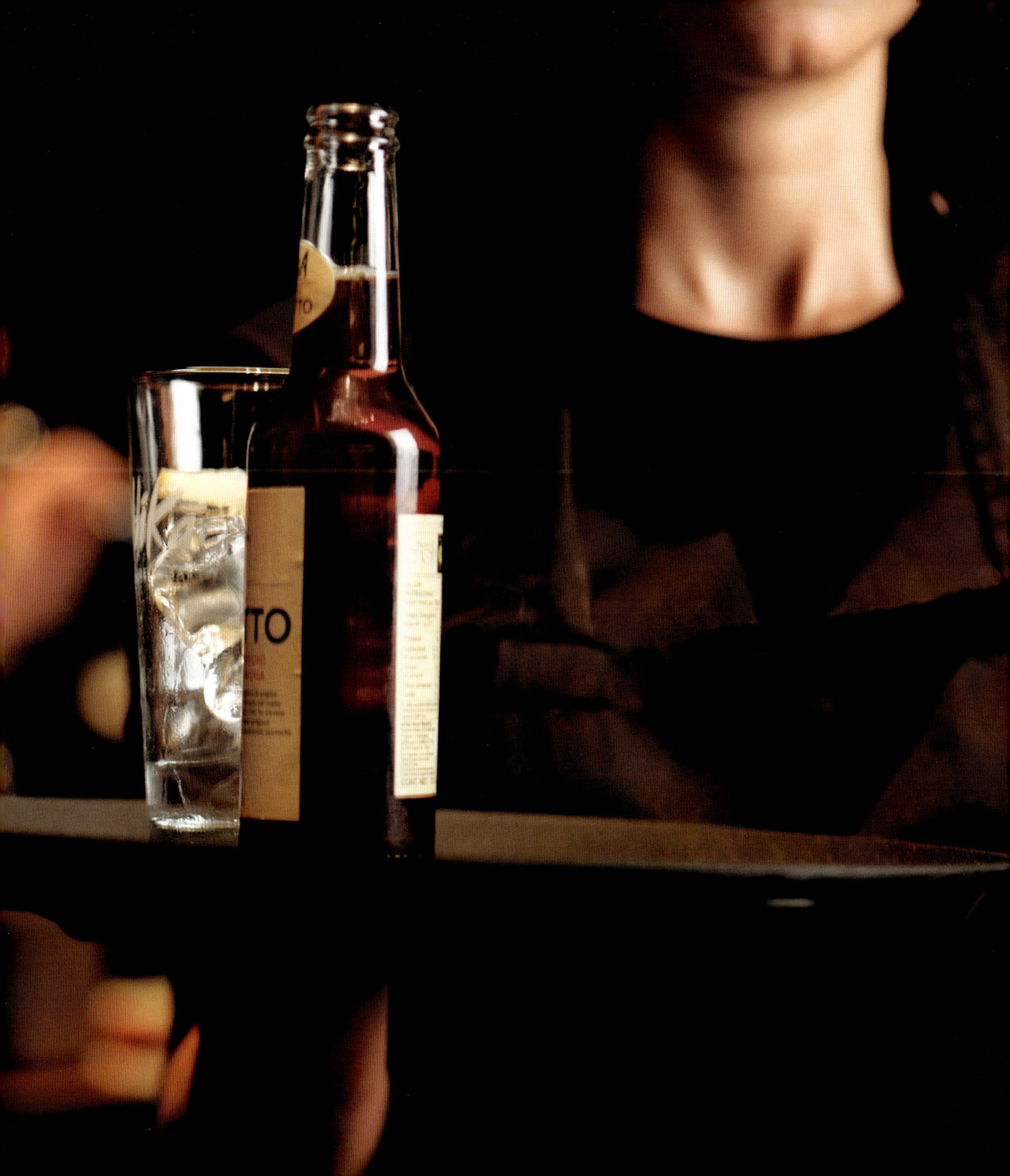

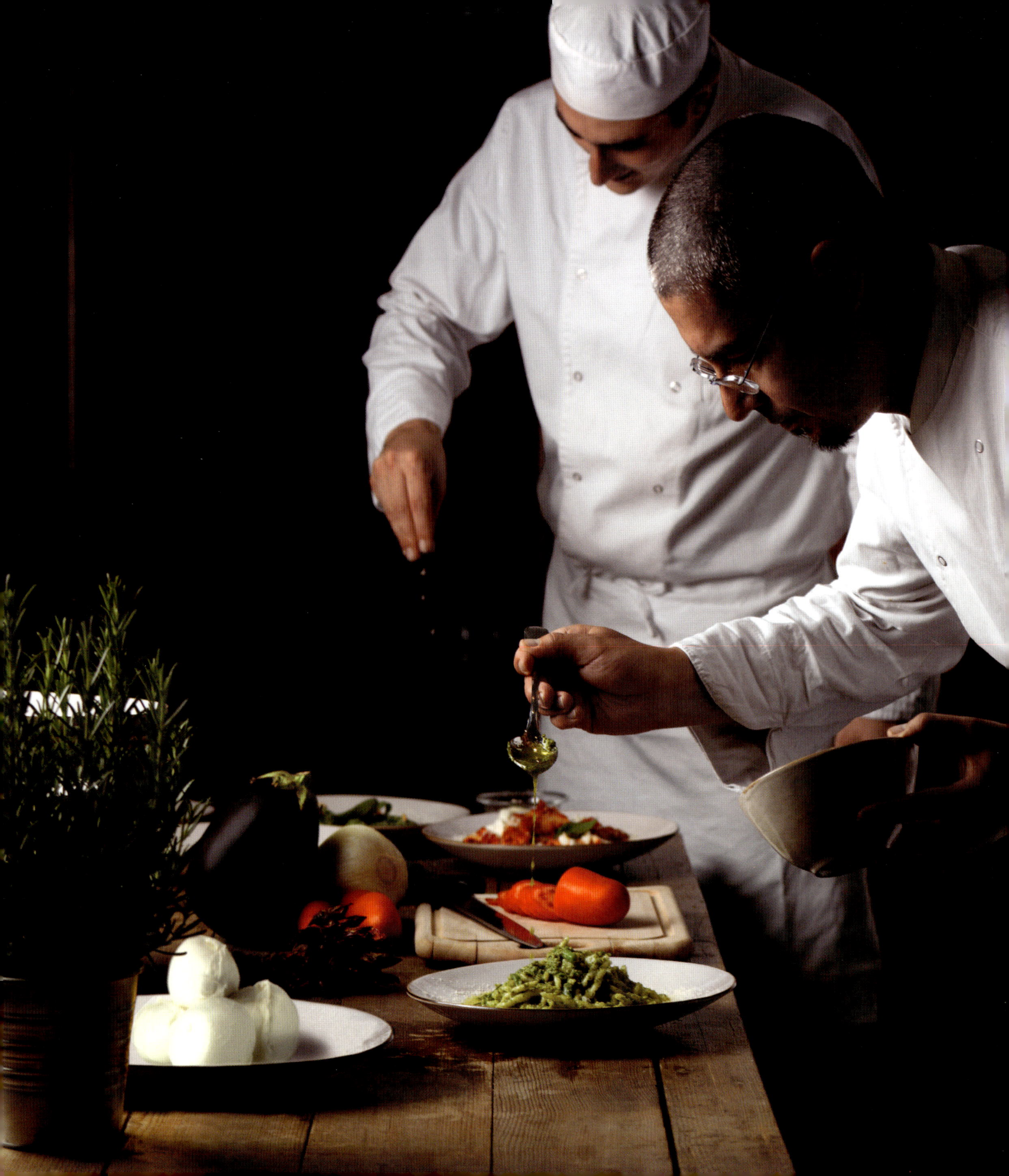

Antipasti

....

Caponata Siciliana

Ciauscolo and N'duja Crostini

Crostini with Porcini Mushrooms,
Grilled Peppers, Olives, and Capers

Eggplant Croquettes

Mozzarella in Carrozza

Potato and N'duja Croquettes

Arancini

Eggplant Parmigiana

Escarole Pie

Potato Pie

Caponata Siciliana

Rich!

Caponata is one of the signatures dishes of Sicilian cuisine. The name comes from *capone*, a local name for a type of fish that was traditionally served in the same type of sweet-and-sour sauce applied to vegetables in caponata. In our restaurants, we serve caponata with slices of paper-thin pane carasau as an antipasto, or as a side dish. The key ingredient in caponata is eggplant, specifically the Sicilian type. Look for firm eggplant with dense flesh. The dish also includes celery, olives, capers, and tomato puree, and our version incorporates raisins and two different types of nuts. Caponata is best served the day after it's made, at room temperature.

Serves 4

2 to 3 medium eggplants
Salt to taste
⅔ cup extra-virgin olive oil
1½ cups (11 ounces) tomato puree *(Reduce)*
2 tablespoons salted capers, soaked and drained
1½ cups chopped celery
2 tablespoons raisins
¼ cup sugar
3 tablespoons white wine vinegar
2 tablespoons pine nuts
2 tablespoons almonds
Fresh basil leaves to taste

Suggested Wine Pairing

Lighea
Producer:
Donnafugata
Grape:
Zibibbo
Region:
Sicily

Preparation

- Trim the eggplants and cut into ½-inch cubes. Place the eggplant in a colander set in the sink and sprinkle with salt. Allow the eggplant to rest for 1 hour, then rinse and dry thoroughly.
- Heat the oil in a pan and sauté the eggplants until golden brown. Remove from the heat.
- Combine the tomato puree, capers, celery, and raisins in a pot. Cook for 15 minutes over medium heat, then add the sugar, vinegar, pine nuts, and almonds.
- Simmer the mixture for 10 minutes, stirring occasionally, then add the eggplant and cook for 5 minutes more.
- Remove from the heat and stir in the basil.

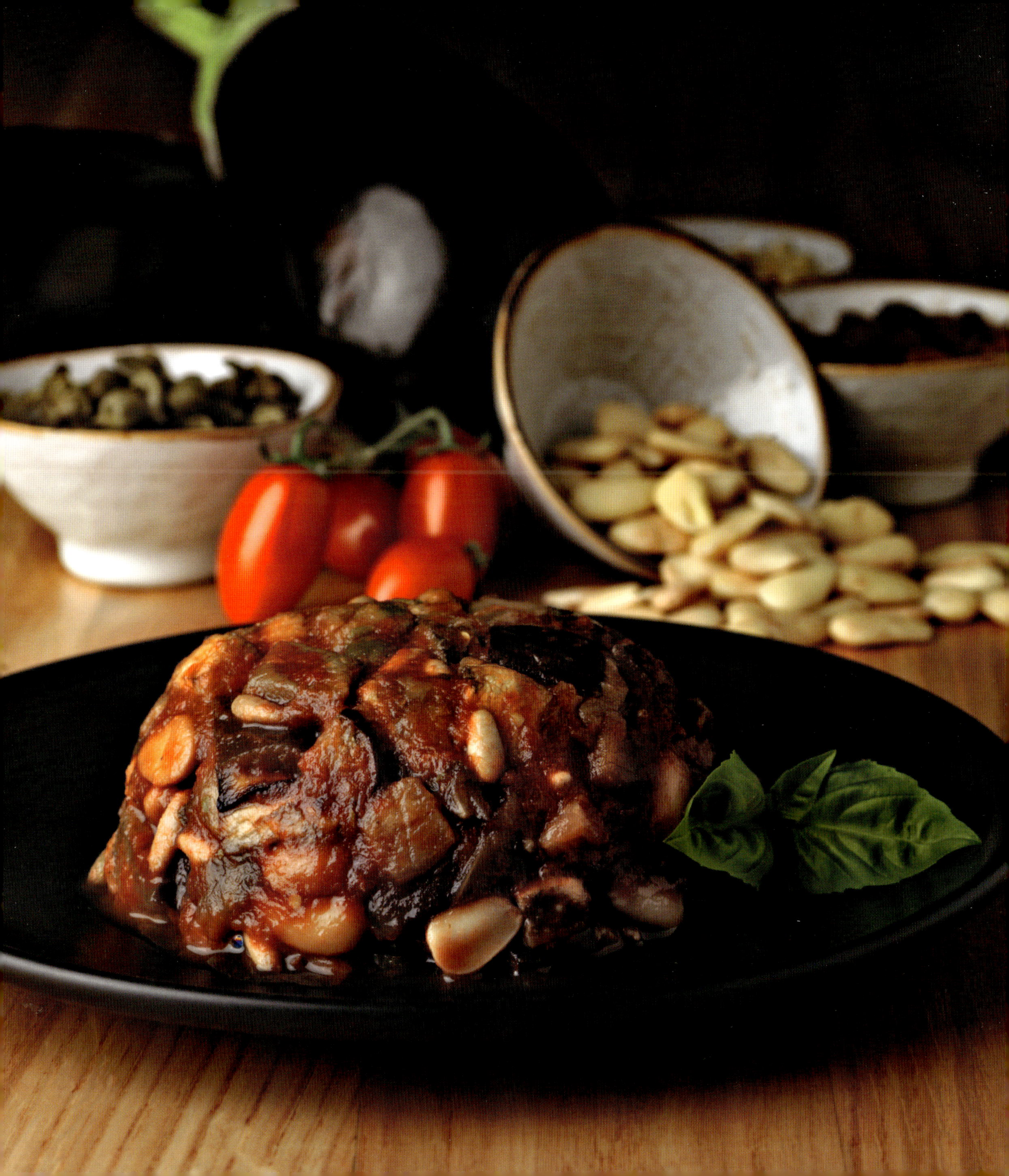

Ciauscolo and N'duja Crostini

These crostini bring out the flavor of two soft, spreadable sausages: Calabria's spicy and bright red n'duja and ciauscolo di Visso IGP, which is light pink and mildly aromatized with spices and wine.

Serves 4 to 6

2 ounces n'duja
½ cup mascarpone
2 tablespoons whole milk
5 to 6 ounces ciauscolo di Visso IGP
6 to 8 (¼- inch thick) slices Altamura bread
½ cup loosely packed arugula
⅓ cup halved grape tomatoes

Suggested Wine Pairing

Trento DOC Perlé
Producer:
Ferrari
Grape:
Chardonnay
Region:
Trentino Alto Adige

Preparation

- Remove the n'duja from its casing and put it in a small bowl with the mascarpone and the milk; stir to combine and set aside. Remove the ciauscolo from its casing and set aside.
- Grill or toast the bread.
- Spread half of the slices of toasted bread with the mascarpone and n'duja mixture and the other half with the ciauscolo di Visso. Alternate the slices on a serving platter or wooden cutting board.
- Arrange the arugula leaves and grape tomatoes on the platter.

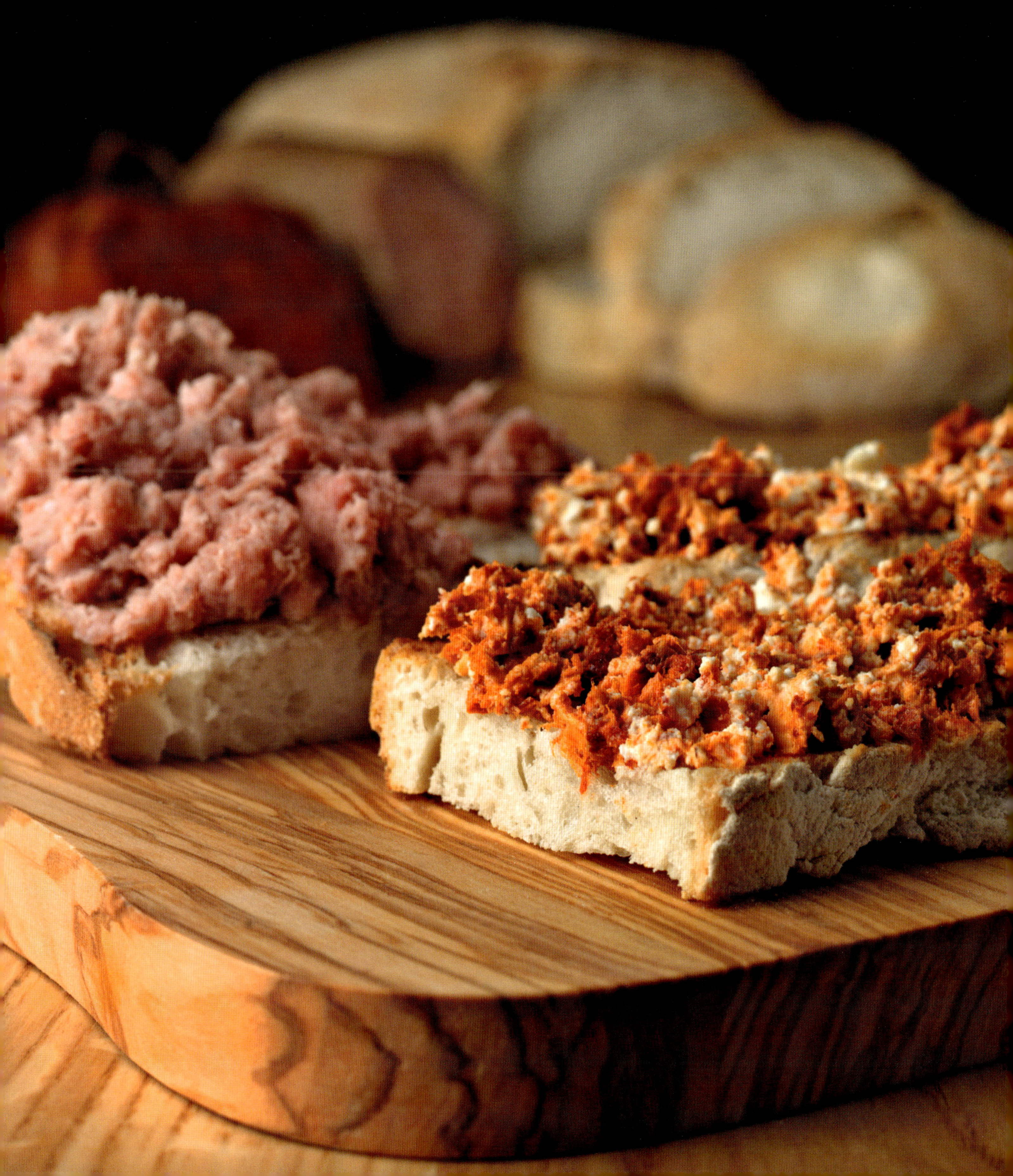

Crostini with Porcini Mushrooms, Grilled Peppers, Olives, and Capers

These vegetarian crostini are easy to prepare and are excellent served before dinner in summer or in winter. Look for elongated Carmagnola ox-horn peppers, which are sweet and particularly meaty. Taggiasca olives from Liguria and capers from Pantelleria are also an excellent choice here.

Serves 4

3 tablespoons extra-virgin olive oil
½ cup diced porcini mushrooms
Salt and black pepper to taste
Fresh thyme leaves to taste
½ cup grilled bell peppers, cut into strips
Fresh basil leaves to taste
2 tablespoons salted capers, soaked and drained
⅓ cup green olives, pitted
2 tablespoons almonds
6 to 9 (¼- inch thick) slices Altamura bread
½ cup loosely packed arugula
⅓ cup halved grape tomatoes
2 to 4 black olives, pitted

Suggested Wine Pairing

Sauvignon Blanc
Producer:
Tenuta Luisa
Grape:
Sauvignon Blanc
Region: Friuli

Preparation

- Heat 1 tablespoon of the olive oil in a small pan over medium heat. Add the mushrooms, season with salt and pepper, and sauté until soft. Stir in the thyme leaves and remove from the heat.

- Toss the pepper strips with 1 tablespoon olive oil and grill them. Toss with basil leaves and set aside.

- In a mortar and pestle or food processor fitted with a metal blade, grind the capers, olives, and almonds. Drizzle in the remaining 1 tablespoon olive oil in a thin stream while grinding. Thin with additional oil if needed to make a thick but spreadable mixture. Set aside.

- Grill or toast the bread. Spread the mushroom mixture on two or three slices of bread, the peppers on two or three slices of bread, and the olive mixture on the remaining two or three slices. Arrange the crostini on a serving platter.

- Arrange some arugula leaves, the tomatoes, and a couple of olives at the center of the serving platter. Serve the crostini warm.

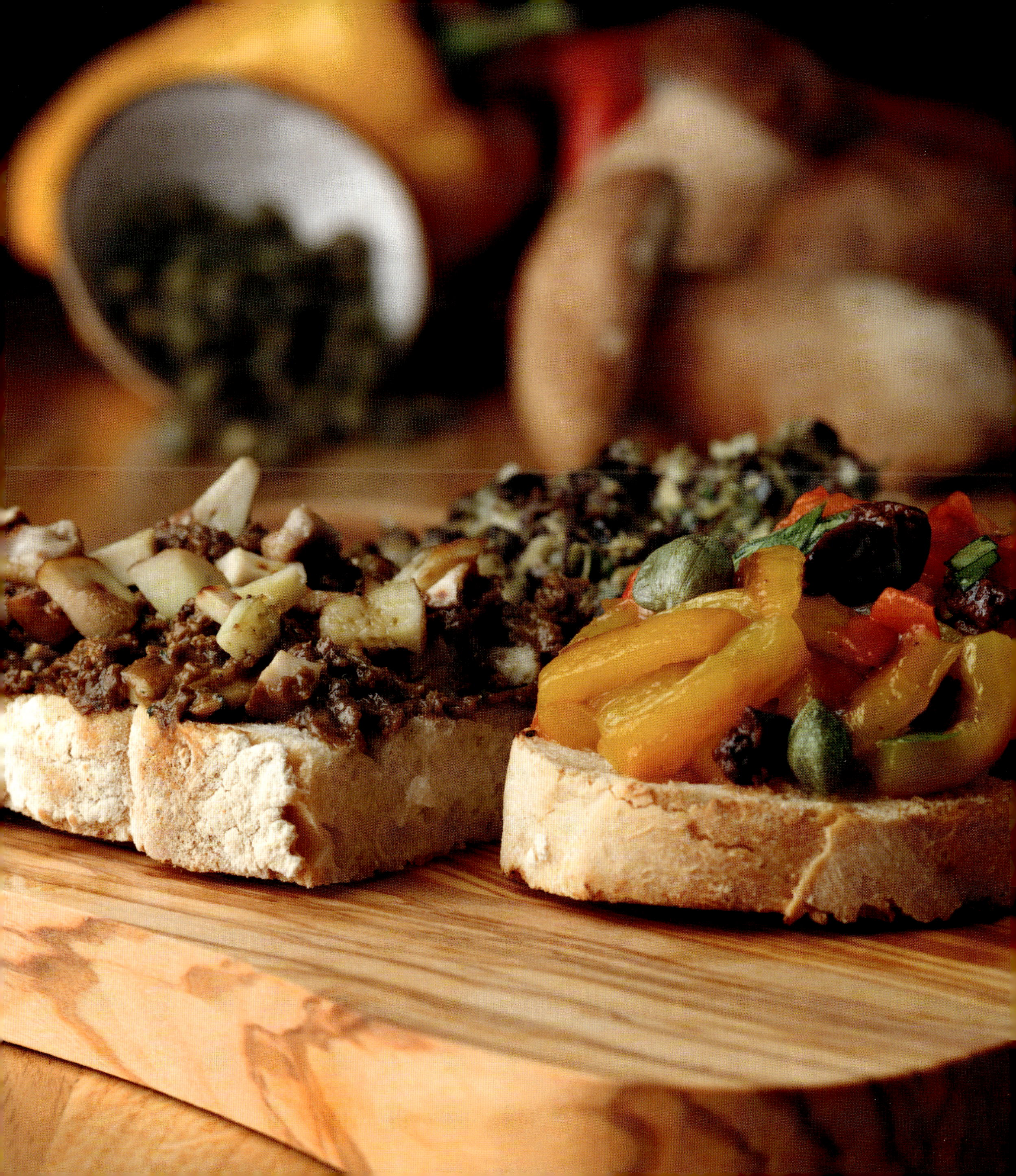

Eggplant Croquettes

These are a delightfully delicious and truly unique antipasto. You can add other aromatic herbs, such as mint, along with the marjoram if you like.

Serves 4

3 to 4 medium eggplants
4 slices stale bread
5 medium eggs
¾ cup grated pecorino Romano
Salt to taste
Fresh marjoram leaves to taste
½ cup unbleached all-purpose flour
½ cup breadcrumbs
1 quart peanut oil

Suggested Wine Pairing

Franciacorta Dosage Zero
Producer:
Ca' del Bosco
Grapes:
Chardonnay, Pinot Bianco, Pinot Nero
Region:
Lombardy

Preparation

- Preheat the oven to 400°F. Place the eggplants on a jelly-roll pan and roast until they are very soft, about 50 minutes. Let stand at room temperature for 5 minutes.

- Soak the bread in water to cover while the eggplants are cooking.

- Peel the eggplants and discard the skin. Wrap the eggplant pulp in cheesecloth or a clean flat-weave dish towel and squeeze as dry as possible.

- Transfer the eggplant pulp to a bowl. Lift the soaked bread out of the soaking water and squeeze dry, then crumble the bread into the bowl with the eggplant pulp. Lightly beat 2 of the eggs and add to the eggplant mixture, along with the grated cheese, salt, and marjoram leaves. Mix with your hands to combine well, then take a piece of the mixture about the size of a walnut and form it into a patty. Set aside on a pan or platter. Repeat with remaining eggplant mixture.

- Beat the remaining 3 eggs in a small bowl. Set the flour in another bowl, and the breadcrumbs in a third bowl. Place the peanut oil in a Dutch oven or other heavy pot with high sides and bring to a temperature of 350°F.

- Dredge each croquette first in the flour, then in the beaten eggs, and last in the breadcrumbs, then fry in the peanut oil until a deep golden brown, about 3 minutes. Use a skimmer to remove the croquettes from the oil and transfer to paper towels to drain briefly. Serve hot.

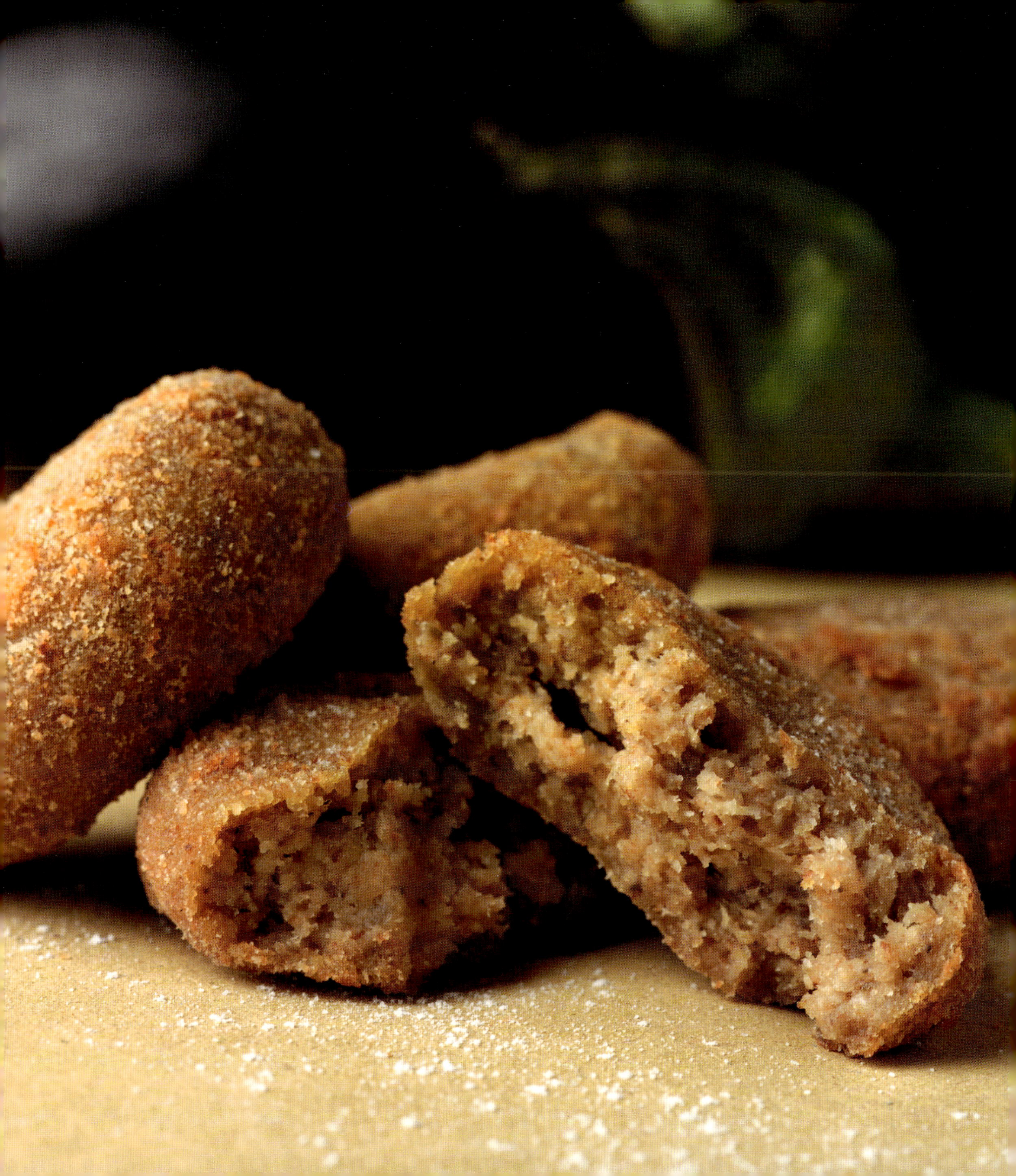

Mozzarella in Carrozza

Mozzarella in carrozza was originally a Neapolitan dish, but it is now popular all across Italy.

Serves 4

7 ounces mozzarella di bufala Campana DOP
⅓ cup shaved pecorino Romano
8 (¼- inch thick) slices Altamura bread, crusts removed
3 medium eggs
3 tablespoons whole milk
Salt to taste
Unbleached all-purpose flour for dredging
1 quart peanut oil

Suggested Wine Pairing

Roero Arneis
Producer:
Fratelli Giacosa
Grape:
Arneis
Region:
Piedmont

Preparation

- Cut the mozzarella into eight slices and allow to drain well.
- Place one slice of mozzarella and about one-fourth of the pecorino shavings between two pieces of bread and press the bread together firmly.
- Repeat with remaining bread and cheese to make 4 sandwiches total.
- Whisk the eggs with the milk and season lightly with salt.
- Place the peanut oil in a Dutch oven or other heavy pot with high sides and heat until very hot. Dredge the sandwiches in flour and then dip them in the egg mixture. Make sure the egg mixture coats the sandwiches and is well and evenly absorbed. Fry the sandwiches in the peanut oil until golden, about 3 minutes. Work in batches if necessary to avoid crowding the pot.
- Transfer the sandwiches to paper towels to drain briefly, then serve.

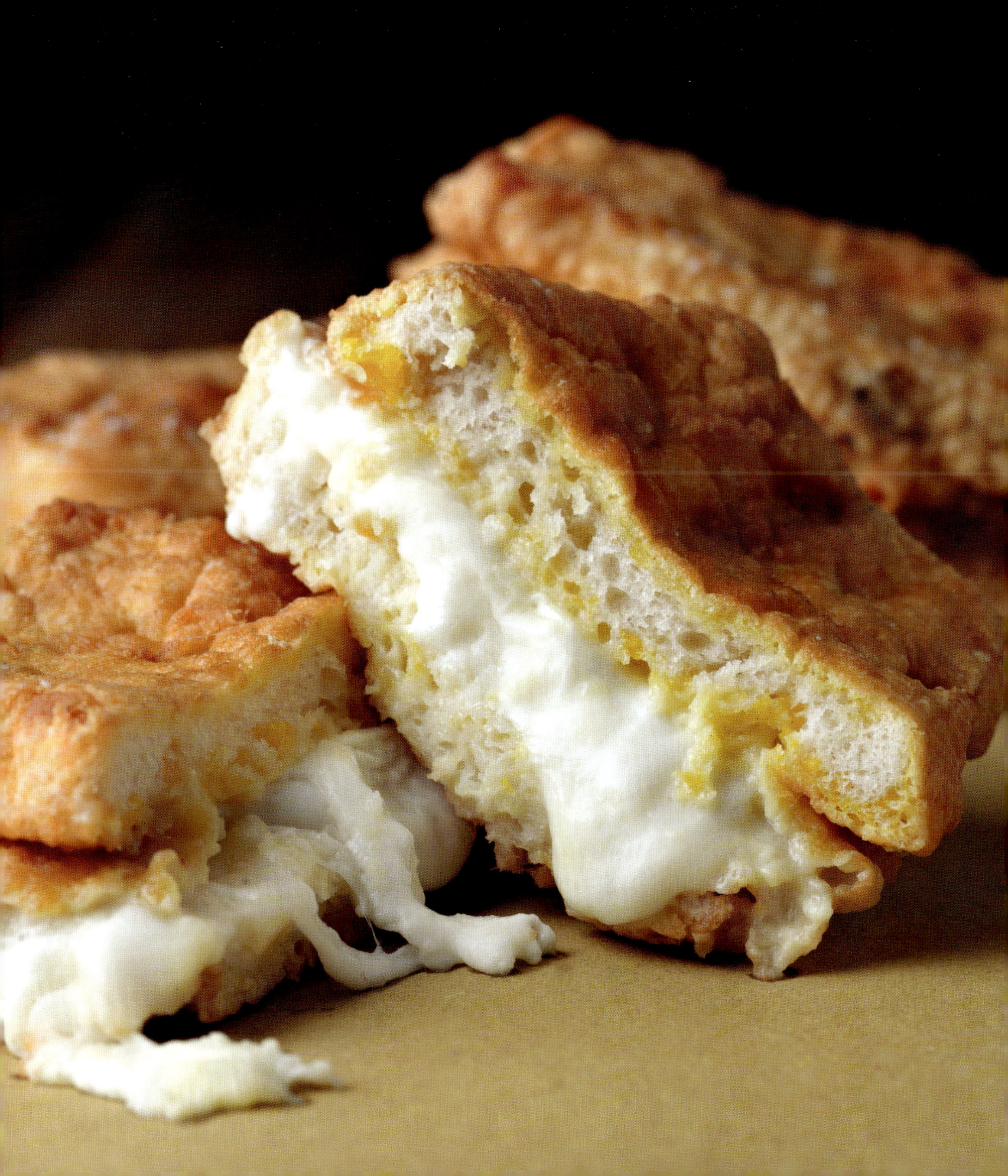

Potato and N'duja Croquettes

Potato croquettes are one of our specialties, and we make them a little spicy by adding delicious n'duja. You want to use starchy potatoes such as russet potatoes here, not the waxy type. You can substitute another type of cheese, such as fontina or Gruyère, for the Parmigiano Reggiano in the filling.

Makes about 30 croquettes

Salt to taste
2 pounds starchy potatoes, such as russet potatoes
5 large eggs
½ cup grated Parmigiano Reggiano
2 ounces n'duja, casing removed
Freshly grated nutmeg to taste
Unbleached all-purpose flour for dredging
¾ cup breadcrumbs
1 quart peanut oil

Suggested Wine Pairing

Verdicchio Classico
Castelli di Jesi
Producer:
Bucci
Grape:
Verdicchio
Region:
Marche

Preparation

- Bring several quarts of water to a boil in a large pot and season with salt. Add the potatoes (unpeeled) and boil until they are tender enough to be pierced with a paring knife. Drain and set aside to cool.

- When the potatoes are cool enough to handle, pass them through a food mill into a large bowl. (The skins will come off—simply discard them.) Add 2 eggs, the grated cheese, n'duja, and nutmeg. Season with salt. Mix until well combined.

- Take a heaping tablespoonful of the mixture and shape it between the palms of your hands into a cylinder about 3½ inches long and 1½ inches in diameter. Repeat with remaining mixture. You should have about 30 croquettes. Lightly beat the remaining 3 eggs in a bowl and arrange the flour in another bowl and the breadcrumbs in a third bowl. Dredge a croquette in flour, then dip in the beaten eggs, and finally coat in the breadcrumbs. Set aside. Repeat with remaining croquettes.

- Place the peanut oil in a Dutch oven or other heavy pot with high sides and heat to 350°F. Fry the croquettes in the peanut oil until deep golden brown, about 3 minutes.

- Use a skimmer to remove the croquettes from the oil and transfer to a plate lined with paper towels to drain briefly.

- Season the croquettes with salt and serve hot.

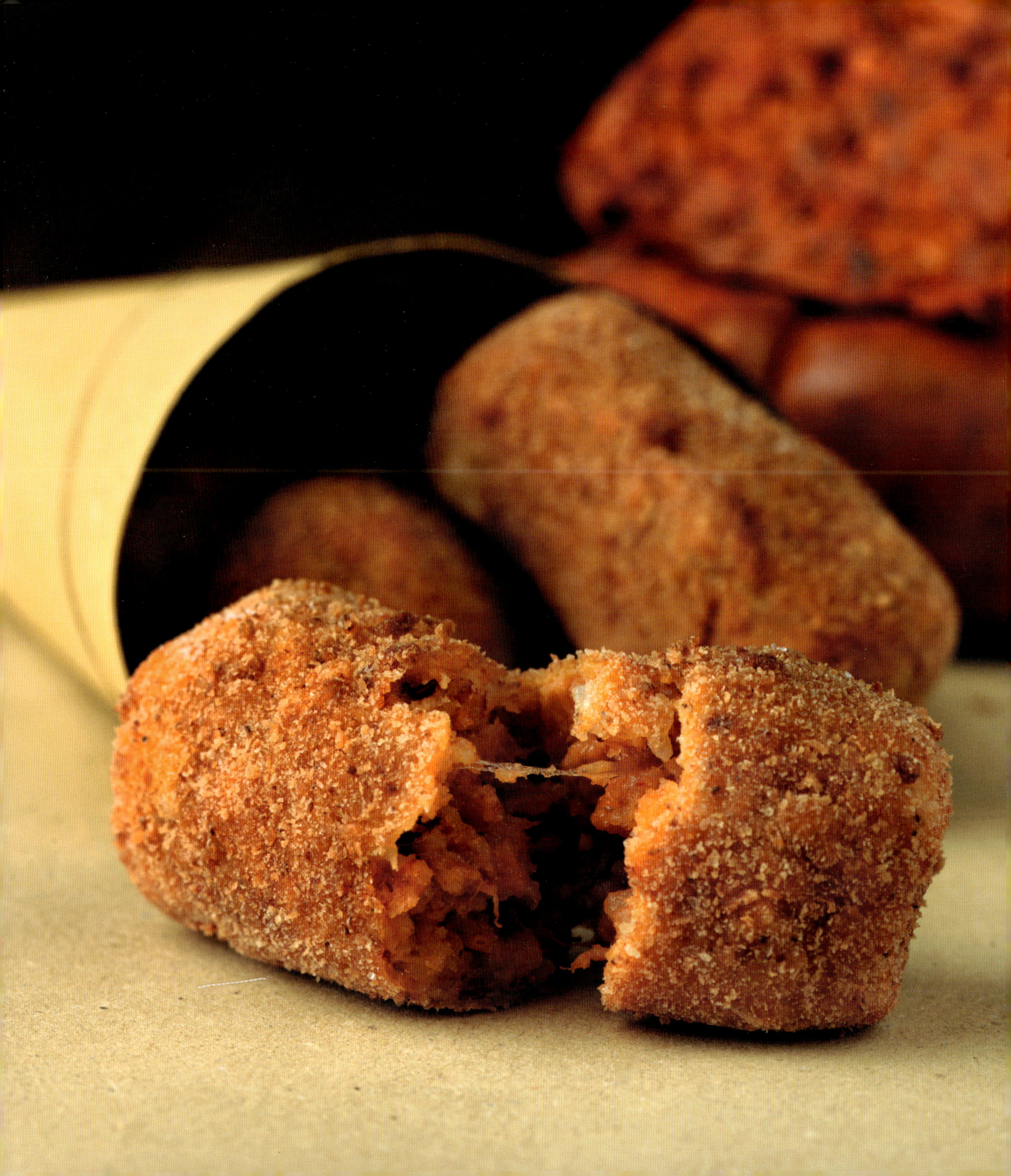

Arancini

Arancini, fried stuffed rice croquettes, are a Sicilian specialty. Their name means "little oranges," in reference to their color. Arancini are served everywhere in Sicily, always steaming hot and fragrant. They are either oval, pear-shaped, or round, and their shape is usually an indication of their filling—prosciutto, cheese, ricotta, or vegetables. For this recipe, we used a pea and Fassona beef ragù filling.

Makes 15 large or 30 small arancini

Salt to taste
3½ cups Roma rice
2 envelopes saffron
2 egg yolks, lightly beaten
½ cup grated Parmigiano Reggiano
2 tablespoons extra-virgin olive oil
9 ounces ground Fassona beef
⅓ cup white wine
1 cup (3½ ounces) peeled tomatoes, drained
Black pepper to taste
½ cup fresh young peas
7 ounces mozzarella di bufala Campana DOP
2 large eggs, lightly beaten
Flour for dredging
Breadcrumbs for dredging
1 quart peanut oil

Suggested Wine Pairing

Alhambra
Producer: Spadafora
Grapes: Catarratto, Inzolia
Region: Sicily

Preparation

- Bring a pot of slightly salted water to a boil, add the rice, and cook until soft.
- Combine the saffron, egg yolks, and grated Parmigiano Reggiano with the rice.
- Transfer the rice mixture to a platter, spread it out into a thin layer, and let cool.
- Heat the olive oil in a pan, then crumble in the ground beef and brown it. Add the wine and the peeled tomatoes. Crush the tomatoes with your spoon. Season with salt and pepper, then cook for 20 minutes over moderate heat. Add the peas and simmer until tender.
- Cut the mozzarella into ¼-inch cubes.
- Pinch off a bit of the rice mixture (the size of a golf ball), and flatten it into a thick disk in the palm of your hand. Make a well in the center and place 1 tablespoon of the meat sauce and a couple of mozzarella cubes in the well. Fold the rice around the cheese and the sauce and shape into a ball. Set aside. Repeat with remaining rice, sauce, and cheese.
- Arrange three shallow bowls, one with the 2 eggs, one with the flour, and the third with the breadcrumbs. Dip a croquette in the beaten egg, dredge in the flour, dip in the beaten egg again, and finally dredge in the breadcrumbs. Repeat with remaining croquettes.
- Place the peanut oil in a heavy pot with high sides. Use a skimmer to lower the arancini into the hot oil. Fry until deep golden brown. Drain on paper towels and serve hot.

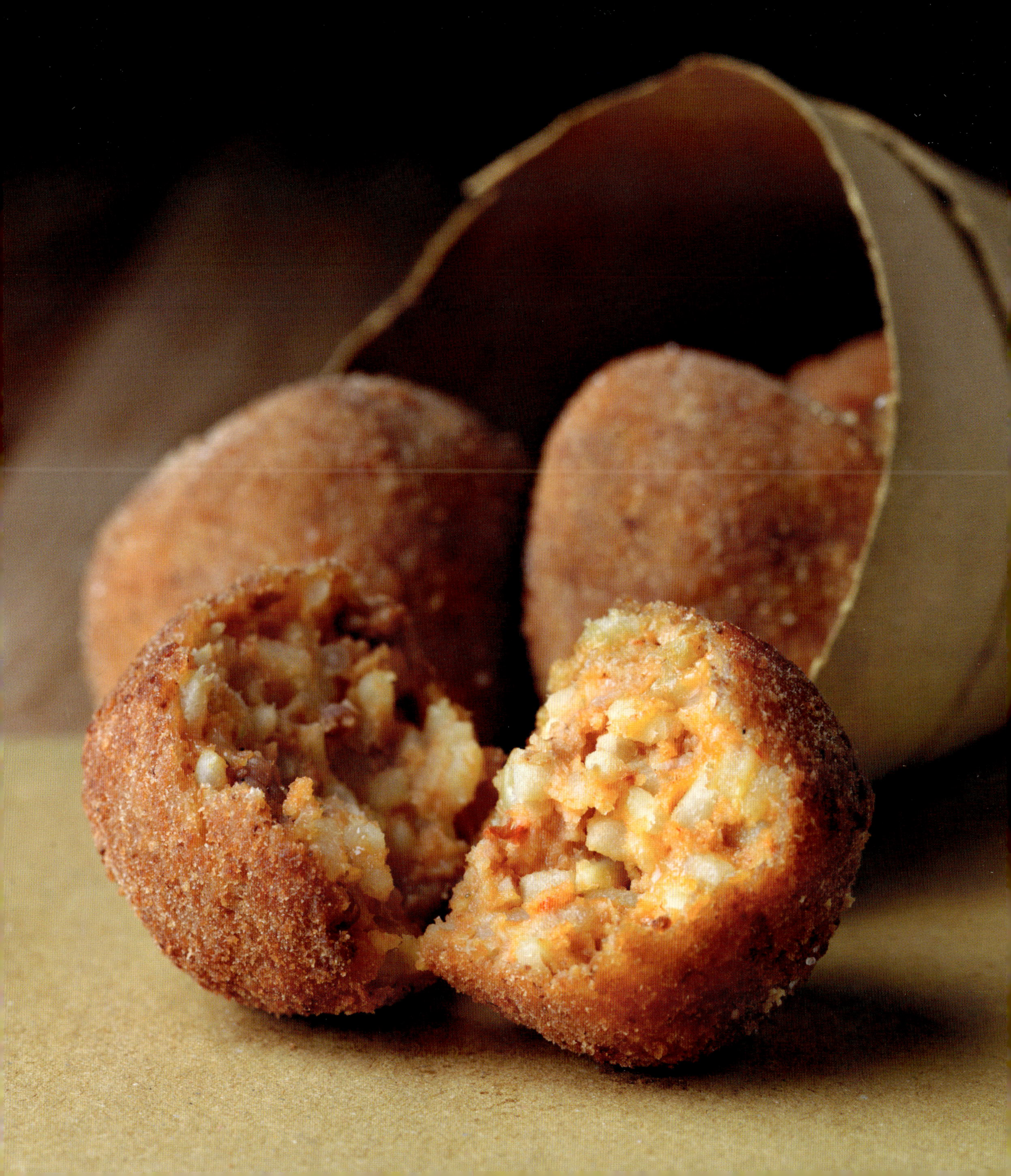

Eggplant Parmigiana

Naples, Parma, and Sicily all claim to have invented this dish. Whatever its origin may be, it is a rich, delicious dish best eaten in summer when eggplants are at their peak. Here's the light version we serve in our restaurants.

Serves 4 to 6

4 to 6 eggplants
Salt to taste
2½ cups (1 pound 5 ounces) peeled tomatoes
3 tablespoons extra-virgin oil
4 basil leaves
¼ cup grated Parmigiano Reggiano
9 ounces mozzarella di bufala Campana DOP, sliced

Suggested Wine Pairing

Monferrato Rosso Mompertone
Producer:
Prunotto
Grapes:
Barbera, Syrah
Region:
Piedmont

Preparation

- Trim and peel the eggplants and cut them lengthwise into ⅛–inch slices.
- Layer the eggplant slices in a baking pan or a container with high sides, seasoning each layer with salt.
- Cover the slices of eggplant with a weight and set aside for about 1 hour, then squeeze them by hand to eliminate as much liquid as possible. Dry with a flat-weave dish towel, then grill until soft.
- To make the tomato sauce, combine the tomatoes, oil, and basil in a pan and simmer over medium heat until the sauce is thick, about 20 minutes.
- Preheat the oven to 400°F.
- Arrange a layer of eggplant slices in a baking dish so that they cover the bottom with no gaps but don't overlap. There is no need to salt them.
- Spread about 2 tablespoons of the tomato sauce over the eggplants.
- Sprinkle some Parmigiano on top and add some slices of mozzarella. Repeat the layering in this order until all the ingredients have been used. End with a sprinkling of Parmigiano Reggiano on top.
- Bake until golden brown on top, about 40 minutes.

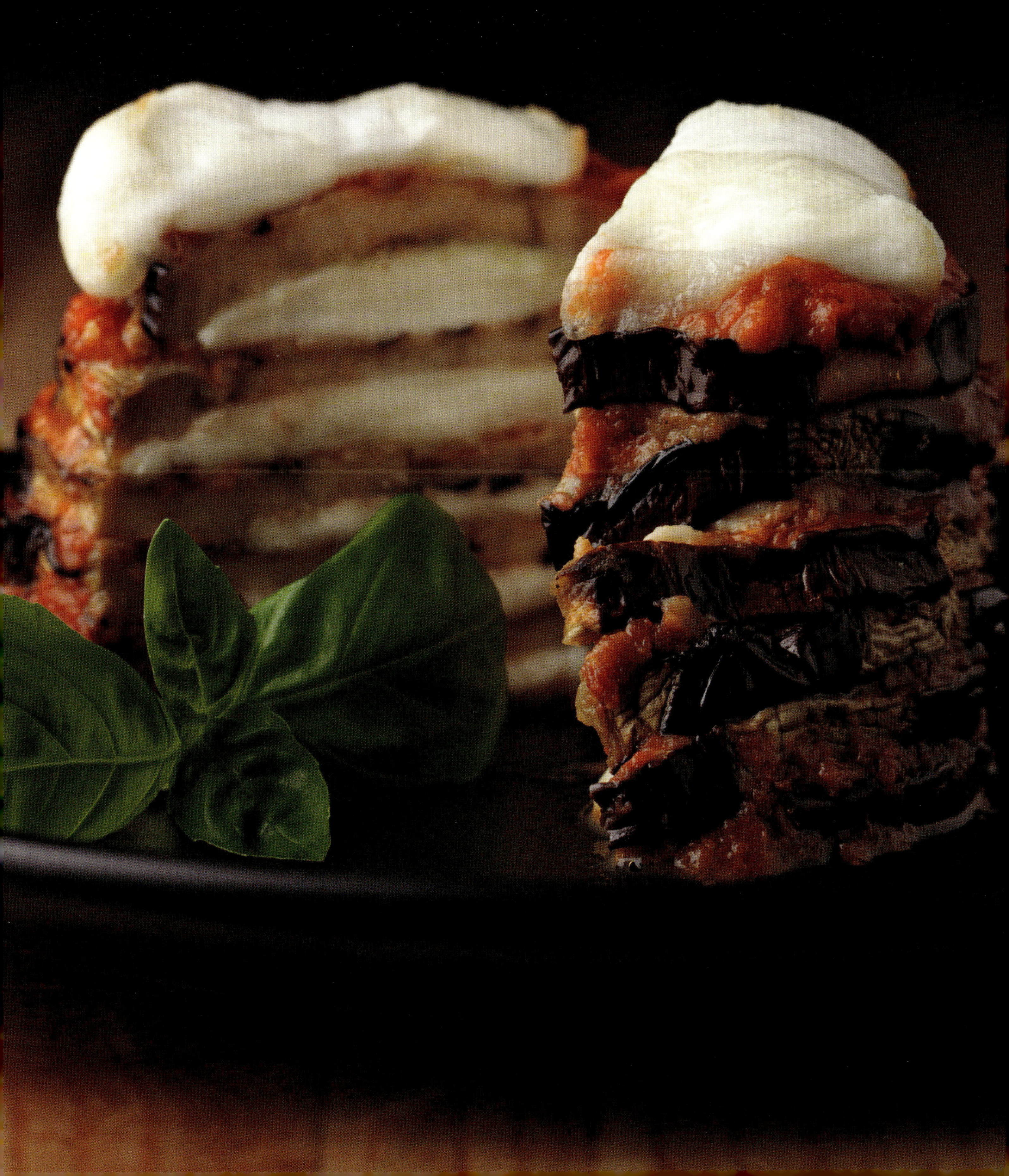

Escarole Pie

Escarole is a light and refreshing vegetable that can be eaten raw (the tender, crunchy heart is especially good this way) or cooked. Cooked escarole makes an excellent filling for pies and pizzas. A member of the chicory family, escarole has long been appreciated for its purifying properties. Its bitter taste goes very well with raisins, pine nuts, and anchovies. In this recipe we've added creamy buffalo milk ricotta to the mix. Look for escarole heads with crisp leaves that are firm and bright green.

Serves 4 to 6

4 pounds (about 4 medium heads) escarole
Salt to taste
⅓ cup extra-virgin olive oil
4 Cetara anchovy fillets, drained
¼ cup pine nuts
½ cup raisins
1 cup buffalo milk ricotta
½ cup plus 2 tablespoons breadcrumbs
12 ounces pastry dough
1 egg yolk, lightly beaten

Suggested Wine Pairing

Gavi la Rocca
Producer:
Ottosoldi
Grape:
Cortese
Region:
Piedmont

Preparation

- Preheat the oven to 350°F.
- Clean and wash the escarole and set the heart aside for the garnish. Bring a large pot of lightly salted water to a boil and add the escarole. Boil about 10 minutes until tender, then remove to a colander. Squeeze out as much water as possible. Chop and set aside.
- In a skillet, heat the olive oil over medium-high heat. Sauté the anchovies in the oil until they begin to break apart, about 1 minute. Add the pine nuts and the raisins, and as soon as the pine nuts are slightly golden, about 2 minutes, add the escarole. Sauté the escarole until the mixture is dry—any water remaining in the greens has evaporated—and the ingredients are combined, about 3 more minutes. Taste and adjust salt if necessary. Set aside to cool.
- Stir the ricotta and the breadcrumbs into the escarole mixture. The mixture should be dry, with a pastelike texture. If the mixture is too wet, add more breadcrumbs.
- Roll out about two-thirds of the pastry dough and cut to fit ramekins or other individual-sized baking dishes. Line the ramekins with the dough, then divide the escarole mixture among the pies.
- Roll out the remaining pastry dough and cut out disks the size of the top of the ramekins. Brush the rim of each bottom crust with the beaten egg yolk, then top each with a disk. Brush each top crust with the egg yolk and pierce with a fork in several places.
- Bake until the crust is golden, about 40 minutes.

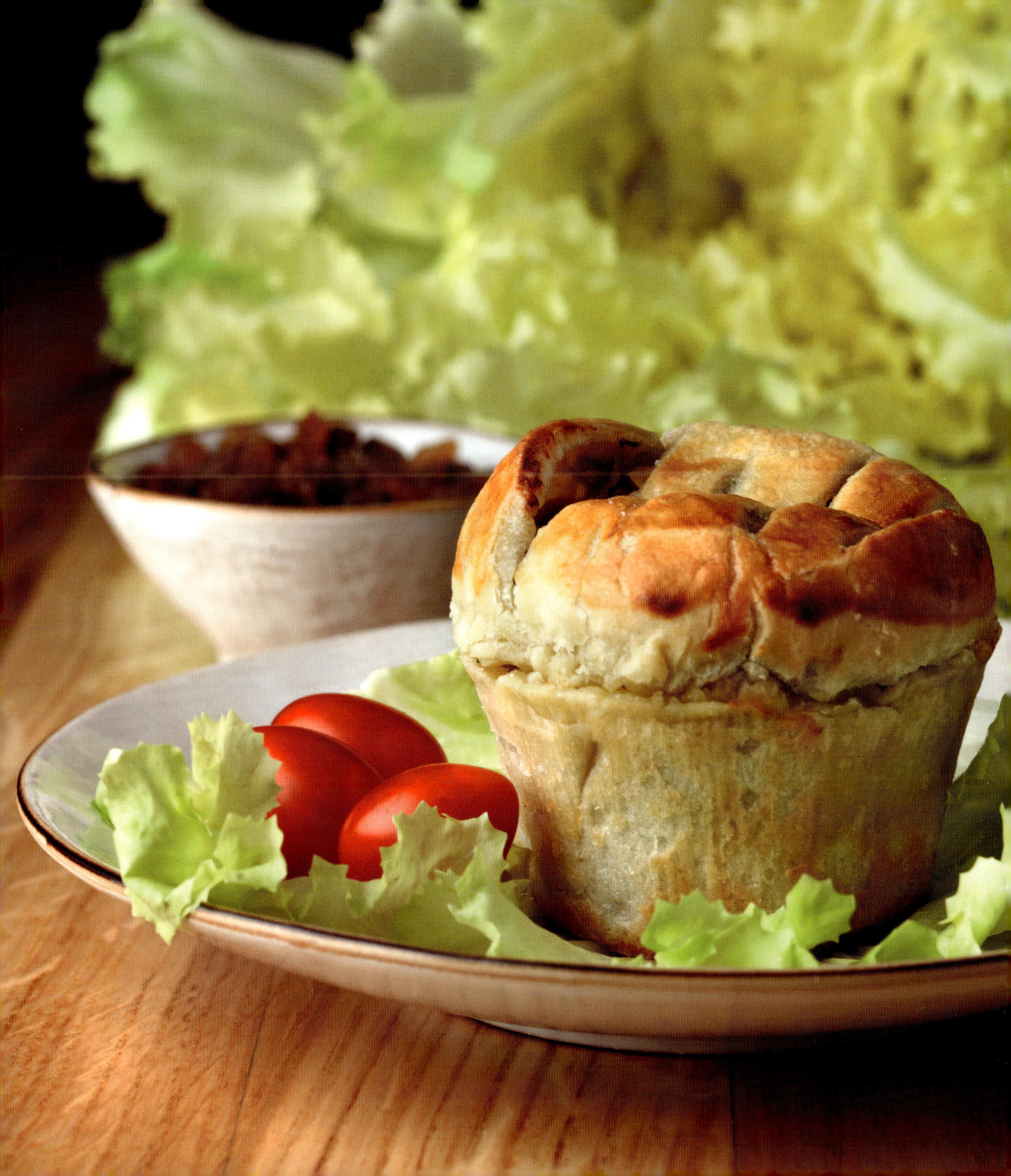

Potato Pie

This potato pie is easy to make and guaranteed to be a hit. You can add all kinds of tasty ingredients to it: speck, smoked bacon, Emmental, and Gorgonzola are all good options.

Use potatoes that are good and starchy, the same type you would use for gnocchi or potato croquettes. Always use a food mill to mash the potatoes—a blender or food processor will make them gummy.

Serves 4 to 6

2 pounds starchy potatoes
½ cup grated Parmigiano Reggiano
2 medium eggs
Salt to taste
Freshly grated nutmeg to taste
9 ounces smoked mozzarella di bufala Campana DOP
3 ounces charcoal-baked ham
½ cup breadcrumbs
Fresh thyme leaves to taste
4 tablespoons unsalted butter

Suggested Wine Pairing

Kerner
Producer:
Zanotelli
Grape:
Kerner
Region:
Trentino Alto Adige

Preparation

- Preheat the oven to 350°F. Boil the potatoes (unpeeled) in salted water until tender and easily pierced with a paring knife, about 30 minutes.
- Drain the potatoes, cool slightly, then peel and pass through a food mill. In a bowl, mix the potatoes with 6 tablespoons of the grated Parmigiano, the eggs, salt, and nutmeg until combined thoroughly.
- Drain the mozzarella and cut it into ½-inch cubes.
- Cut the ham into ½-inch cubes. Fold the mozzarella and the ham into the potato mixture.
- Toast the breadcrumbs in a dry pan over low heat until golden and fragrant. Stir thyme leaves into the breadcrumbs, then spread in a shallow bowl to cool.
- When the breadcrumbs are cool, combine them with the remaining 2 tablespoons Parmigiano.
- Butter 4 to 6 individual ramekins (or a large baking dish if you prefer).
- Fill the ramekins with the potato mixture and sprinkle the breadcrumb mixture on top.
- Bake until golden and crisp, about 20 minutes.

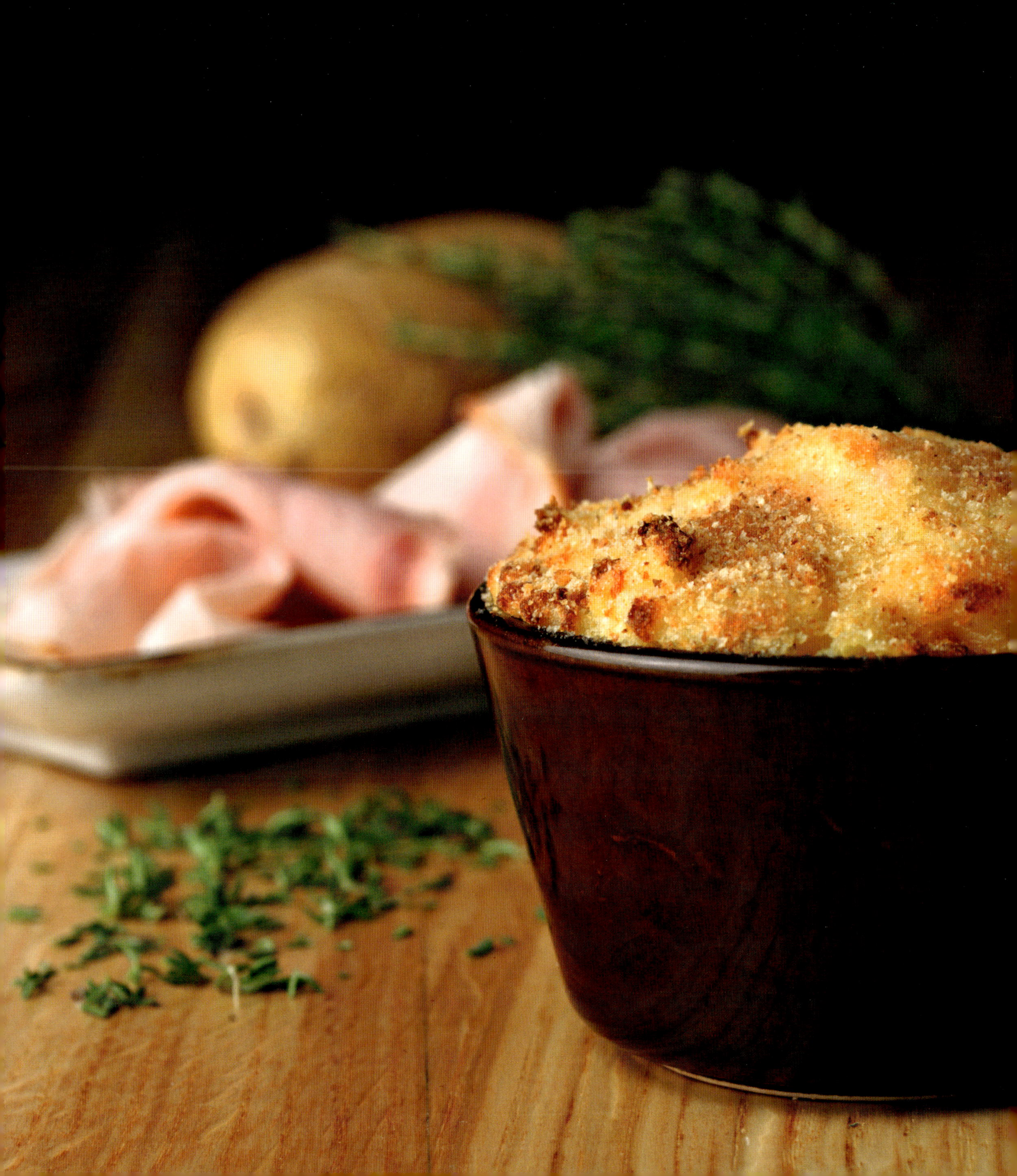

MOZZARELLA BAR   PIZZA E CUCINA

ROME,
Campo dei Fiori

© Luigi Filetici

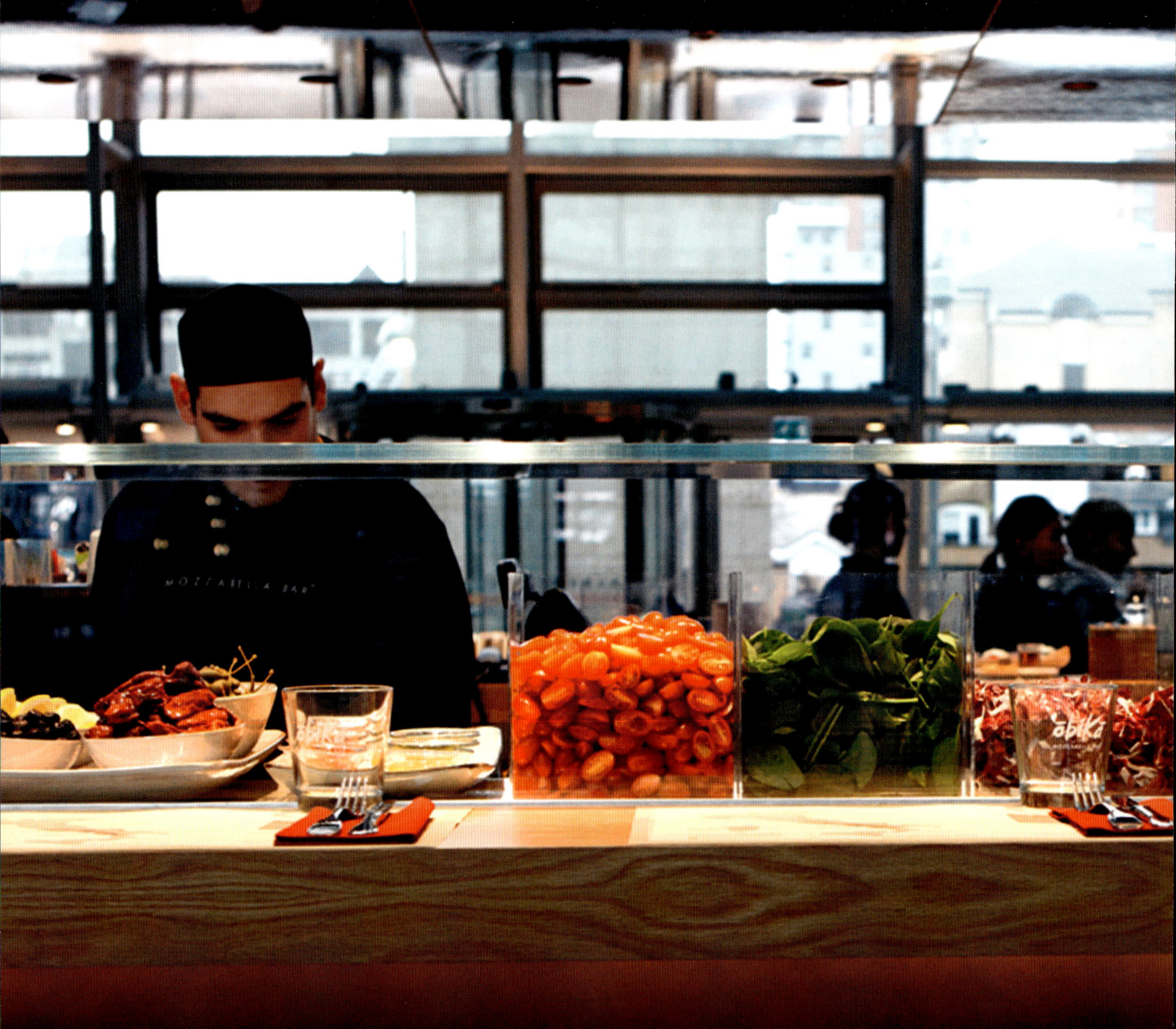
obikā

Insalate

Prosciutto Cotto, Walnuts, and Parmigiano Reggiano

Blu di Bufala, Baby Spinach, Apples, and Walnuts

Grilled Squash, Buffalo Milk Caciocavallo, and Pumpkin Seeds

Smoked Trout with Herbs, Avocado, Mâche, Arugula, and Grape Tomatoes

Bresaola di Fassona, Stracchino, Spinach, and Grape Tomatoes

Barley, Carrots, and String Beans

Prosciutto Cotto, Walnuts, and Parmigiano Reggiano

Mâche—also known as lamb's lettuce or corn salad—is an extremely tender green that makes a fresh and delicious salad. It grows wild in the meadows of the Po Valley. Mâche's fresh, sweet taste is ideal with our tender prosciutto cotto—baked ham made in a wood-burning oven—and Parmigiano Reggiano, seasoned with a light mustard, oil, and lemon juice emulsion.

Serves 4

1½ ounces (⅓ cup loosely packed) mâche
¾ ounce (¼ cup loosely packed) arugula
2 ounces prosciutto cotto
1½ tablespoons extra-virgin olive oil
½ teaspoon mustard
1½ tablespoons lemon juice
Salt to taste
1 tablespoon Parmigiano Reggiano shavings
3 walnuts, shelled

Suggested Wine Pairing

Torre di Ceparano
Producer:
Fattorie Zerbina
Grape:
Sangiovese di Romagna
Region:
Emilia Romagna

Preparation

- Thoroughly wash the mâche and the arugula. (Sometimes soil clings to the roots of mâche very tenaciously.) Remove and discard any thick stems and spin dry in a salad spinner.
- Cut the prosciutto cotto into ¼-inch slices.
- Arrange the mâche and arugula on a large glass or ceramic platter and top with the sliced prosciutto cotto.
- To make the dressing, whisk the oil, mustard, and lemon juice in a small bowl. Season with salt.
- Dress the salad just before serving. Garnish with the Parmigiano Reggiano shavings and the walnuts.

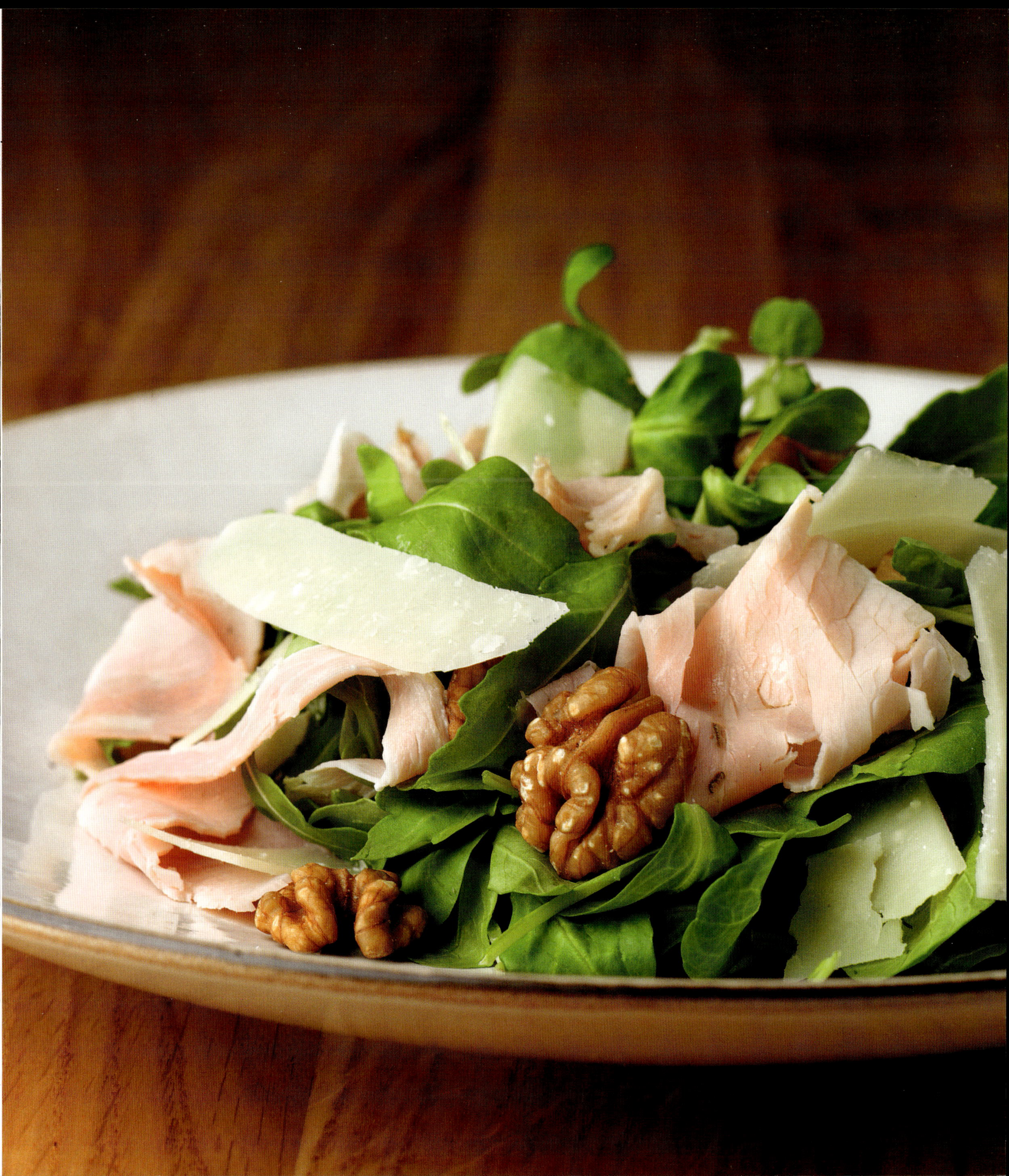

Blu di Bufala, Baby Spinach, Apples, and Walnuts

The star of this salad is blu di bufala, a creamy and crumbly herb-laced cheese with a strong aroma and a unique flavor that brings out all the sweetness of the buffalo milk. To make our salad even more special, we add walnuts and juicy Golden Delicious apples. Chioggia radicchio is the type with a round head. Spinach for salad should be as young and tender as possible, and we always use organic spinach.

Serves 4

2 ounces (½ cup loosely packed) baby spinach
¾ ounce (⅓ cup loosely packed) arugula
¾ ounce (⅓ cup loosely packed) Chioggia radicchio
Juice of ½ lemon
½ medium Golden Delicious apple
1½ tablespoons extra-virgin olive oil
¾ tablespoon balsamic vinegar
Salt to taste
1 ounce blu di bufala
3 walnuts, shelled

Suggested Beer Pairing

Pink Ipa
Producer:
Almond 22
Description:
Blend of malts
Region:
Abruzzo

Preparation

- Wash the spinach, arugula, and radicchio and spin dry in a salad spinner. Remove and discard any tough stalks or stems. Julienne the radicchio. Transfer to a salad bowl.
- Prepare a bowl of cold water and add the lemon juice to it. Core the apple and slice very thinly. Transfer the apple slices to the acidulated water to keep them from browning.
- In a small bowl, whisk the oil and vinegar. Salt to taste.
- Just before serving, dress the lettuce with the oil and vinegar mixture and toss. Cut the cheese into strips or cubes and add those and the walnuts to the bowl. Drain the apple slices and add those as well.

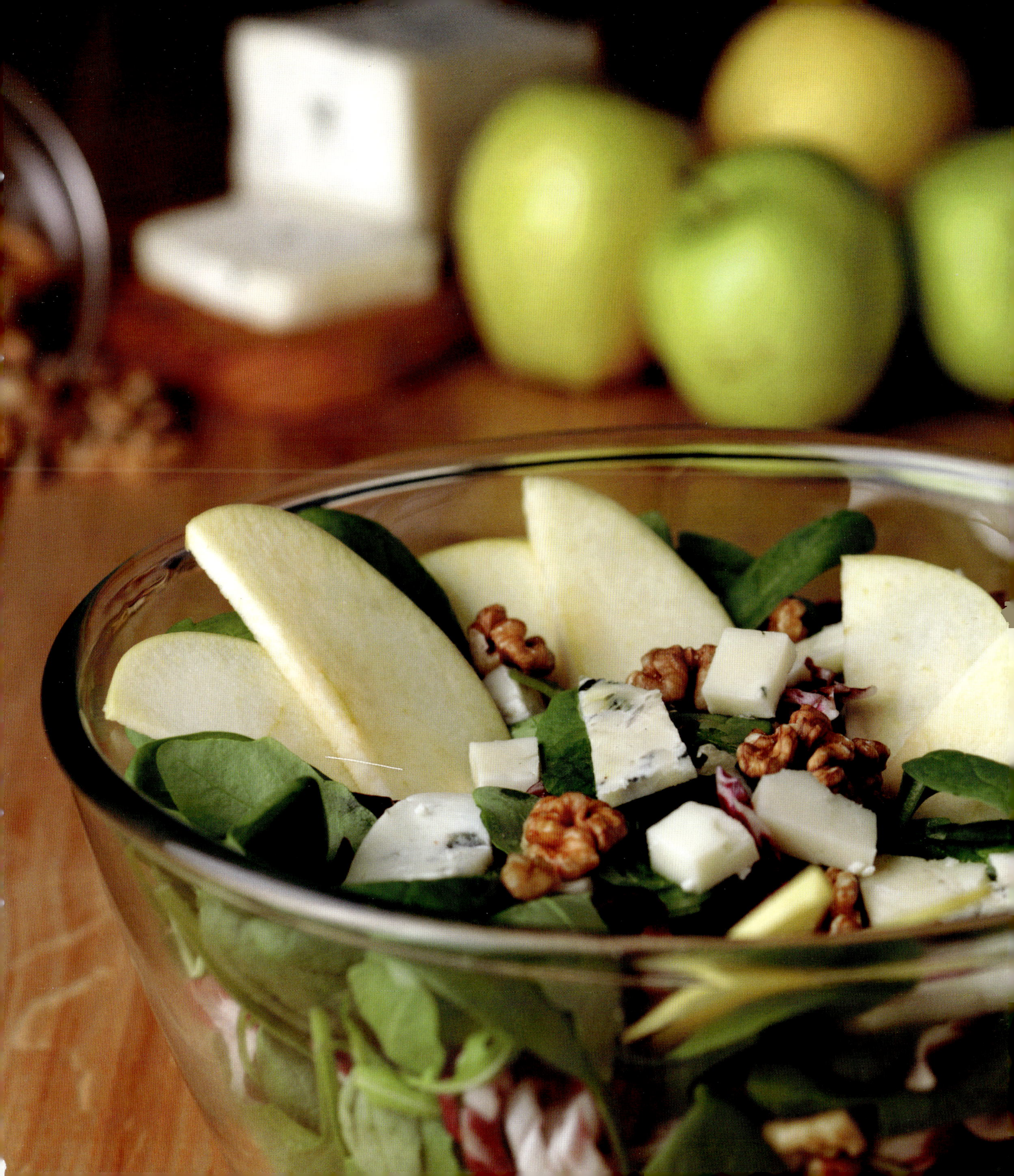

Cinzia Ceci Giovinazzi

The family of Cinzia Ceci Giovinazzi, the head of the company, has been connected to the land for generations. They have grown wheat and cultivated vineyards, but are now best known for lush olive groves.

The farm is in the Andria-Barletta province. Cinzia Ceci makes extremely high-quality organic extra-virgin olive oil that is protected under DOP status.

For the harvest, mechanical tree shakers are used in conjunction with more traditional methods, such as manually using rods to lightly jostle the branches and drop olives without damaging the trees. This keeps the olives in the best condition possible.

OPPOSITE:
Cinzia Ceci Giovinazzi, head of the family company, with her chief of operations, Giuseppe Mastrodonato.

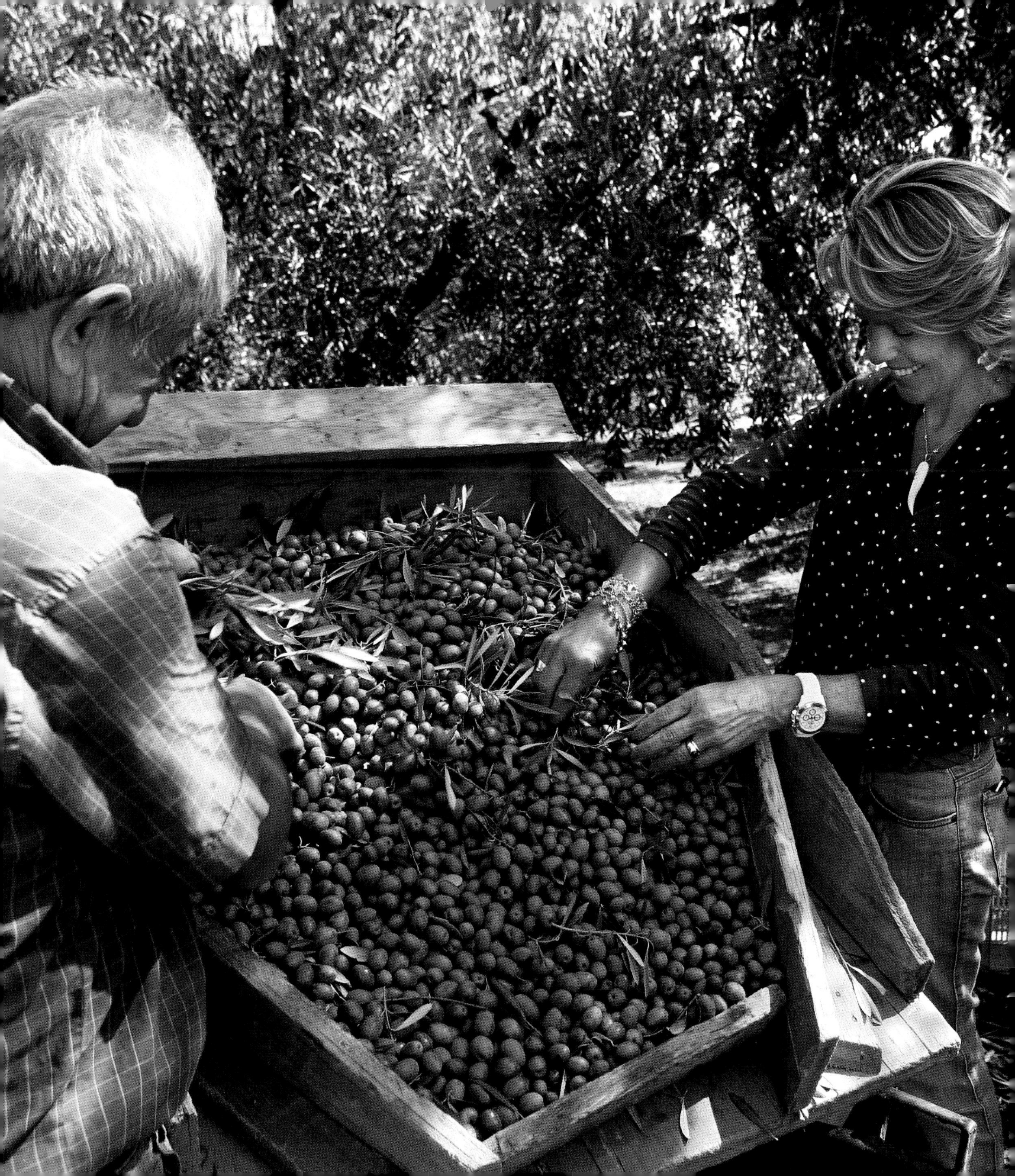

Grilled Squash, Buffalo Milk Caciocavallo, and Pumpkin Seeds

Here's a delicious salad that's perfect for winter: the sweet taste of winter squash is perfect with the slightly aromatic and spicy taste of our caciocavallo, which is aged eighteen months. Ragusano DOP is a pasta filata (stretched curd) cheese made with raw whole cow's milk. It is made during the period of the year when the pastures in the Hyblaean Mountains are in full bloom.

Serves 4

7 ounces winter squash
Salt to taste
2 tablespoons extra-virgin olive oil
Fresh thyme leaves to taste
2 ounces (½ cup loosely packed) mâche
1 (⅓ cup tightly packed) Chioggia radicchio
Apple cider vinegar to taste
1½ ounces caciocavallo Ragusano DOP, shaved
1 teaspoon pumpkin seeds
Croutons to taste

Suggested Wine Pairing

Pinot Nero
Producer:
St Michael Eppan
Grape:
Pinot Nero
Region:
Trentino Alto Adige

Preparation

- Peel and seed the squash, then wash it and cut it into ¼-inch slices.
- Salt the squash and either grill it until soft, about 5 minutes per side, or bake it at 400°F until soft, about 20 minutes.
- Drizzle the squash with about 1 teaspoon of the olive oil, season with salt and thyme, and set aside to cool.
- Thoroughly wash the mâche and the radicchio. (Sometimes soil clings to the roots of mâche very tenaciously.) Remove and discard any thick stems and spin dry in a salad spinner. Julienne the radicchio.
- Arrange the mâche and radicchio on a large serving platter. Top with the squash and the caciocavallo. Scatter the pumpkin seeds on top. Whisk together the remaining 1 tablespoon plus 2 teaspoons olive oil and the vinegar. Season with salt and toss with the salad. Scatter the croutons on top and serve.

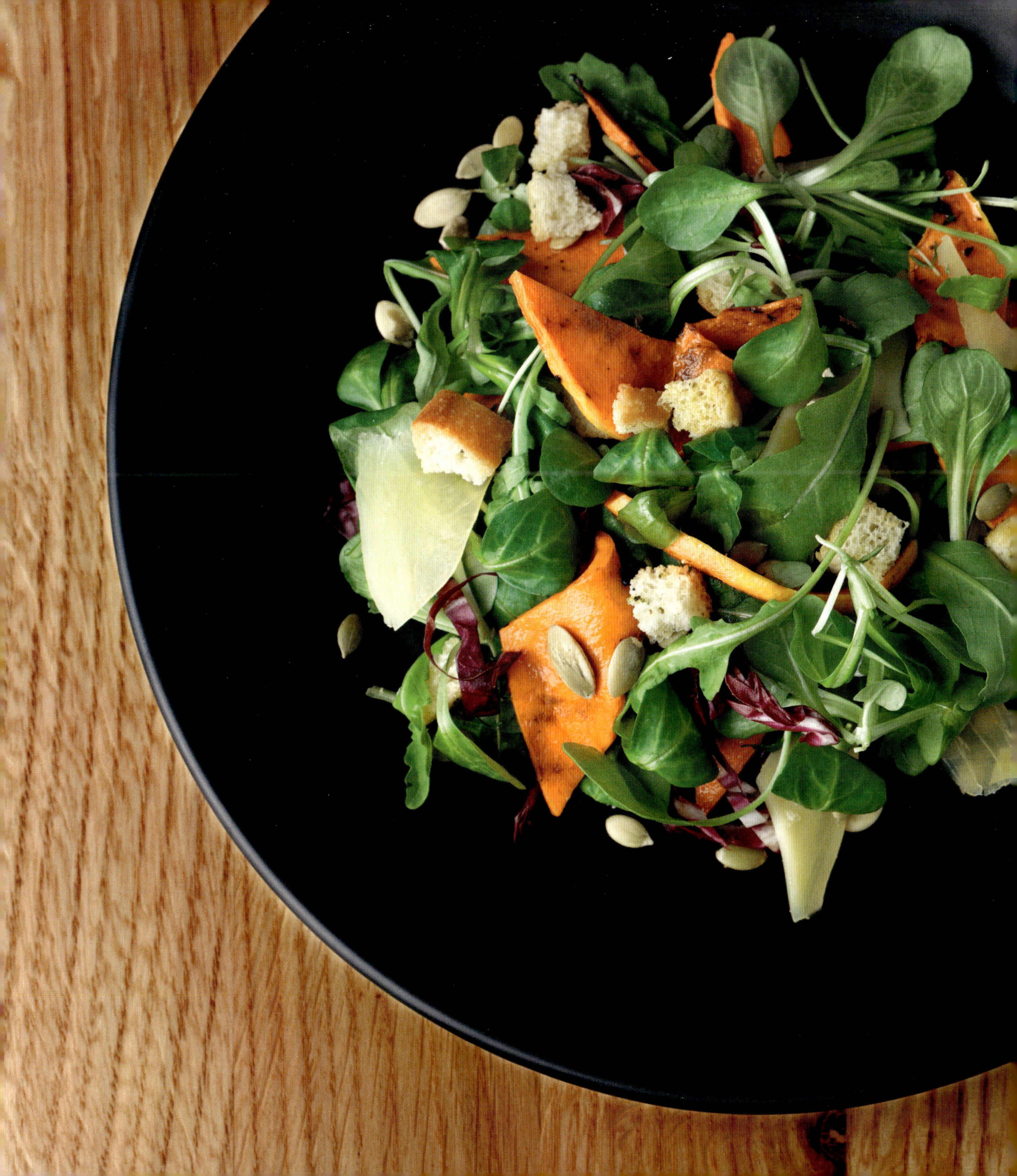

Smoked Trout with Herbs, Avocado, Mâche, Arugula, and Grape Tomatoes

The smoked trout we use for this salad is made from the very finest rainbow trout bred in pure fresh water. The fillets are rubbed with a mixture of aromatic herbs and then smoked. The tender lean trout is ideal with the sweet, nutty taste of the avocado and the sharp flavor of arugula.

Serves 4

Juice of ½ lemon
½ ripe avocado
1 ounce (¼ cup loosely packed) mâche
1½ ounces (⅓ cup loosely packed) arugula
2½ ounces smoked trout with herbs, thinly sliced
½ cup grape tomatoes, halved
Thin lemon slices for garnish
1½ tablespoons extra-virgin olive oil
Salt to taste

Suggested Wine Pairing

Mimo Rosé
Producer: Cantalupo
Grape: Nebbiolo
Region: Piedmont

Preparation

- Prepare a large bowl of cold water and add the lemon juice. Peel and pit the avocado, cut into strips, and drop into the acidulated water to keep the flesh from browning.

- Thoroughly wash the mâche and the arugula. (Sometimes soil clings to the roots of mâche very tenaciously.) Remove and discard any thick stems and spin dry in a salad spinner.

- Arrange the greens on a platter.

- Drain the avocado slices and arrange on top of the greens. Top with the smoked trout. Garnish with the tomatoes and slices of lemon. Season with the oil and salt.

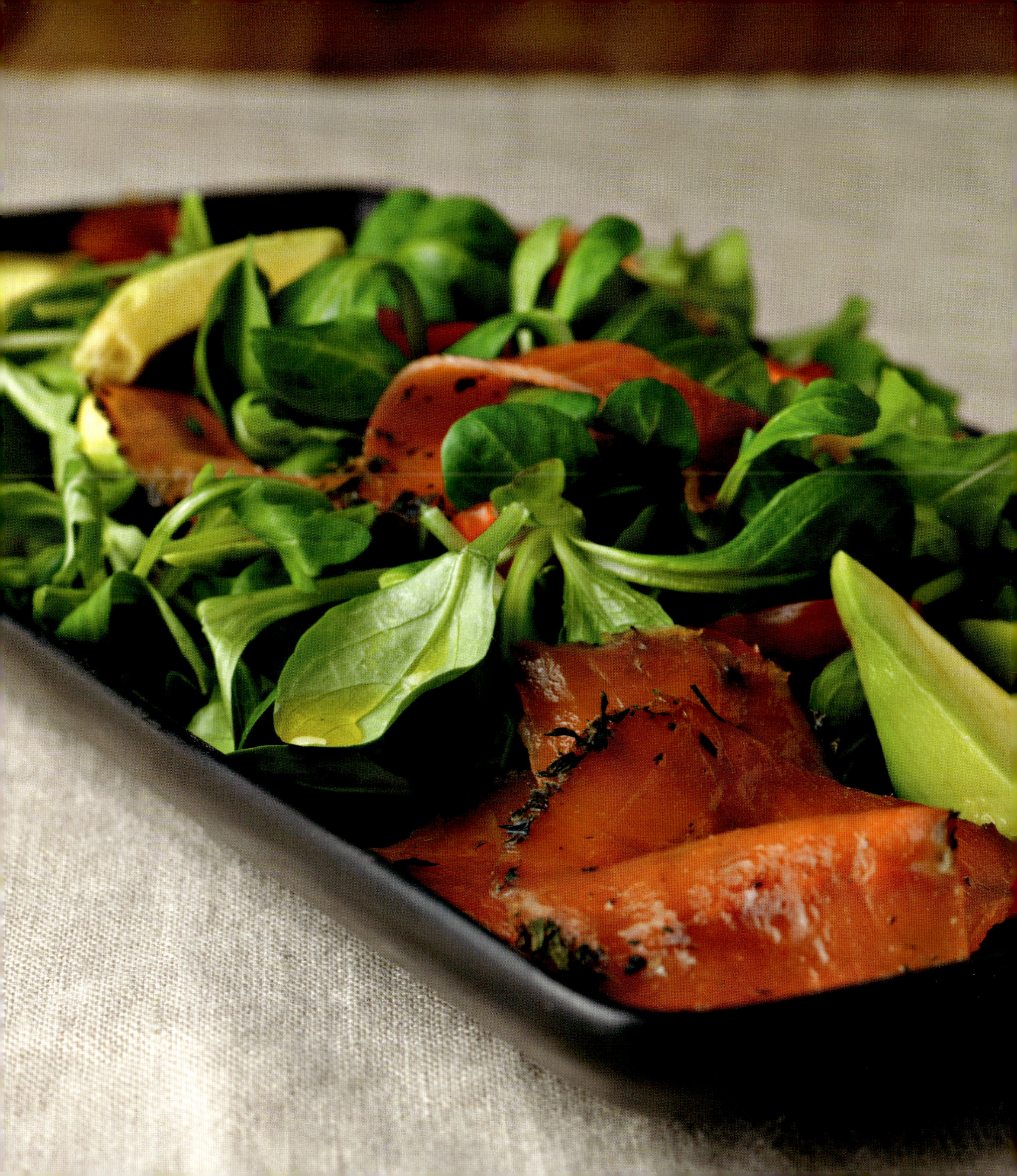

Bresaola di Fassona, Stracchino, Spinach, and Grape Tomatoes

A very fine Piedmontese breed of cattle is used to make Fassona beef. The animal's muscular fasciae are particularly developed, and this produces tender, lean, and flavorful meat. We use this meat to make our delicious bresaola, with just the right salting and aging techniques, and when we pair it with stracchino and baby spinach, the result is a truly rich, tasty salad.

Serves 4

1 ½ ounces (⅓ cup loosely packed) baby spinach
1 ounce (¼ cup loosely packed) mâche
1 ½ ounces bresaola di Fassona
⅓ cup grape tomatoes, halved
2 ounces stracchino
1 ½ tablespoons extra-virgin olive oil
Lemon juice to taste
Salt and black pepper to taste

Suggested Wine Pairing

Inferno
Producer:
Nino Negri
Grape:
Chiavennasca (Nebbiolo)
Region:
Lombardy

Preparation

- Thoroughly wash the spinach and the mâche. (Sometimes soil clings to the roots of mâche very tenaciously.) Remove and discard any thick stems and spin dry in a salad spinner.
- Arrange the greens on a large platter.
- Slice the bresaola ½ inch thick and place on top of the greens.
- Garnish with the tomatoes. Cut the stracchino into cubes (this is difficult because it is very soft—you may have more luck simply scooping out bits with a spoon) and scatter over the salad.
- For the dressing, in a small bowl, whisk together the oil, lemon juice, and salt and pepper.
- Just before serving, dress the salad.

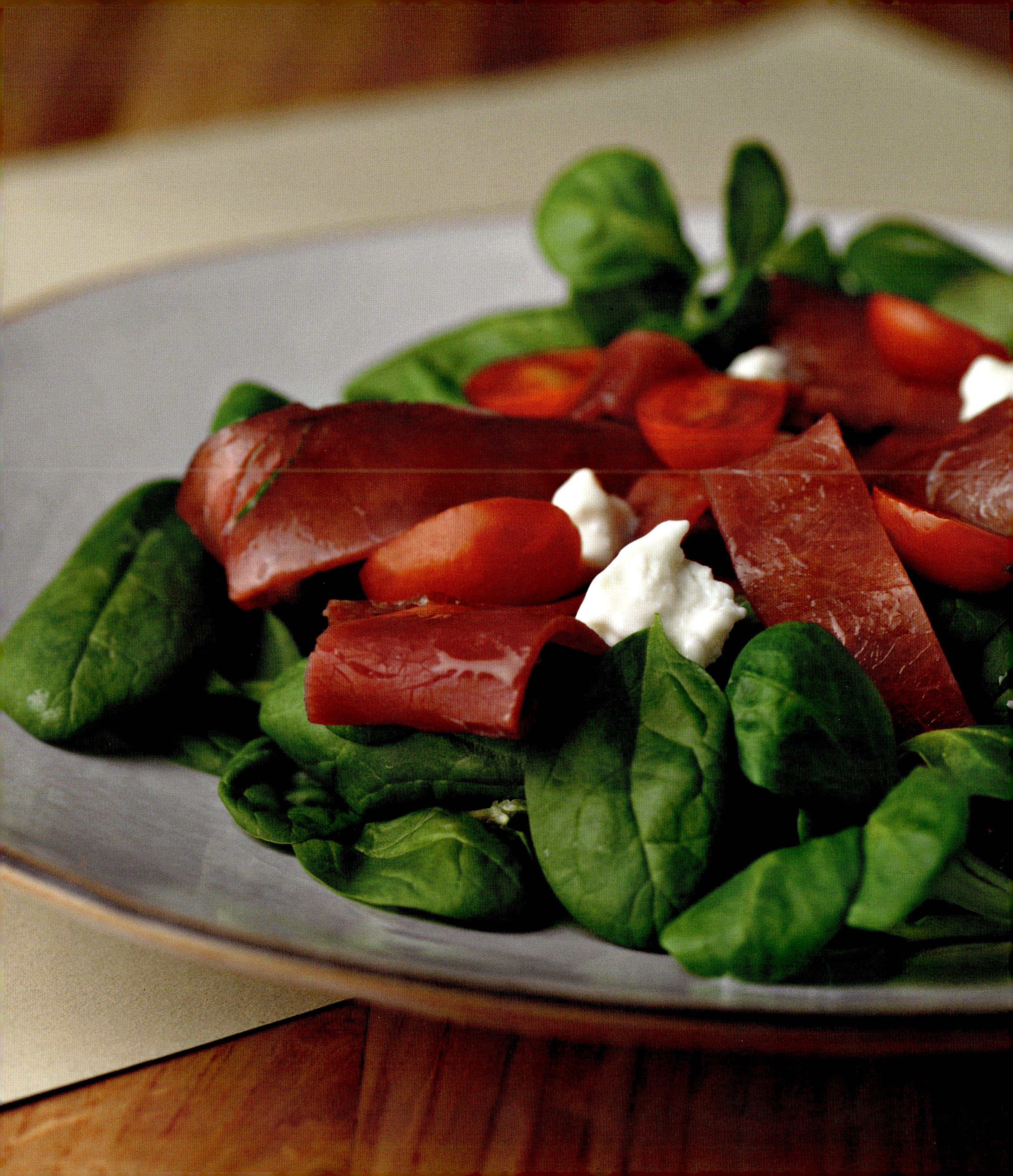

Barley, Carrots, and String Beans

Barley is a nutritious grain that's quite refreshing. It's especially delicious in the summer paired with carrots, string beans, and arugula in a light salad like this one.

Serves 4

1 tablespoon pine nuts
1 tablespoon almonds
Fresh mint leaves to taste
Fresh basil leaves to taste
1 tablespoon salted capers, soaked and drained
Zest of ½ orange
1½ tablespoons extra-virgin olive oil
2 tablespoons pearl barley
Salt to taste
½ cup string beans, trimmed
¼ cup diced carrots
1 ounce (¼ cup loosely packed) mâche
1 ounce (¼ cup loosely packed) arugula
½ cup grape tomatoes, halved

Suggested Wine Pairing

Pinot Bianco
Producer:
Alois Lageder
Grape:
Pinot Bianco
Region:
Trentino Alto Adige

Preparation

- In a mortar and pestle or food processor fitted with a metal blade, grind the pine nuts, almonds, mint, basil, capers, and zest. Drizzle in the olive oil in a thin stream while grinding.
- Rinse the barley, then bring a pot of salted water to a boil and boil the barley, string beans, and carrots together until all are tender, about 20 minutes. Drain, toss with the pine nut mixture, and set aside to cool.
- Thoroughly wash the mâche and the arugula. (Sometimes soil clings to the roots of mâche very tenaciously.) Remove and discard any thick stems and spin dry in a salad spinner.
- Arrange the greens on a platter.
- Top the greens with the barley mixture. Garnish with the tomatoes.

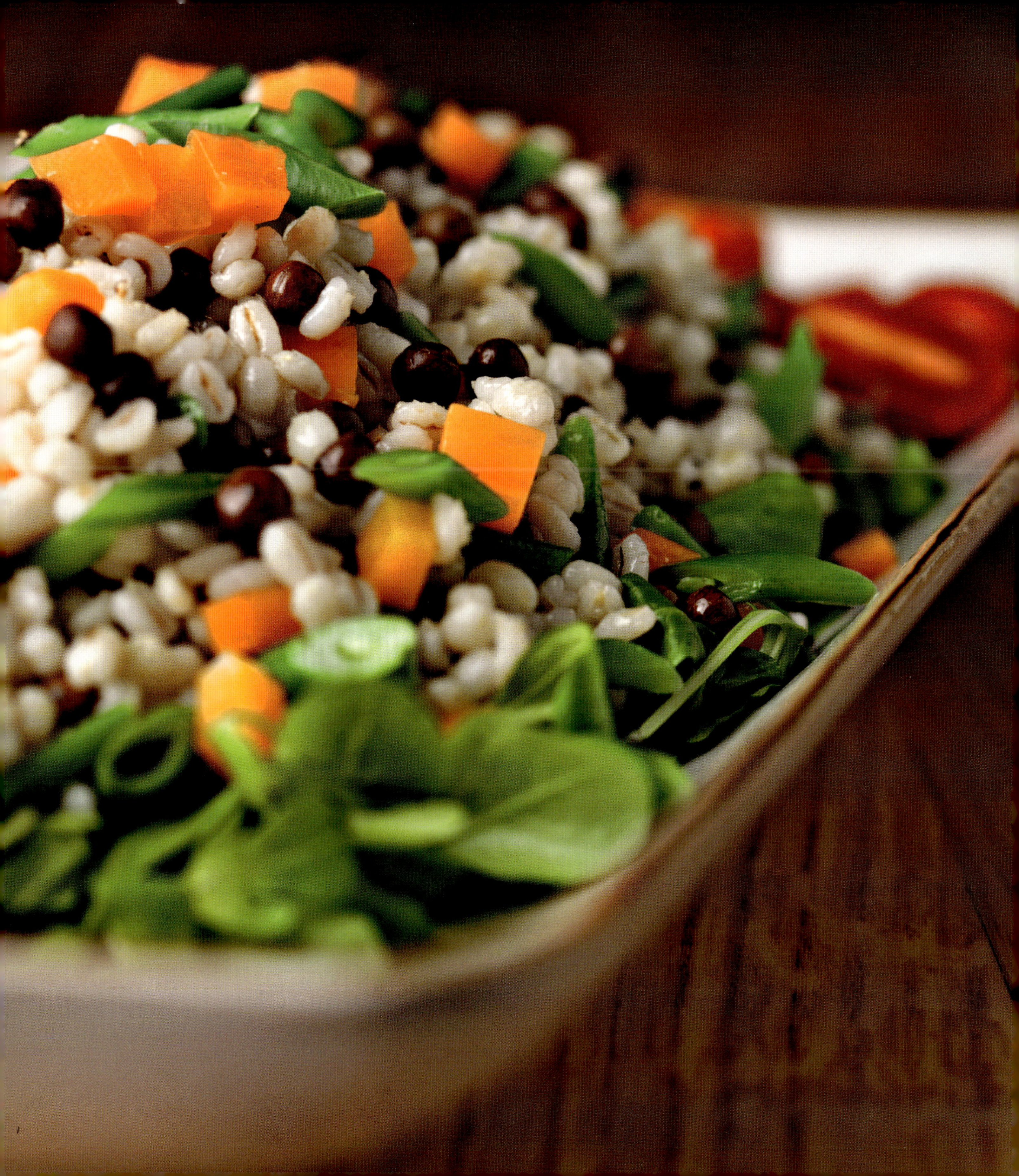

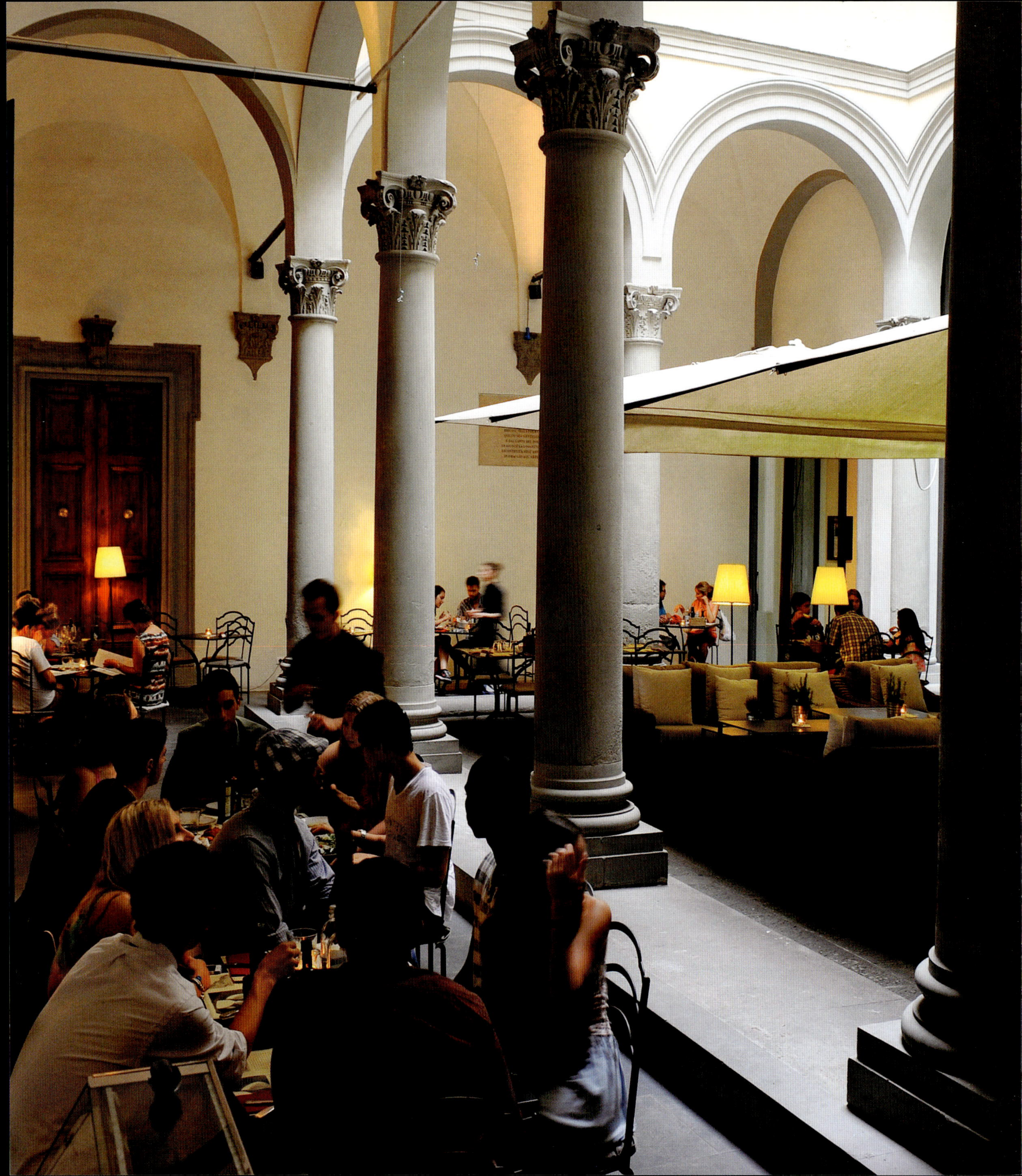

FLORENCE,
Via de' Tornabuoni

© Luigi Filetici

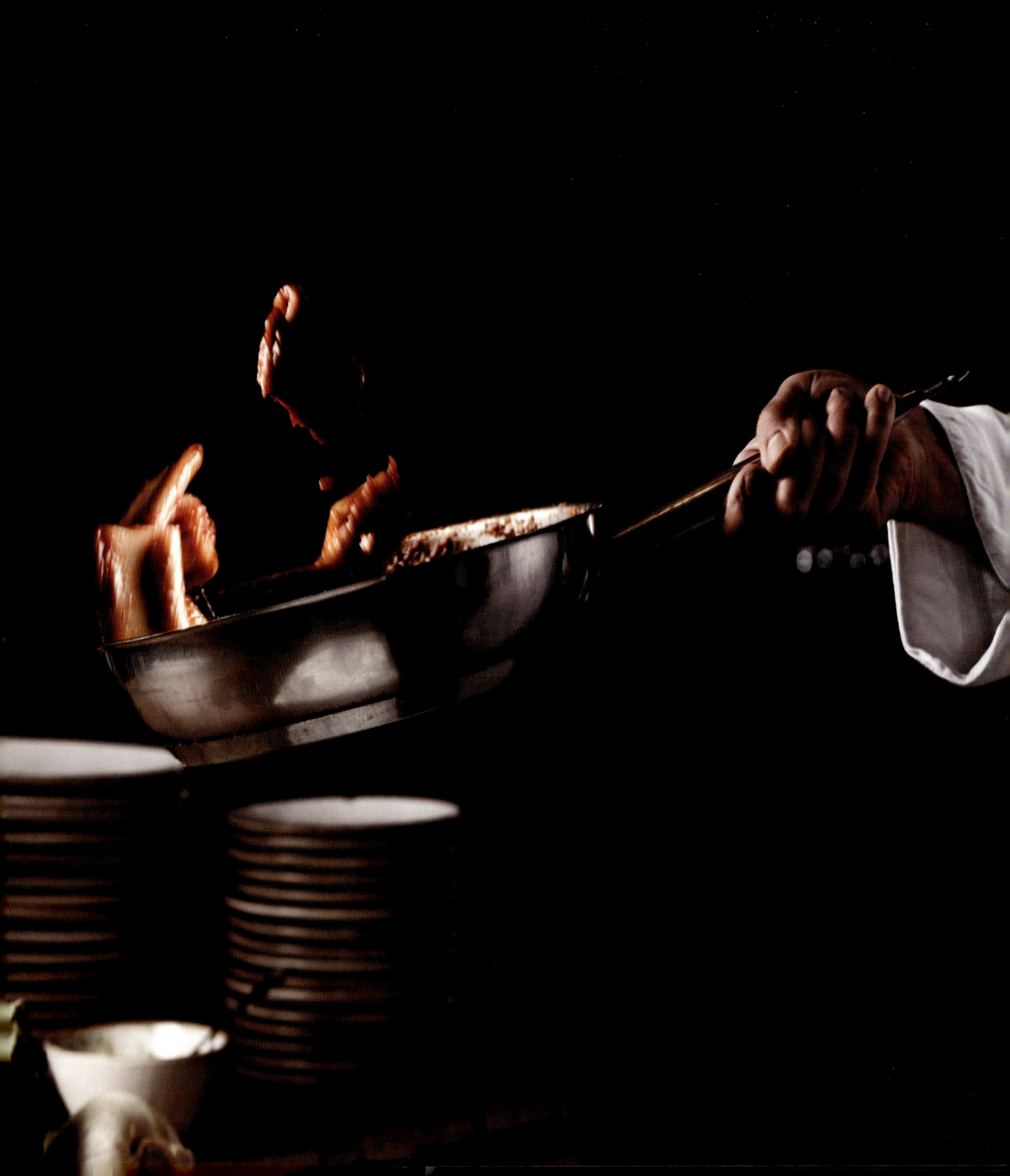

Paste

Schiaffoni alla Sorrentina

Trofie with Pesto, Potatoes, and String Beans

Linguine with Yellowfin Tuna

Scialatielli alla Nerano

Tortiglioni with Sea Urchin

Pasta all'Uovo

Pappardelle with Sausage and Fennel

Pumpkin Ravioli with Amaretto Cookies

Ravioli with Ricotta and Eggplant

Lasagne with String Beans and Pesto

Lasagne with Chianina Ragù

Cannelloni with Zucchini and Stracciatella

Potato Gnocchi

Gnocchi with Blu di Bufala and Spinach

Gnocchi with N'duja and Tomatoes

Orecchiette with Garden Peas and Sugar Snap Peas

Orecchiette with Broccoli and Provolone

Fregola with Tuna and Tomatoes

Schiaffoni alla Sorrentina

Schiaffoni, also known as paccheri, are wide tubes of pasta from the Campania region. They are served with a sauce made with San Marzano tomatoes protected under DOP status, which are firm, tasty, and bright red. We use La Motticella tomato puree, an organic product that is still processed by hand, for the sauce and Gentile brand pasta. This pasta is made according to traditional artisanal methods from Gragnano, meaning that it is made from durum wheat and uses bronze dies, which results in a pasta with a rough surface so that the sauce adheres properly.

Serves 4 to 6

3 tablespoons extra-virgin olive oil, plus more for drizzling
2¾ cups (1 pound 9 ounces) La Motticella tomato puree
Salt to taste
1 pound artisanal schiaffoni or paccheri
7 ounces torn mozzarella di bufala Campana DOP
8 fresh basil leaves, cut into strips
¼ cup grated Parmigiano Reggiano

Suggested Wine Pairing

Costa d'Amalfi Tramonti Rosso
Producer:
Tenuta San Francesco
Grapes:
Aglianico, Tintore, Piedirosso
Region:
Campania

Preparation

- Heat the oil in a wide and shallow skillet. Add the tomato puree and cook over a high heat for 3 minutes.
- Meanwhile, bring a large pot of water to a boil. Salt the water, add the pasta, stir, and cook, stirring frequently, until al dente. Reserve about ½ cup of the pasta cooking water. Drain the pasta in a colander.
- Transfer the pasta to the skillet with the tomato sauce.
- Toss the pasta and sauce over medium-high heat until combined. If the sauce is too thick, add some of the reserved pasta cooking water, a tablespoon or two at a time, until it is the correct consistency.
- Add the mozzarella and the basil and toss to combine.
- Transfer the pasta to a heated serving bowl, sprinkle on the grated cheese, and drizzle with a little additional olive oil.

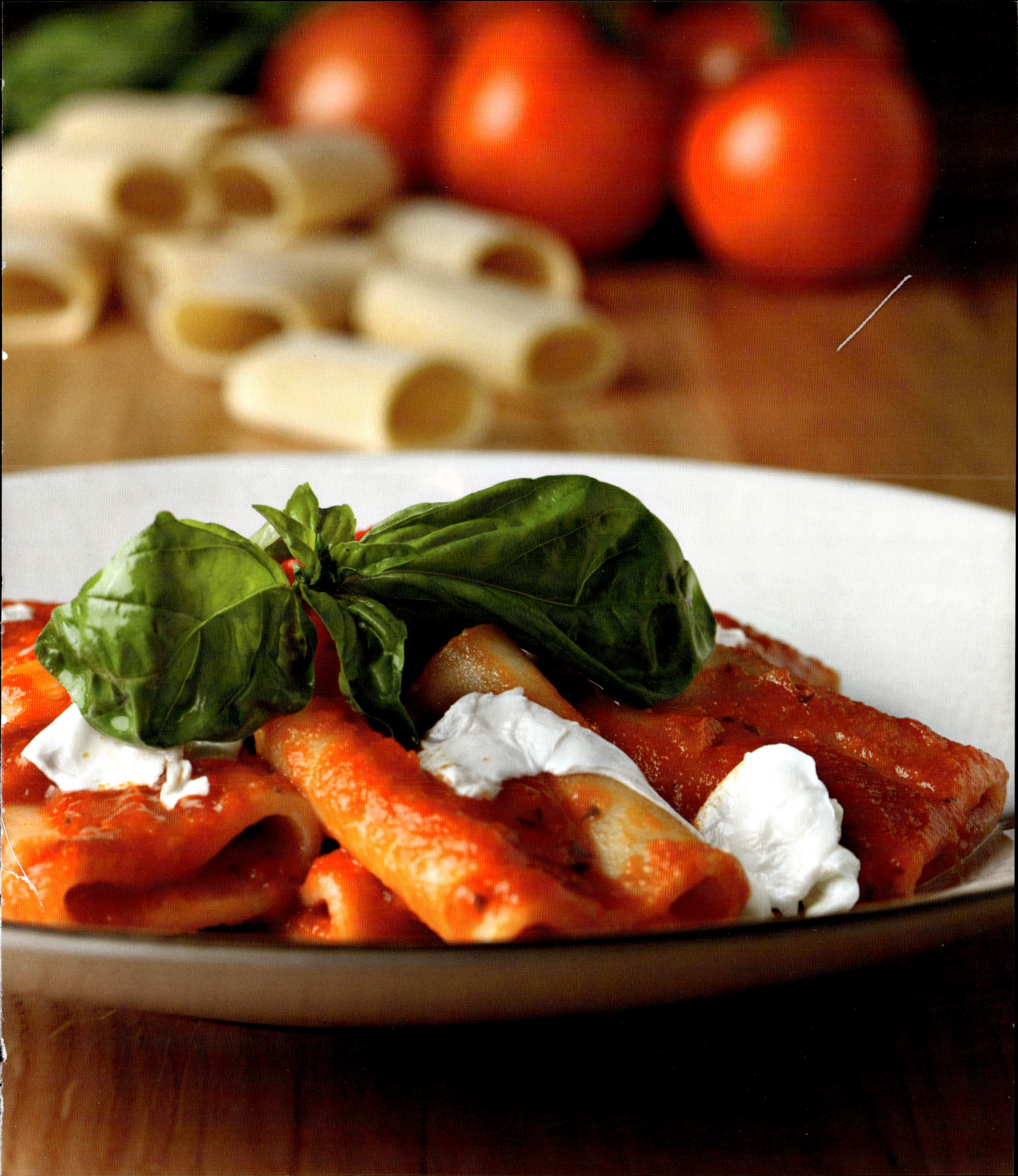

Gentile Pasta

Flavor, passion, and tradition are the features that distinguish the two small businesses run by the Zampino family: Pastificio Gentile (founded in 1876) and Conserve San Nicola dei Miri in Gragnano. Both businesses embrace the same philosophy: offering top-notch products made artisanally.

Since 1876, Gentile pasta has been produced according to the traditional slow-drying method, which brings out the flavor and fragrance of its high-quality durum wheat flour and results in pasta with terrific firmness to the bite.

The company makes a multitude of pasta shapes, including fusilli that are produced completely by hand by artisans who wrap the pasta around iron rods to create the typical spiral shape.

OPPOSITE:
Alberto Zampino, head of sales and business for the family-owned company, and his brother, Pasquale, head of production, shown with Silvio Ursini at the Gragnano pasta factory.

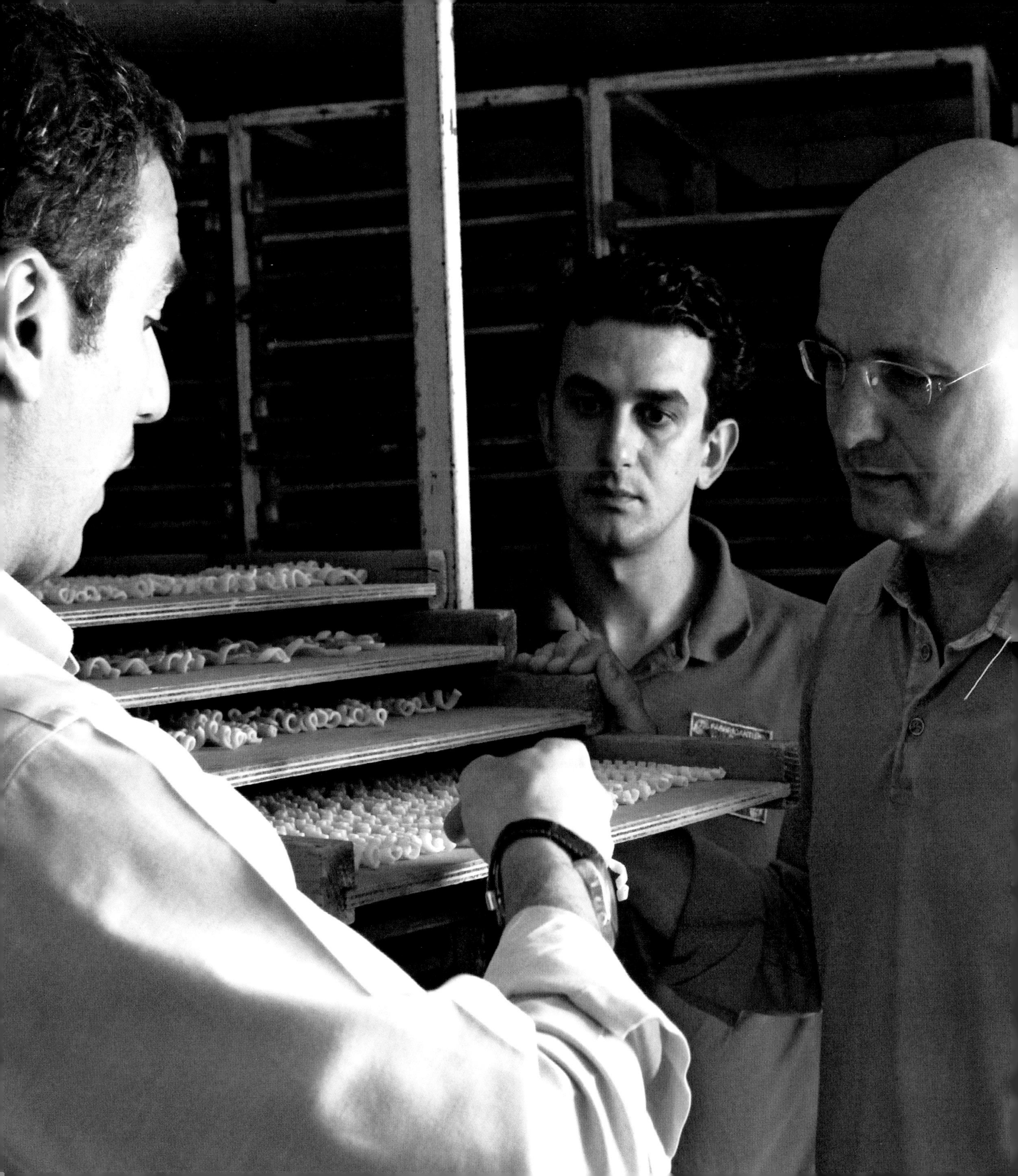

Trofie with Pesto, Potatoes, and String Beans

This recipe combines two of Liguria's most famous specialties: pesto and trofie. Trofie are a type of pasta made from durum wheat flour and water. For the pesto, use only young basil leaves with a delicate aroma. The extra-virgin olive oil must be mildly fruity. Only the finest pine nuts should be used, and both the Parmigiano Reggiano and the Sardinian pecorino should be aged. Our only break from tradition is to eliminate the garlic, which makes our pesto easier to digest.

Serves 4 to 6

¼ cup fresh basil leaves
½ cup diced Parmigiano Reggiano, plus shavings for garnish
2 tablespoons diced Sardinian pecorino
2 tablespoons pine nuts
3 tablespoons extra-virgin olive oil
1 cup string beans, trimmed
Coarse sea salt to taste
7 ounces potatoes, peeled and diced
1 pound 3 ounces fresh trofie

Suggested Wine Pairing

Vermentino
Producer:
Vio Bio
Grape:
Vermentino
Region:
Liguria

Preparation

- Reserve a few basil leaves for garnish. In a mortar and pestle or food processor fitted with a metal blade, grind the basil.
- Add the diced Parmigiano and the pecorino, the pine nuts, and the oil. Blend the ingredients until you obtain a smooth sauce. Be careful not to overheat the pesto or the basil will oxidize and the sauce will darken.
- Cut the string beans into thirds. Bring a pot of water to a boil, salt it, and add the string beans. Cook for 10 minutes.
- Add the potatoes and the trofie to the cooking water and cook until all are tender.
- Reserve about ½ cup of the pasta cooking water. Drain the pasta and the vegetables and transfer to a serving dish. Whisk 1 to 2 tablespoons of the pasta cooking water into the pesto until creamy, then toss the pesto with the pasta and vegetables.
- Garnish with the reserved basil leaves and Parmigiano Reggiano shavings.

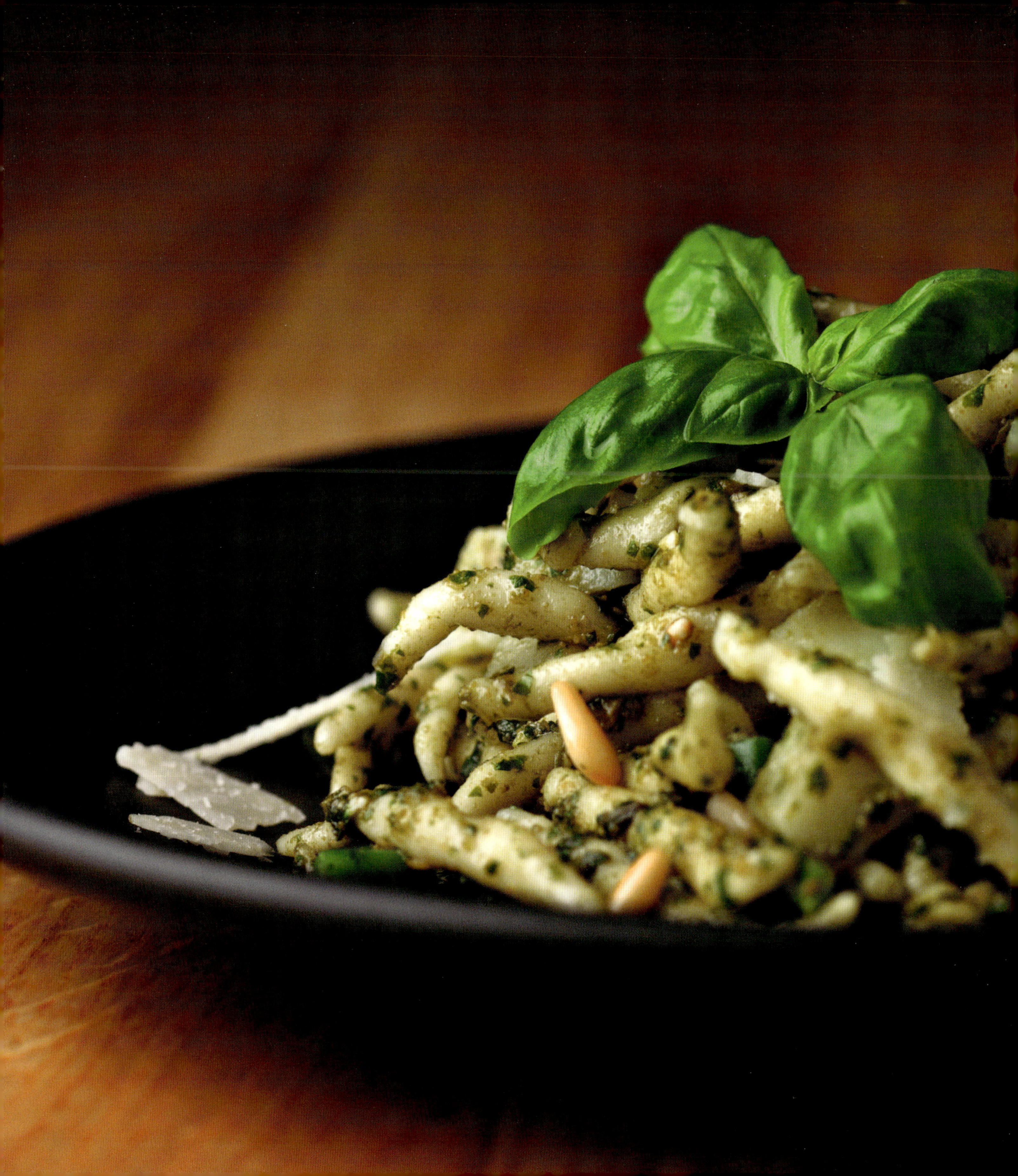

Linguine with Yellowfin Tuna

Fresh tuna and linguine are a wonderful match. Although there is plenty of delicious canned tuna available from Italy, this dish will really only be top-notch with fresh tuna, preferably the meaty yellowfin variety.

Serves 4 to 6

2½ cups (1 pound 5 ounces) La Motticella peeled tomatoes
1 pound yellowfin tuna
¼ cup extra-virgin olive oil, plus more for drizzling
2 sprigs rosemary
Red pepper flakes to taste
⅓ cup white wine
¼ cup salted capers, soaked and drained
½ cup pitted Gaeta olives
Coarse sea salt to taste
1 pound Gragnano linguine
Chopped fresh parsley to taste

Suggested Wine Pairing

Flor di Uis
Producer:
Vie di Romans
Grape:
Malvasia Istriana Friulano Riesling
Region:
Friuli

Preparation

- Drain the tomatoes and cut them into strips. Set aside. Cut the tuna into ½-inch cubes. Heat the oil in a pan and sauté the tuna with 1 sprig of rosemary and a pinch of red pepper flakes.
- Add the wine and simmer until it evaporates, then add the capers.
- Add the olives and the tomatoes and cook over high heat for 15 minutes.
- Bring a large pot of water to a boil and salt it. Cook the linguine in the boiling water until al dente. Drain the pasta in a colander and transfer to the pan with the tuna sauce. Toss to combine.
- Sprinkle on the parsley, drizzle with a little oil, and garnish with the remaining rosemary sprig. Serve warm.

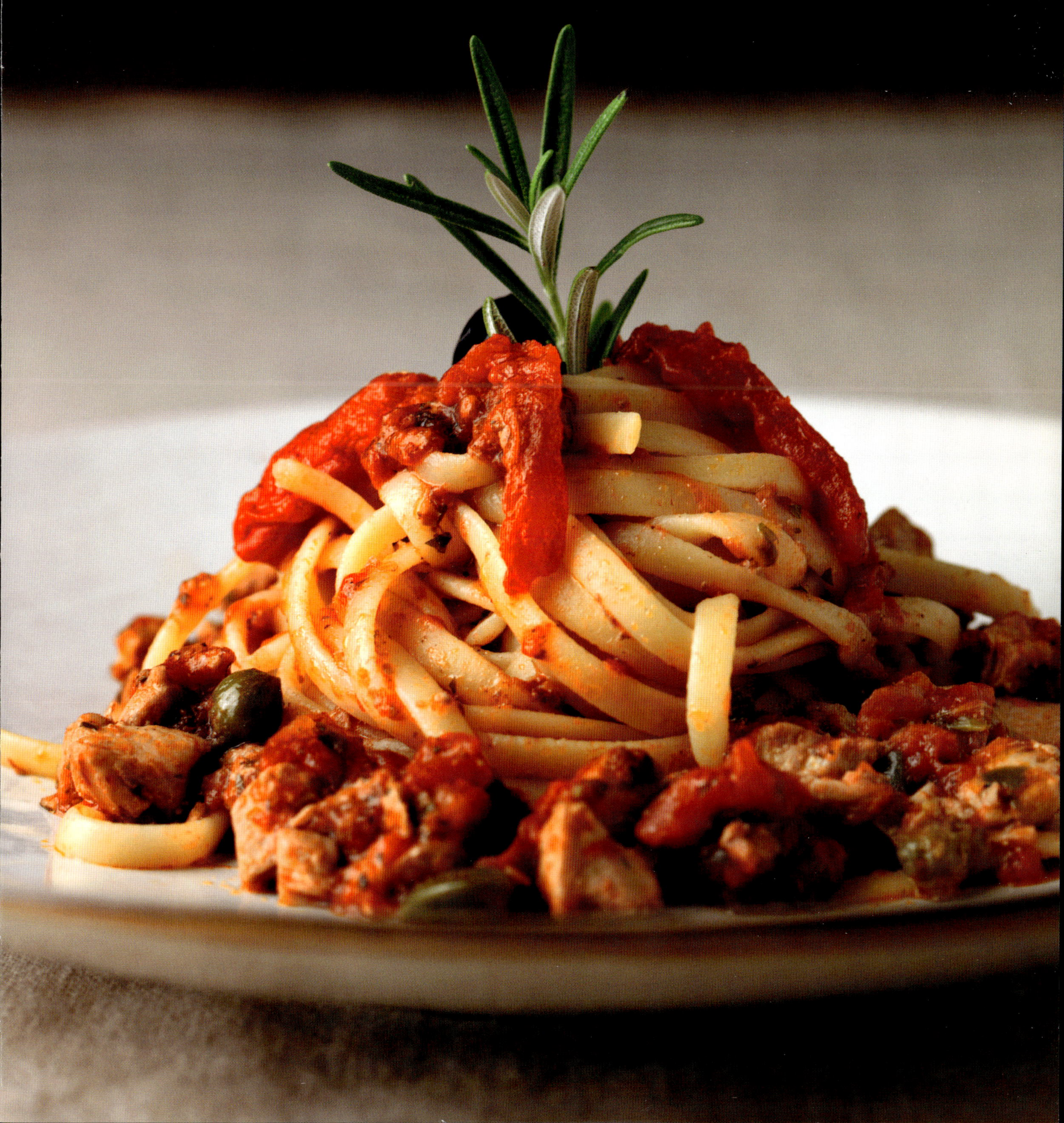

Scialatielli alla Nerano

Nerano is a lovely town overlooking the Sorrento coast, and this is the classic dish from the area. There are a thousand versions of this dish, and ten thousand secrets to making it "just right." We give it a touch of freshness by adding Nerano mint and make it creamier by adding eggs.

Scialatielli is a fresh flour-and-water pasta from the Amalfi Coast shaped like thick linguine that is often served with grated cheese and basil and works wonderfully here as well.

Serves 4 to 6

4 cups extra-virgin olive oil
4 cups zucchini, thinly sliced into rounds
Coarse sea salt to taste
1 pound 5 ounces Gragnano scialatielli
Chopped fresh mint to taste
3 large eggs
½ cup grated pecorino Romano, plus more for serving
Black pepper to taste
Fresh mint leaves for garnish

Suggested Wine Pairing

Terre di Tufi
Producer:
Terruzzi & Puthod
Grapes:
Vernaccia, Chardonnay, Sauvignon Blanc
Region:
Tuscany

Preparation

- Heat the olive oil in a large skillet and fry the zucchini until golden brown. Drain on paper towels. Wipe out any excess oil from the skillet.

- Bring a large pot of water to a boil and salt it. Cook the scialatielli in the boiling water until al dente. Reserve about ½ cup pasta cooking water and drain the pasta in a colander. Transfer the scialatielli to the pan with the fried zucchini and add the chopped mint.

- Beat the eggs with the ½ cup pecorino and then add the mixture to the pasta.

- Toss over low heat. (You don't want to cook the eggs.) If the pan looks dry, add a tablespoon or two of the reserved pasta cooking water.

- Season with pepper and additional grated pecorino and garnish with a few whole mint leaves.

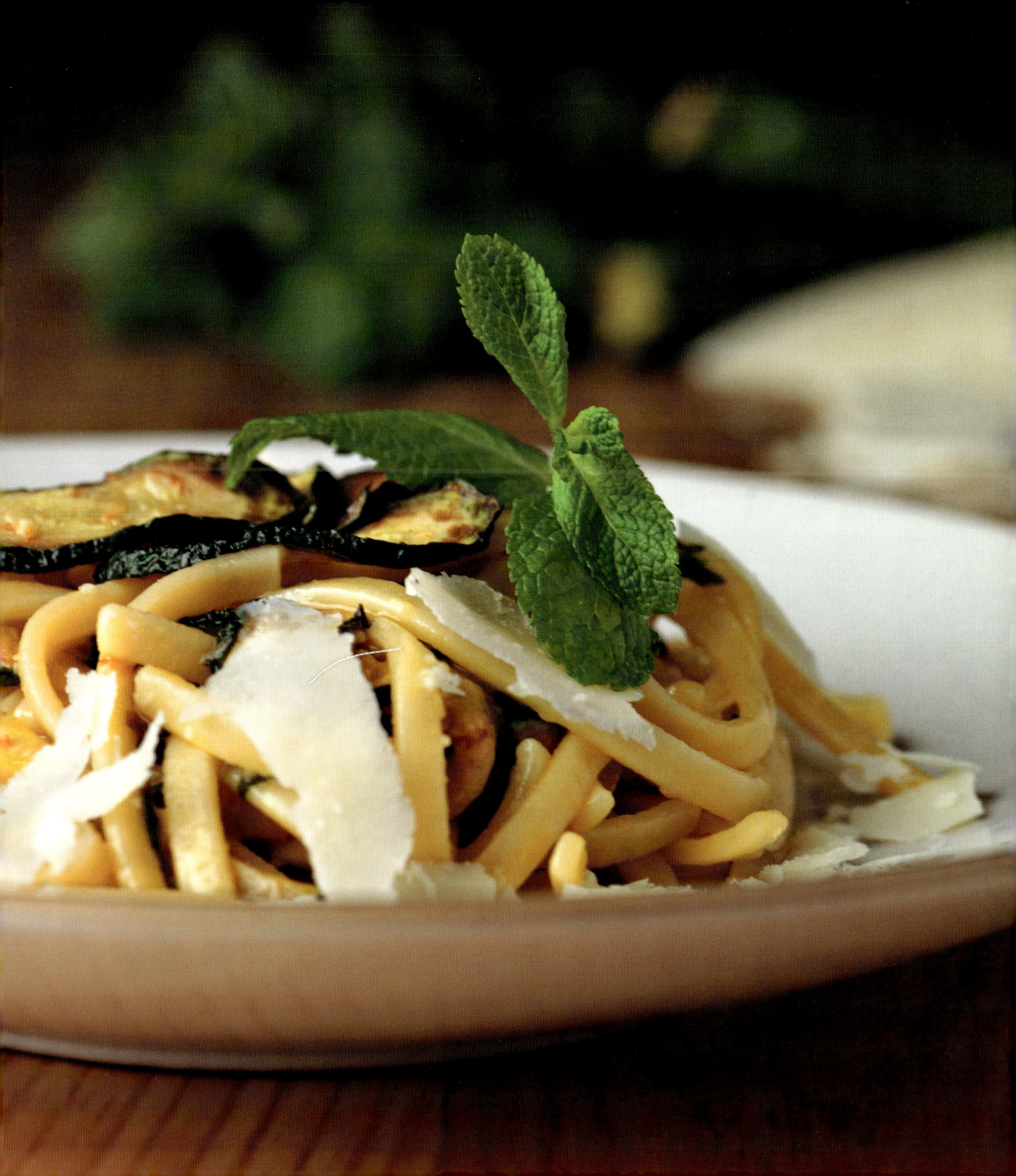

Tortiglioni with Sea Urchin

This recipe comes from our restaurant in Tokyo. It combines the products of the land, like buffalo milk ricotta, with a treasure from the sea. Sea urchin is a delicacy. Its color ranges from green to orange and it tastes of the sea with a hazelnut aftertaste.

Serves 4 to 6

7 ounces buffalo milk ricotta
¾ cup plus 2 tablespoons whole milk
8½ ounces sea urchin
Salt and black pepper to taste
Coarse sea salt to taste
1 pound Gragnano tortiglioni
¼ cup grated Parmigiano Reggiano
Extra-virgin olive oil to taste
Chopped Bronte pistachios to taste
Fresh flat-leaf parsley for garnish

Suggested Wine Pairing

Cabreo
Producer:
La Pietra
Grape:
Chardonnay
Region:
Tuscany

Preparation

- Combine the ricotta and milk in a large bowl.
- Stir in the sea urchin and season with salt and pepper.
- Meanwhile, bring a large pot of water to a boil and add coarse sea salt. Cook the pasta until al dente. Reserve about ½ cup pasta cooking water.
- Drain the pasta, transfer to a pan, add the ricotta mixture, and toss briefly over low heat. The ricotta mixture should be heated through but not cooked. The dish should be extremely creamy. If it seems too stiff, stir in a tablespoon or two of the reserved pasta cooking water.
- Serve with the grated Parmigiano and a drizzle of oil and garnish with the pistachios and parsley.

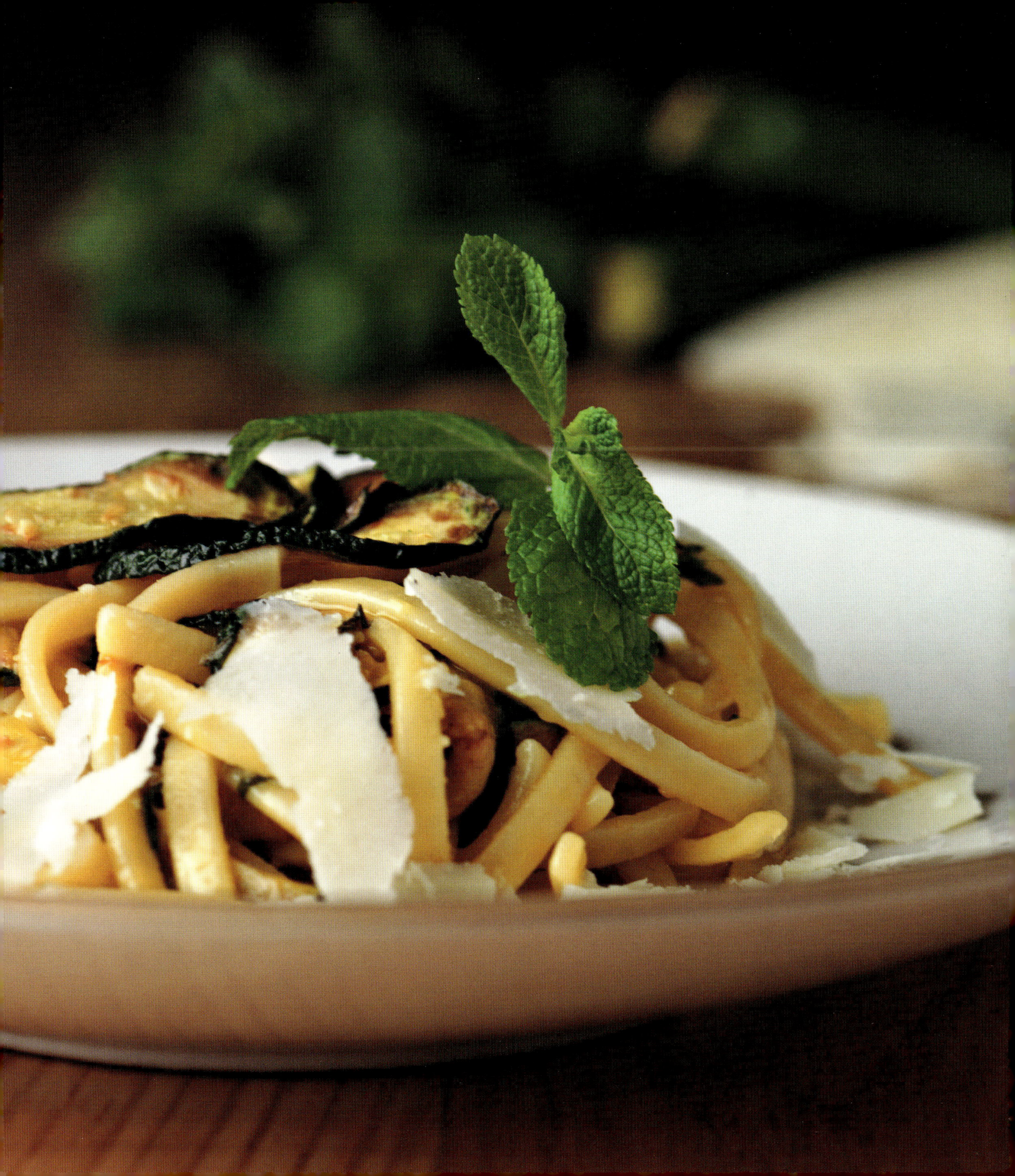

Tortiglioni with Sea Urchin

This recipe comes from our restaurant in Tokyo. It combines the products of the land, like buffalo milk ricotta, with a treasure from the sea. Sea urchin is a delicacy. Its color ranges from green to orange and it tastes of the sea with a hazelnut aftertaste.

Serves 4 to 6

7 ounces buffalo milk ricotta
¾ cup plus 2 tablespoons whole milk
8½ ounces sea urchin
Salt and black pepper to taste
Coarse sea salt to taste
1 pound Gragnano tortiglioni
¼ cup grated Parmigiano Reggiano
Extra-virgin olive oil to taste
Chopped Bronte pistachios to taste
Fresh flat-leaf parsley for garnish

Suggested Wine Pairing

Cabreo
Producer:
La Pietra
Grape:
Chardonnay
Region:
Tuscany

Preparation

- Combine the ricotta and milk in a large bowl.
- Stir in the sea urchin and season with salt and pepper.
- Meanwhile, bring a large pot of water to a boil and add coarse sea salt. Cook the pasta until al dente. Reserve about ½ cup pasta cooking water.
- Drain the pasta, transfer to a pan, add the ricotta mixture, and toss briefly over low heat. The ricotta mixture should be heated through but not cooked. The dish should be extremely creamy. If it seems too stiff, stir in a tablespoon or two of the reserved pasta cooking water.
- Serve with the grated Parmigiano and a drizzle of oil and garnish with the pistachios and parsley.

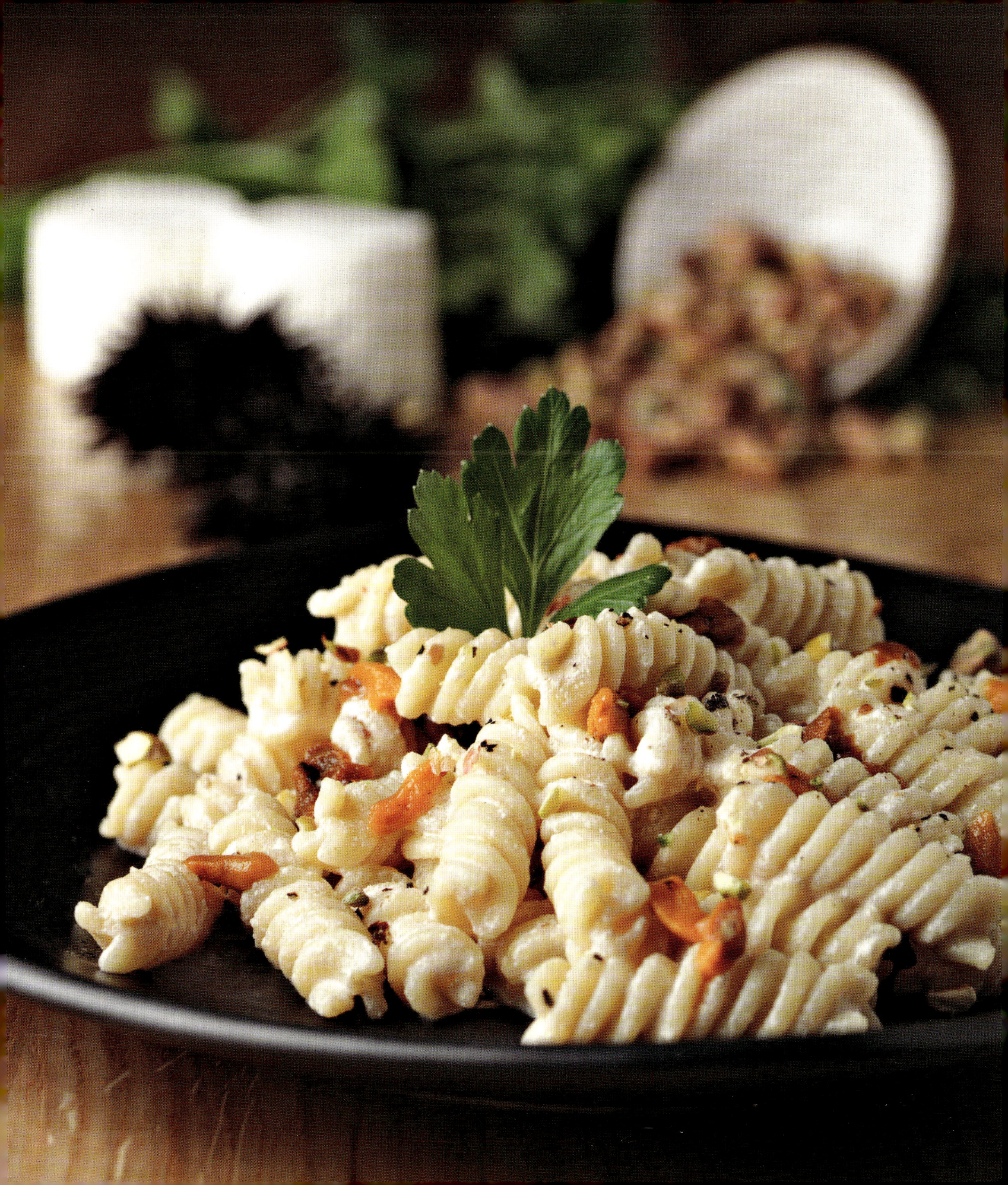

Pasta all'Uovo

The success of our fresh pasta, from lasagne to cannelloni, from ravioli to pappardelle, lies in the egg pasta dough, which we make fresh every day using only organic eggs laid by free-range chickens. We highly recommend the eggs laid by Paolo Parisi's Livornese chickens.

Here are a few tips for making pasta at home: Use a large wooden board, as the roughness of the surface will make it easier to knead the pasta. Make a well in the center of the flour and add the eggs to the well, then beat them lightly with a fork in the well before kneading. Keep the dough in a draft-free area both when you're kneading it and when it's resting, as air can dry out the pasta and make it stiff and hard to handle.

Makes 1 pound 12 ounces of egg pasta

4 cups unbleached all-purpose flour
5 large eggs
Salt to taste

Preparation

- Mound the flour on a large wooden board. Make a well in the center, sprinkle salt into the well, and then add the eggs to the well. Lightly beat the eggs with a fork, then gradually incorporate the flour. Knead the dough until smooth and firm. Shape the dough into a ball, wrap it in plastic wrap, and let it rest for 1 hour. Clean the work surface thoroughly.

- Divide the dough into two pieces. Rewrap one piece and set aside. Roll out the other piece with a rolling pin to a ¼-inch-thick disk. Repeat with the other half of the dough. At this point you can start making the pasta shapes you need:

- **For tagliatelle, tagliolini, and pappardelle:** Roll up the sheet into a loose cylinder and then slice into strips ¼ to ½ inch wide for tagliatelle, ⅛ inch wide for tagliolini, and 1 inch wide for pappardelle. Unroll the strips of pasta and arrange them on a flat-weave dish towel or surface lightly dusted with flour.

- **For quadrucci:** Overlap several ¼ inch wide strips of pasta dusted with flour and cut into ¼-inch squares.

- **For lasagne and cannelloni**: Use a pastry cutter to cut 6-by-8-inch rectangles. Use the same rectangles to make cannelloni by placing the filling on the rectangle and then rolling it.

- **For maltagliati:** Any leftover pasta dough can be cut into small irregular shapes to be served in soups.

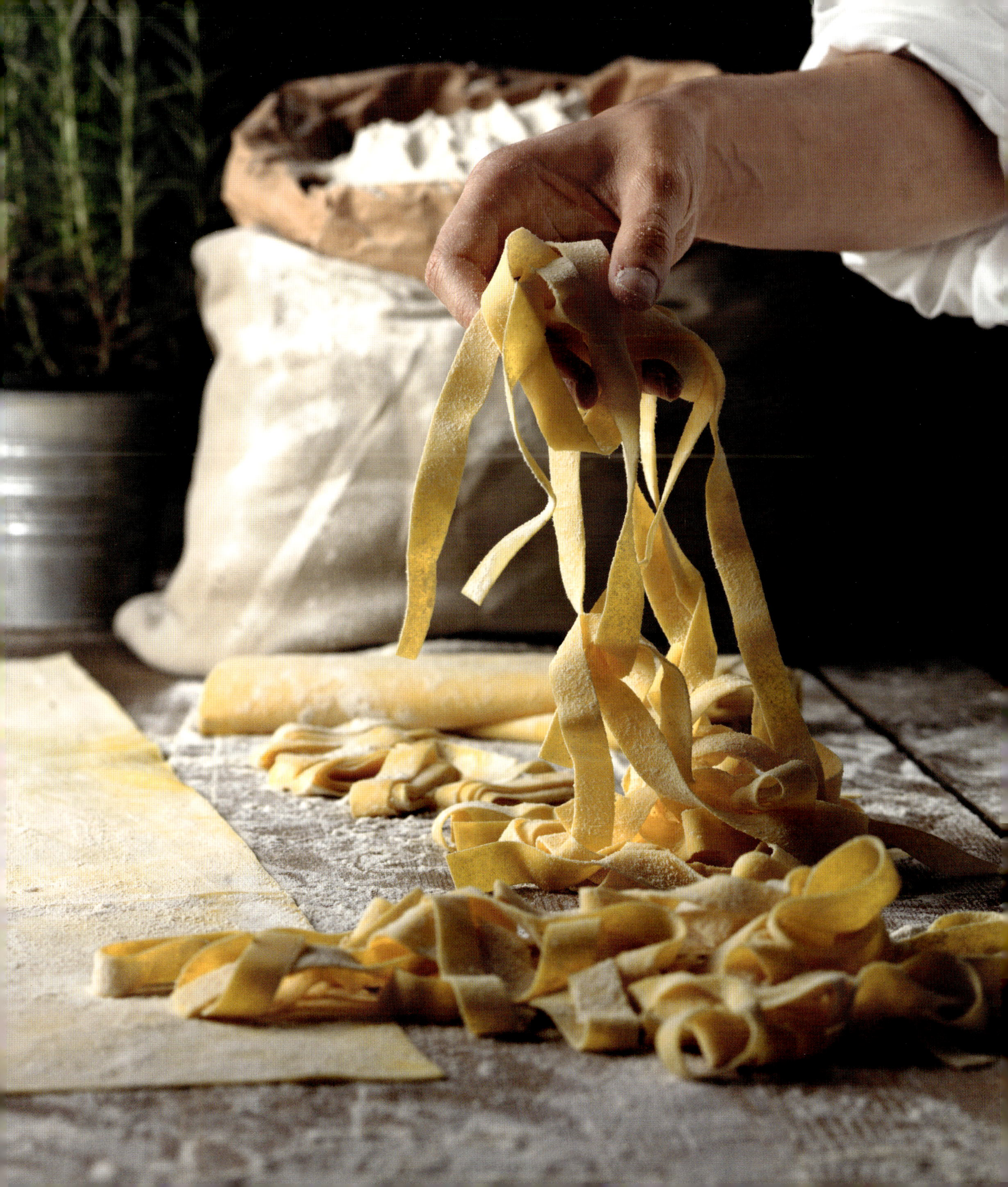

Pappardelle with Sausage and Fennel

This sausage and fresh fennel sauce is easy to assemble and takes much less time to make than the wild boar meat sauce that is traditionally served over pappardelle.

Serves 4 to 6

2 tablespoons extra-virgin olive oil
1 pound fennel sausage
1/3 cup plus 2 tablespoons dry white wine
1/2 cup tomato paste
1 3/4 cups (14 ounces) La Motticella tomato puree
Coarse sea salt to taste
1 pound 5 ounces pappardelle (see page 132)
Black pepper to taste
Fresh fennel fronds for garnish
1/3 cup grated pecorino Romano

Preparation

- Heat the oil in a pan. Remove the casing from the sausage and crumble it into the pan.
- When the sausage starts to brown, stir in the white wine, the tomato paste, the tomato puree, and 1/2 cup water.
- Cook the sauce over medium heat for 20 minutes.
- Bring a large pot of water to a boil and salt it. Cook the pappardelle. They will cook very quickly and rise to the surface when ready. Drain the pasta, transfer it to the pan with the sauce, and toss over medium heat until combined, 1 to 2 minutes.
- Season with pepper, garnish with fresh fennel, and serve with the grated pecorino.

Suggested Wine Pairing

Lianti
Producer:
Capichera
Grape:
Carignano del Sulcis
Region:
Sardinia

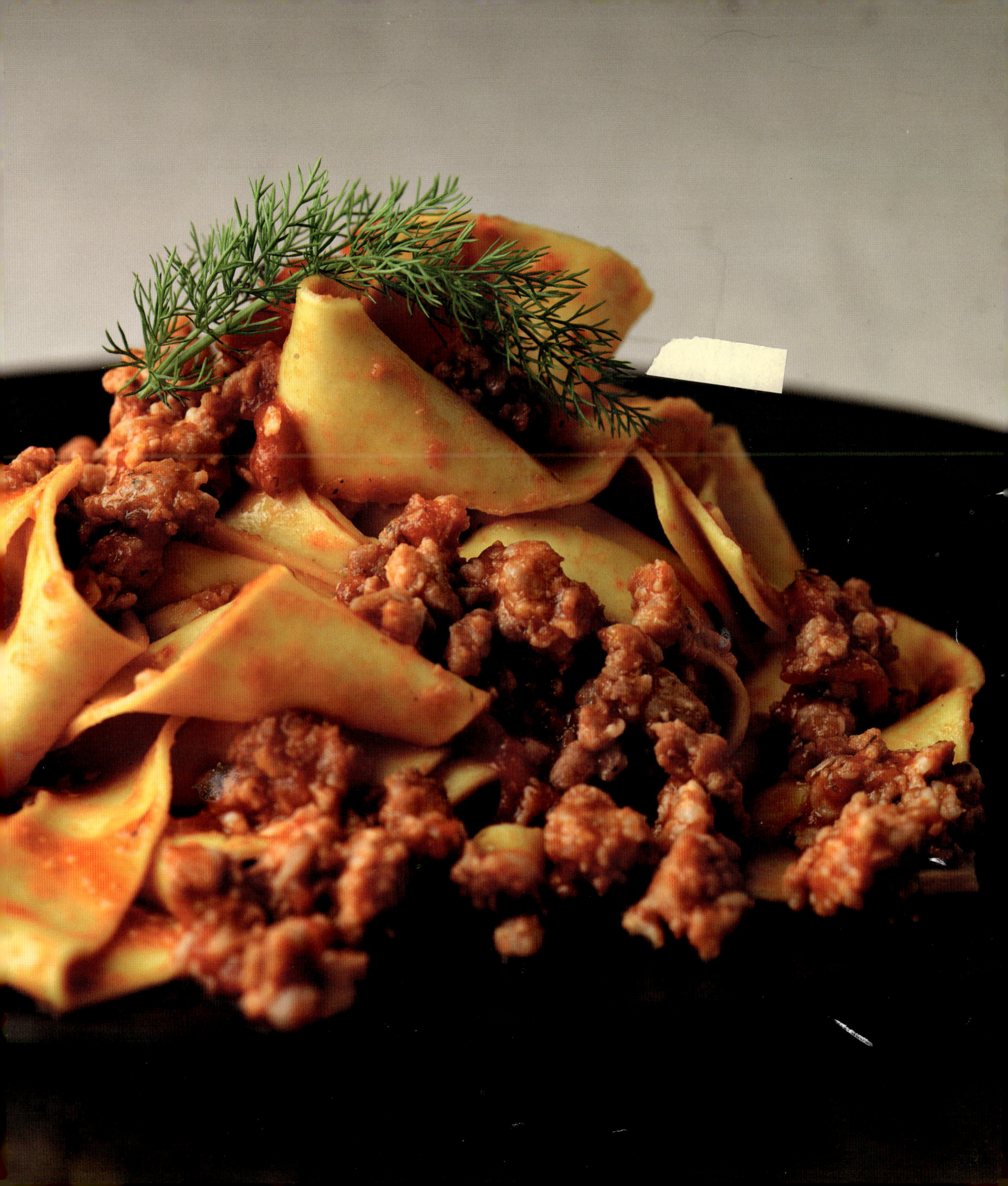

Pumpkin Ravioli with Amaretto Cookies

This delicate pasta dish has its roots in northern Italy, in the area around the city of Mantua and the Emilia region. The pumpkin plays an essential role in the stuffing and we suggest using the Marina di Chioggia variety with bumpy green skin. Its firm, sweet flesh is a perfect match for Mantua's famed lightly spiced mostarda (Italy's answer to chutney), which gives the dish its unique sweet-and-sour flavor.

Serves 4 to 6

1 (3-pound) Marina di Chioggia pumpkin
½ cup crumbled amaretto cookies
½ cup Cremona apple mostarda, chopped
¾ cup grated Parmigiano Reggiano
Freshly grated nutmeg to taste
Salt to taste
1 pound 2 ounces egg pasta dough (see page 132)
Coarse sea salt to taste
8 tablespoons (1 stick) unsalted butter, melted
Fresh sage leaves to taste
Black pepper to taste

Suggested Wine Pairing

Riesling
Producer:
St Paul
Grape:
Riesling
Region:
Trentino Alto Adige

Preparation

- Preheat the oven to 320°F. Cut the pumpkin into thick slices. Remove and discard the seeds and filaments. Bake until soft but not charred, about 1 hour.

- Let the pumpkin cool, then remove the rind. Dice about ½ cup of the cooked pumpkin and set aside. Puree the remaining pumpkin with a food mill.

- Reserve 1 to 2 teaspoons crumbled amaretto cookies and stir the rest into the pumpkin puree, then add the mostarda, about half of the grated Parmigiano, and nutmeg. Combine the ingredients well, add salt to taste, and refrigerate for a few hours.

- When you're ready to make the ravioli, divide the egg pasta dough into four pieces. Keep three pieces wrapped, and roll out one piece of dough ⅛ inch thick. Cut into wide strips. Starting one inch from the end of the strip and slightly closer to the bottom, place tablespoons of the filling 1½ inches apart down the strip the long way. Fold the strip of pasta in half the long way and press together the edges and in between each spoonful of filling to seal. Use a pastry cutter to cut the ravioli into squares. Repeat with remaining dough and filling.

- Bring a large pot of water to boil and add coarse sea salt. Cook the ravioli until they float to the top of the cooking water, 4 to 5 minutes.

- Arrange the ravioli on a serving platter in layers, drizzling melted butter and the reserved cooked pumpkin in between the layers. Top with sage, pepper, the remaining Parmigiano, and the reserved crumbled amaretto cookies.

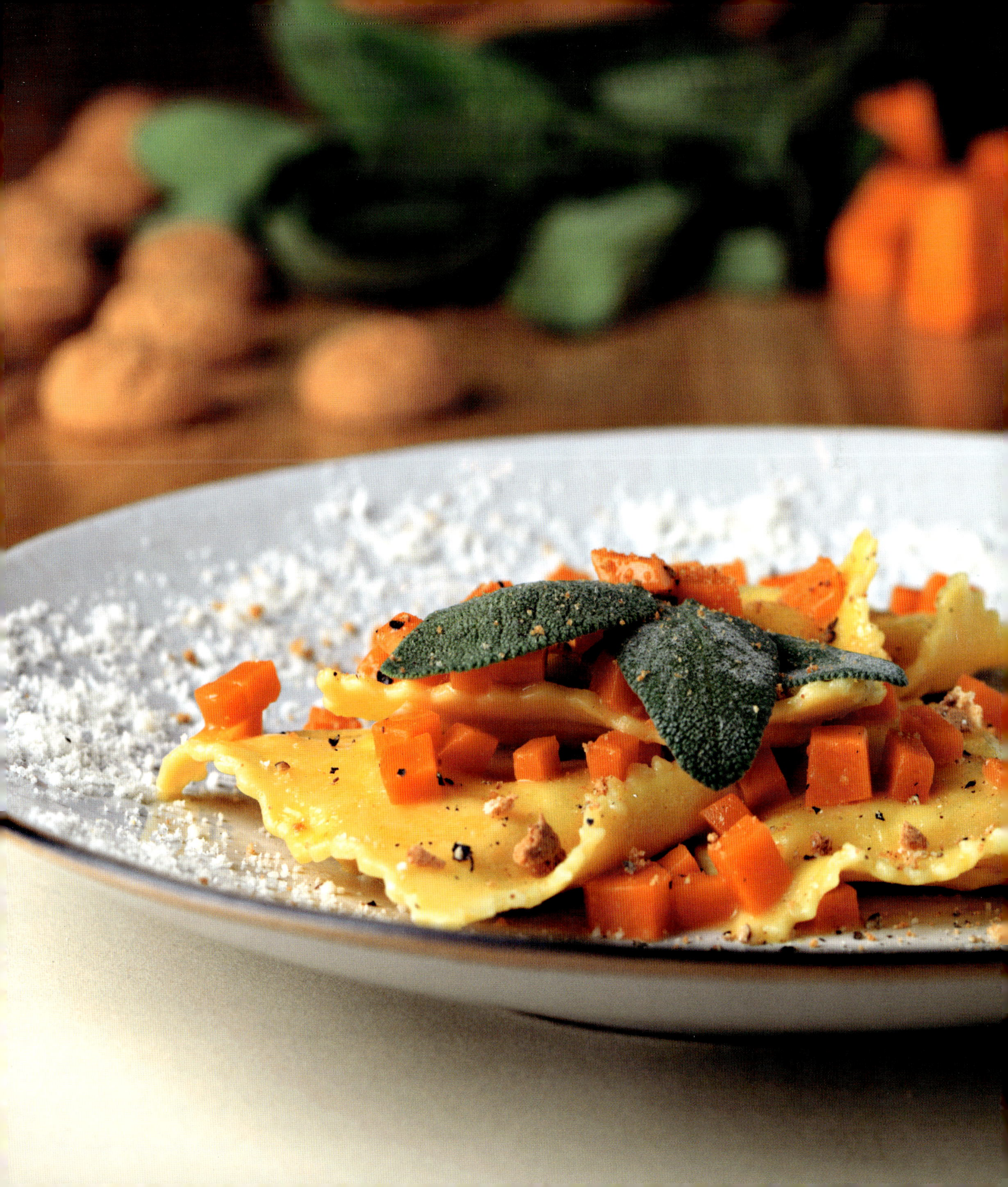

Ravioli with Ricotta and Eggplant

This ideal summer dish includes a tasty, delicate filling made with buffalo milk ricotta and eggplant. We recommend using light purple round eggplants, as their flesh is tender, firm, and not particularly bitter, and they have very few seeds.

Serves 4 to 6

3 to 4 medium eggplants
11 ounces buffalo milk ricotta
1 egg yolk
½ cup grated Parmigiano Reggiano
10 fresh basil leaves
9 ounces egg pasta dough (see page 132)
2 tablespoons extra-virgin olive oil, plus more for drizzling
1¾ cups grape tomatoes, cut into strips
Coarse sea salt to taste
Black pepper to taste

Suggested Wine Pairing

Etna Rosso
Producer:
Benanti, Serra della Contessa
Grape:
Nerello Mascalese, Nerello Cappuccio
Region:
Sicily

Preparation

- Preheat the oven to 400°F. Place the eggplants on a jelly-roll pan lined with parchment paper and bake until soft, about 40 minutes.
- Set the eggplants aside to cool. When they are cool enough to handle, peel them and squeeze out any excess liquid.
- With a fork, mash the eggplant, then blend in the ricotta, the egg yolk, and about half of the grated Parmigiano. Chop 4 of the basil leaves and stir them in. Blend well. Transfer the filling to a pastry bag.
- When you're ready to make the ravioli, roll out the dough ⅛ inch thick. Cut into wide strips. Use a pastry bag to dot the eggplant mixture about 1½ inches apart down one side of a strip.
- Fold the strip of pasta in half the long way and press together the edges and in between each spoonful of filling to seal, ensuring that there is no air trapped inside the ravioli. Use a fluted pastry wheel or ravioli stamp to cut the ravioli. Repeat with remaining dough and filling.
- Heat the oil in the pan and cook the tomatoes until softened. Chop 2 basil leaves and stir into the tomato mixture.
- Meanwhile, bring a large pot of water to a boil and add coarse sea salt. Cook the ravioli until they float to the top of the cooking water, 4 to 5 minutes. Drain and transfer to a serving bowl. Top with the tomato mixture.
- Sprinkle on the remaining Parmigiano and season with pepper and a drizzle of oil. Garnish with the remaining 4 basil leaves.

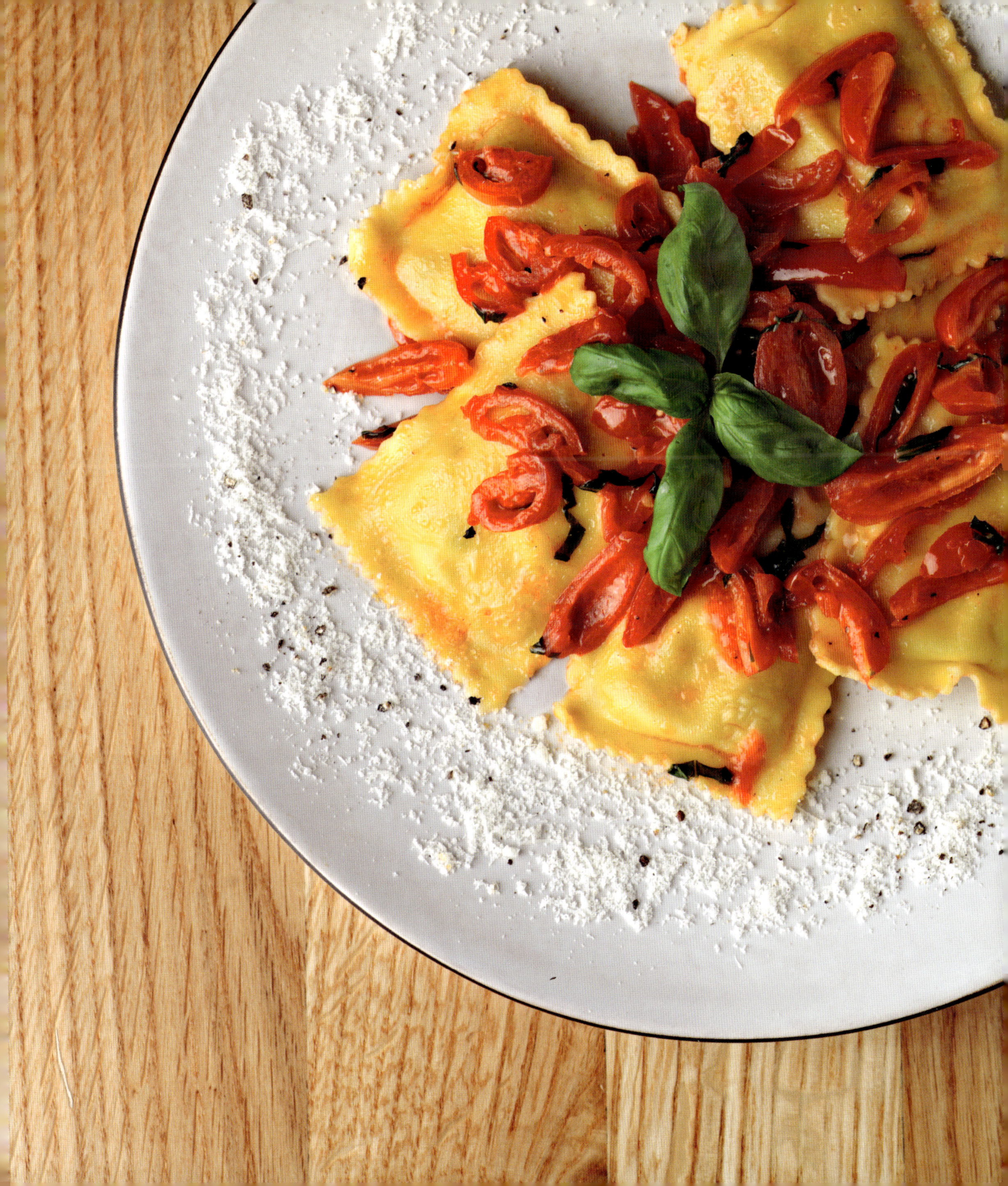

Lasagne with String Beans and Pesto

The recipe for this vegetarian dish comes from our Los Angeles restaurant. It incorporates some truly superb cheeses, and. the basil and string beans make it a great seasonal summer dish.

Serves 4 to 6

11 ounces string beans
Coarse sea salt to taste
14 ounces fresh lasagne (see page 132)
1 quart thin béchamel
7 ounces fresh goat cheese
9 ounces buffalo milk ricotta
¾ cup grated Parmigiano Reggiano
1 cup basil pesto (see page 124)

Suggested Wine Pairing

Pigato
Producer:
Lupi
Grape:
Pigato
Region:
Liguria

Preparation

- Preheat the oven to 350°F. Trim the string beans and cut in half at an angle.
- Bring a large pot of water to a boil, salt to taste, and cook the string beans until very al dente, 5 to 8 minutes. Remove the string beans with a slotted spoon and let the water return to a boil. Cook the lasagne until it floats to the top of the water, drain, and set aside.
- Spread about ¼ cup of the béchamel in the bottom of a rectangular glass or ceramic baking dish. Top with a layer of lasagne without overlapping them.
- Top the pasta with another layer of béchamel, some string beans, some goat cheese, some ricotta, some Parmigiano, and a few tablespoons of pesto. Repeat in this order until all the ingredients have been used up. You should have enough for 3 or 4 layers in all.
- Bake until heated through and browned on top, about 40 minutes. Let the pasta stand for 5 minutes before serving

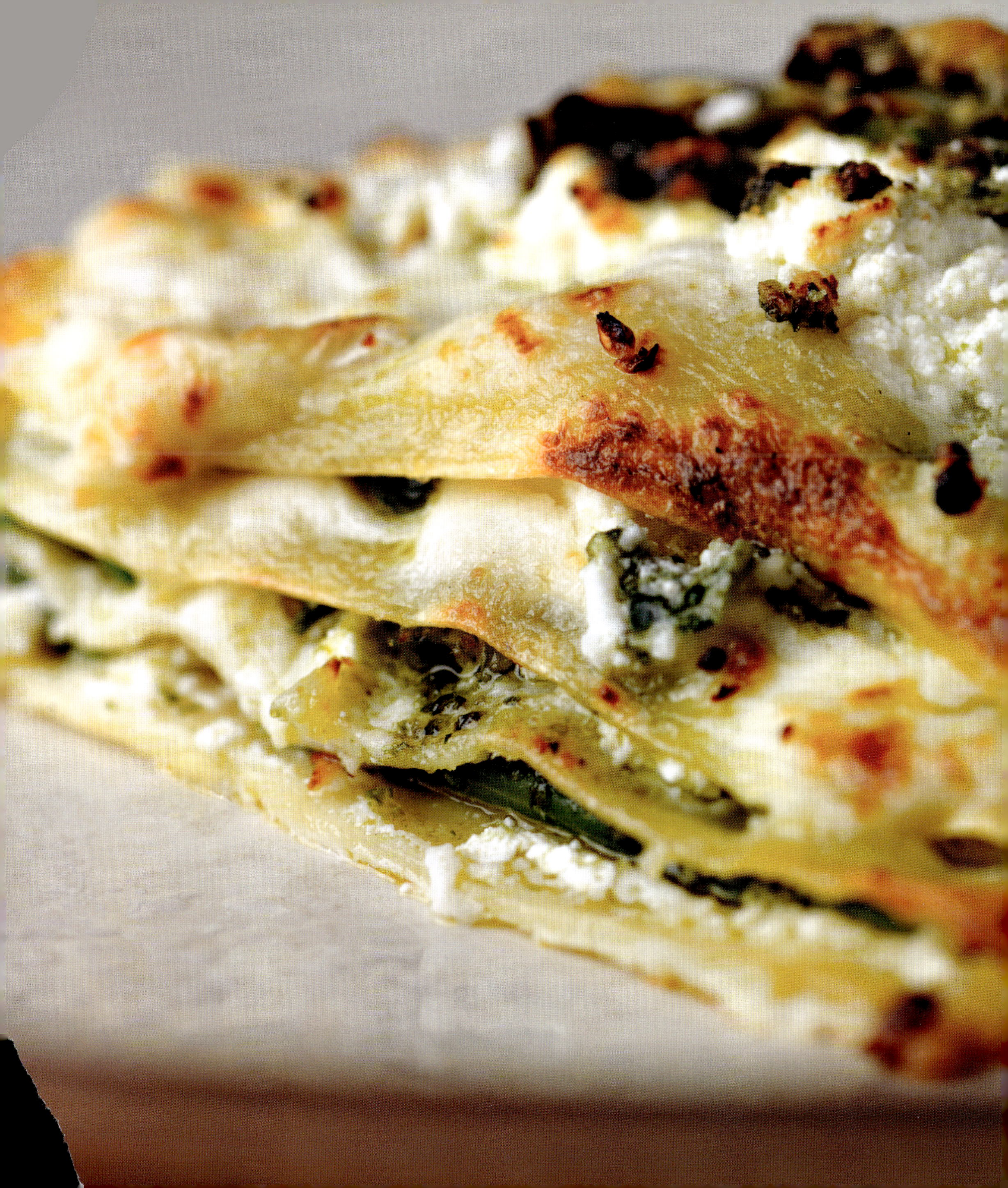

Lasagne with Chianina Ragù

We chose to give this traditional recipe from the Emilia region a unique, light touch by using lean Chianina beef in the meat sauce. This breed of cattle gets is name from Val di Chiana and is protected under IGP status, so that the area of production, birth, breeding, butchering, and quality are all closely regulated.

Serves 4 to 6

⅓ cup extra-virgin olive oil
¾ cup minced carrots
¾ cup minced celery
Minced fresh rosemary to taste, plus more for serving
1 pound 2 ounces ground Chianina beef
⅓ cup plus 2 tablespoons dry red wine
1 cup tomato puree
¾ cup plus 2 tablespoons beef stock
Salt and black pepper to taste
¾ cup plus 2 tablespoons whole milk
Coarse sea salt to taste
14 ounces lasagne (see page 132)
1 quart béchamel
14 ounces mozzarella di bufala Campana DOP, diced
1 cup grated Parmigiano Reggiano, plus more for serving

Suggested Wine Pairing

Therra
Producer:
PoderNuovo a Palazzone
Grapes:
Sangiovese, Montepulciano, Cabernet Sauvignon, Merlot
Region: Tuscany

Preparation

- Heat the olive oil in a saucepan and add the carrots, celery, and rosemary. Crumble in the beef and cook over high heat until browned, about 5 minutes.
- Add the wine and let it evaporate.
- Add the tomato puree, the stock, and a pinch of salt and pepper.
- Turn the heat down to a very gentle simmer, cover the saucepan, and let the sauce simmer for 2 hours, stirring occasionally. At the end of the cooking time, stir in the milk.
- Bring a large pot of water to a boil, add coarse sea salt, and cook the lasagne until it floats to the top of the water. Drain and set aside.
- Preheat the oven to 350°F. Spread about 3 tablespoons of meat sauce and 3 tablespoons of béchamel on the bottom of a rectangular glass or ceramic baking dish. Top with a layer of lasagne, then add another layer of béchamel, meat sauce, some of the mozzarella, and a sprinkling of Parmigiano. Repeat in that order until all the ingredients have been used up.
- Bake the lasagne until heated through and browned on top, about 50 minutes. Let stand for 5 minutes. Sprinkle with additional Parmigiano and rosemary and serve.

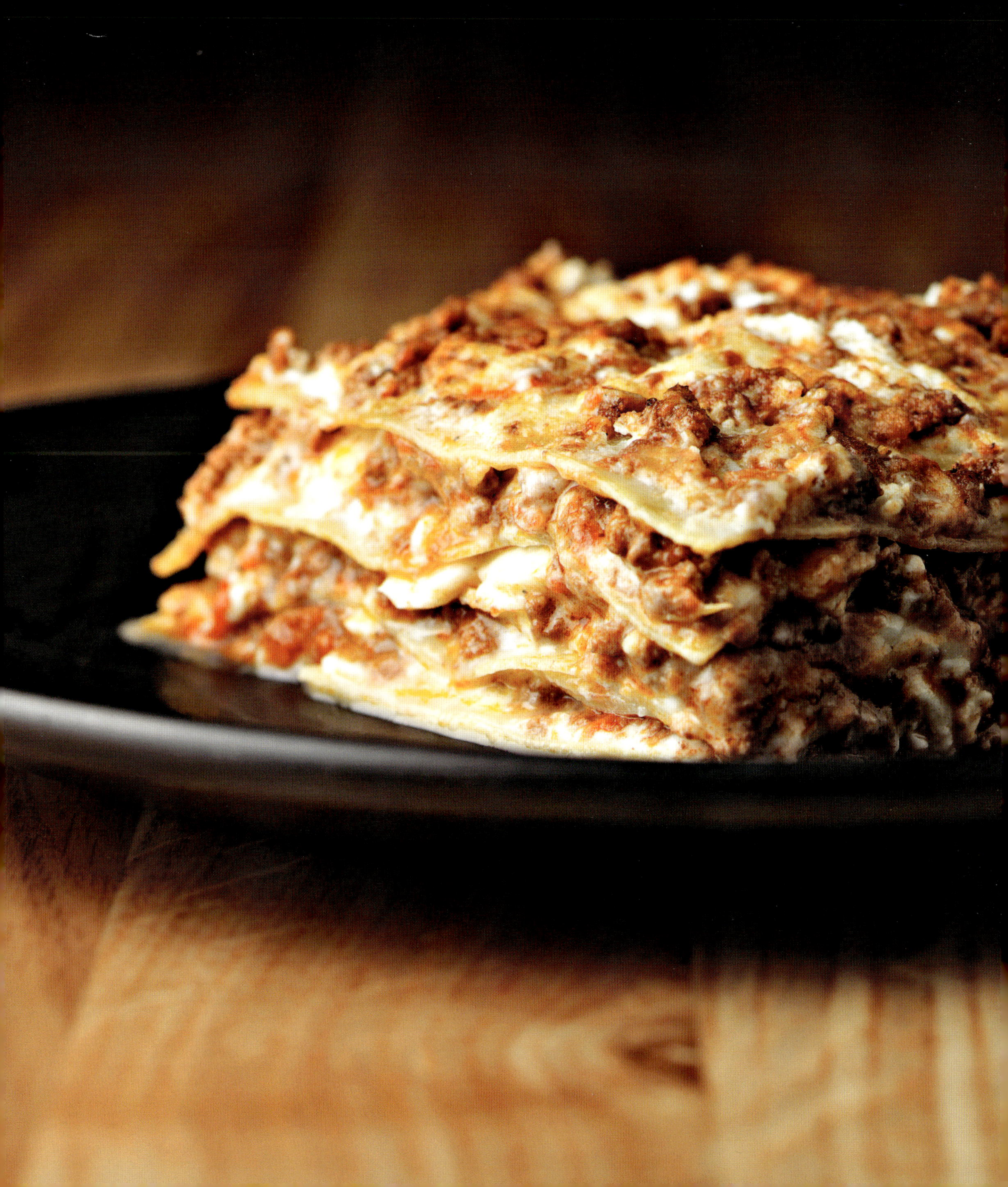

Cantine PoderNuovo a Palazzone

Podernuovo a Palazzone is both a place and a project. It was founded by father and son duo Paolo and Giovanni Bulgari. Ever committed to the quest for the beautiful and the well-made through their famous, prestigious family business, in 2004 they launched a new business and reestablished a vineyard that had been long abandoned, thereby creating this innovative farm nestled in the Sienese hills. The Bulgari family has long nurtured a passion for excellence and for nature that has led them to investigate and develop the potential of various types of terroir, which have rewarded them with three harmonious red wines. Giovanni Bulgari, CEO of Podernuovo a Palazzone and the company's inspirational leader, is extremely conscious of the environment, which he sees as the crucial starting point in creating his wine. The company works to limit carbon dioxide emissions, as well as to handle its grapes using methods that are respectful of nature.

OPPOSITE:
Since 2004, Giovanni Bulgari has devoted himself to this business along with his father, Paolo.

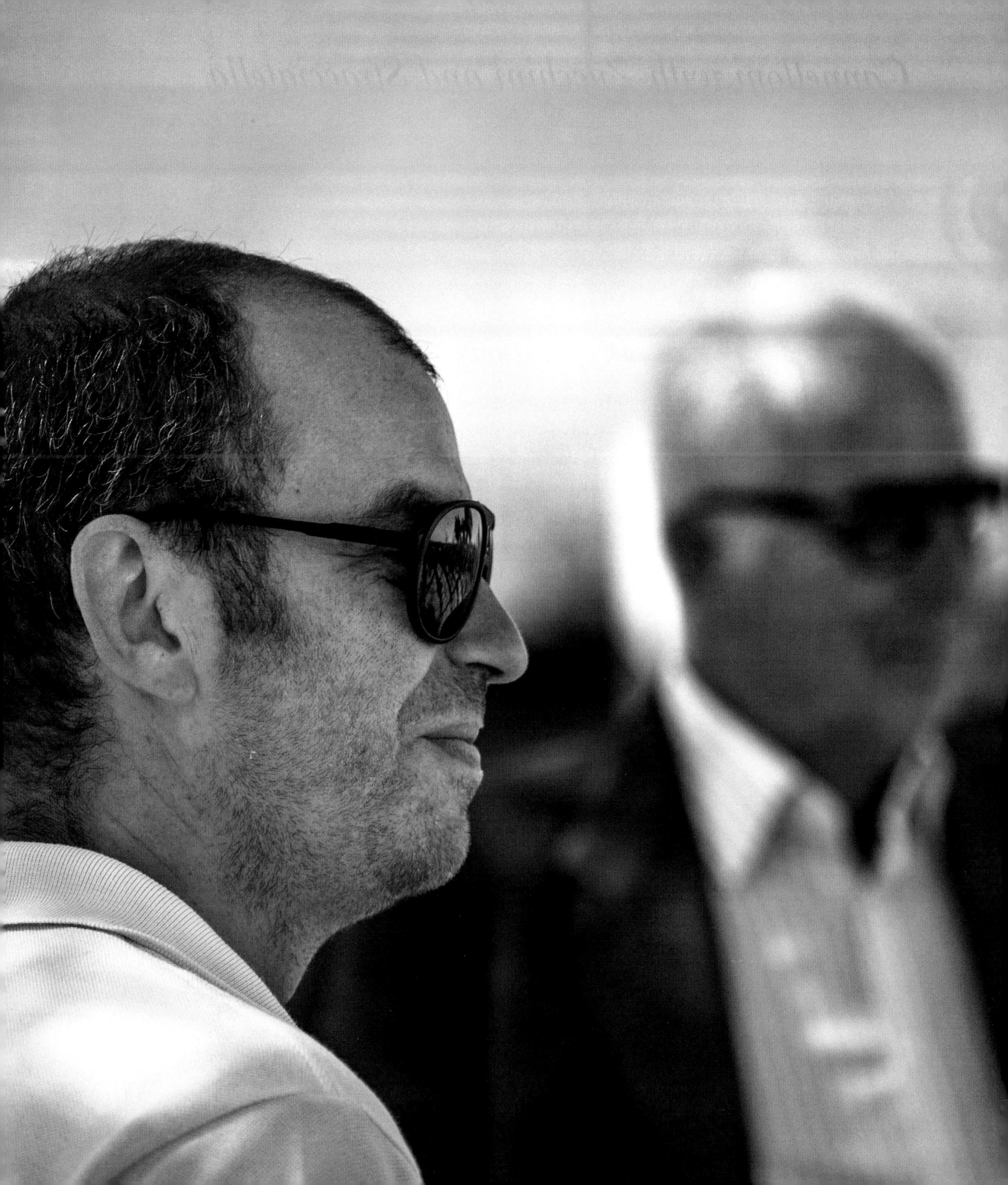

Cannelloni with Zucchini and Stracciatella

Cannelloni, along with lasagne, is one of Italy's most famous baked pastas. Cannelloni is a homey dish, originally made by skillful grandmothers to celebrate Sundays spent with the whole family. Although they are somewhat complicated to make, they are always a hit.

In this recipe, we combine tasty Sardinian pecorino cheese with creamy burrata from Puglia and excellent Romanesco zucchini (the variety with light green ribs running lengthwise) seasoned with thyme.

Serves 4 to 6

3 tablespoons extra-virgin olive oil
1 pound 12 ounces Romanesco zucchini, diced
Thyme sprigs to taste
Salt and black pepper to taste
9 ounces burrata
9 ounces buffalo milk ricotta
½ cup plus 1 tablespoon grated Parmigiano Reggiano
Coarse sea salt to taste
14 ounces cannelloni (see page 132)
2¼ cups béchamel
½ cup grated early Sardinian pecorino

Suggested Wine Pairing

Leone
Producer: Tasca d'Almerita
Grapes: Catarratto, Pinot Bianco, Traminer, Sauvignon blanc
Region: Sicily

Preparation

- Heat the oil in a saucepan over medium-high heat and add the diced zucchini with the sprigs of thyme. Cook, stirring occasionally, until the zucchini are a deep golden brown. Remove from heat and season with salt and pepper. Set aside to cool.

- When the zucchini have cooled, remove and discard the thyme. Transfer the zucchini to a bowl. Tear the burrata into pieces and add to the zucchini. Stir in the ricotta and ½ cup Parmigiano.

- Bring a large pot of water to a boil, add coarse sea salt, and cook the cannelloni. Drain and arrange in a single layer on flat-weave dish towels. Blot the tops.

- Preheat the oven to 350°F. Spread about ½ cup of béchamel in the bottom of a baking dish. Place the cheese mixture in a pastry bag fitted with a wide tip. Place a cooked egg noodle on the work surface and pipe a thick strip of filling down the center. Loosely roll the noodle and arrange it seam-side down in the baking dish on top of the béchamel. Repeat with remaining cannelloni and filling, arranging the cannelloni in a single layer. It's fine if they are pressed tightly against each other, but don't stack them.

- Drizzle the remaining béchamel over the top of the cannelloni. Sprinkle any remaining filling over them and sprinkle on the remaining tablespoon Parmigiano.

- Bake until the top is browned, about 20 minutes, then sprinkle the cannelloni with the pecorino and serve.

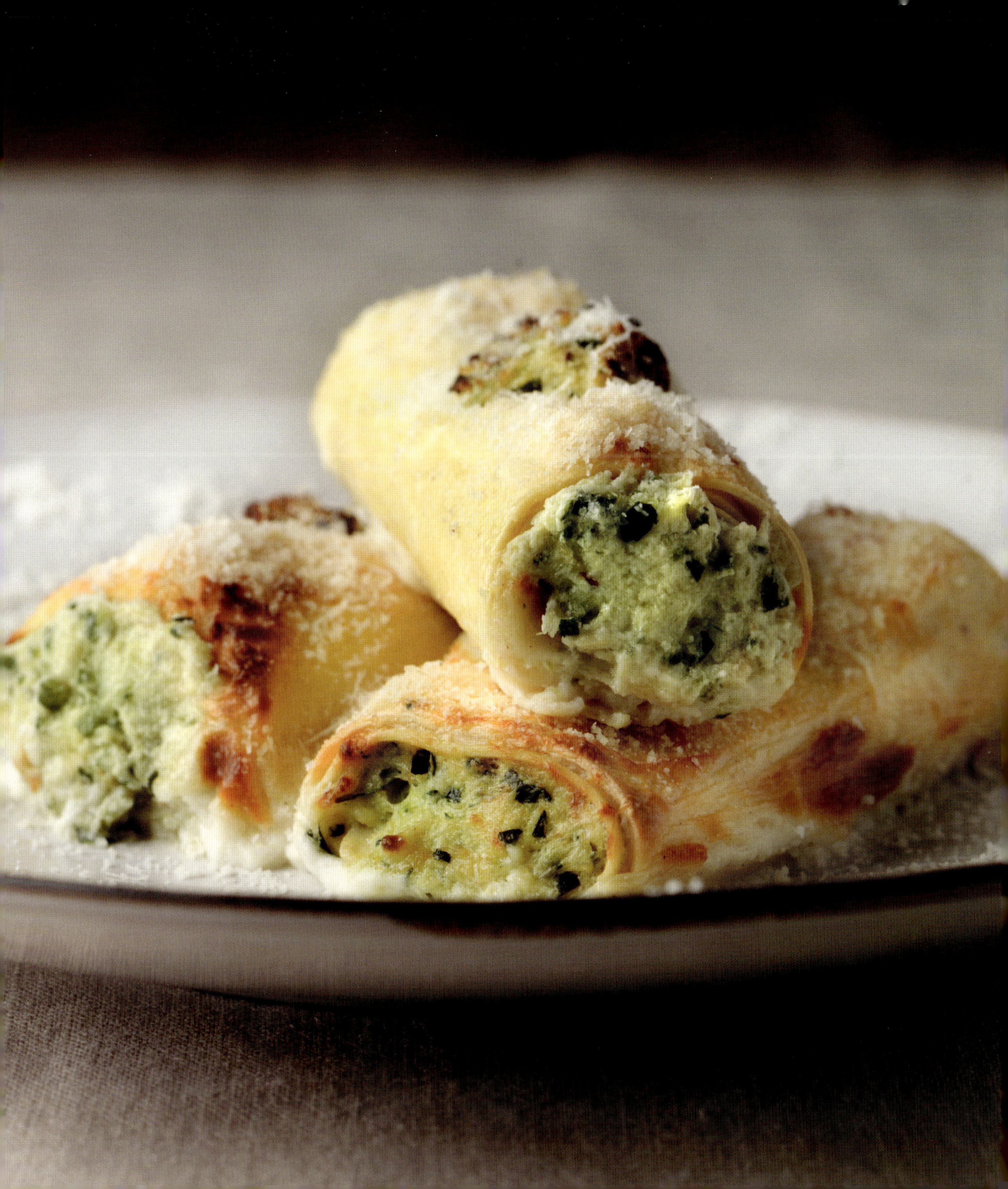

Potato Gnocchi

Though potato gnocchi are the most famous type of gnocchi, the word simply means dumplings, and gnocchi can also be made with wheat flour, rice flour, semolina flour, stale bread, or root vegetables. For potato gnocchi, russet potatoes are a good choice as they are starchier and absorb less flour, so the gnocchi will be softer and more flavorful. The less flour you use, the softer the gnocchi—the goal is gnocchi that melt in your mouth. Don't use more than 30 percent flour (by weight). After you've made this recipe a few times, you'll never need to weigh your flour and your potatoes—you'll have no trouble creating a dough that's delightfully soft but won't disintegrate while cooking.

Serves 4 to 6

1 pound 12 ounces starchy potatoes, such as russet potatoes
2 cups unbleached all-purpose flour
1 small egg
1 tablespoon plus 1 teaspoon salt

Preparation

- Wash the potatoes, then put them (unpeeled) in a large pot. Add cold water to cover by a couple of inches. Bring to a boil, then simmer uncovered until done, about 40 minutes.
- While the potatoes are still warm, peel them and puree them through a food mill. Discard the peels.
- Mound the flour and the potato puree on a wooden work surface. Make a well in the center and break the egg into the well. Add the salt and beat the egg.
- Gradually work in the ingredients, then knead until you have a smooth, compact dough with no lumps.
- Form the dough into a ball, wrap in plastic wrap, and let rest for at least 30 minutes in a cool dry place. Thoroughly clean the work surface.
- Lightly flour the work surface and jelly-roll pans or platters where you will place the finished gnocchi. Pinch off a piece of the dough about the size of an egg and rewrap the rest. Briefly knead the piece of dough, then roll it into a rope ¾ inch to 1 inch in diameter. Use a knife to cut the gnocchi about 1 inch long. Let stand on the floured pan.
- To cook the gnocchi, bring a large pot of water to a boil. Season with coarse sea salt and add the gnocchi. When they float to the surface, they are cooked. Remove with a skimmer or slotted spoon to a colander.
- Toss with one of the following sauces.

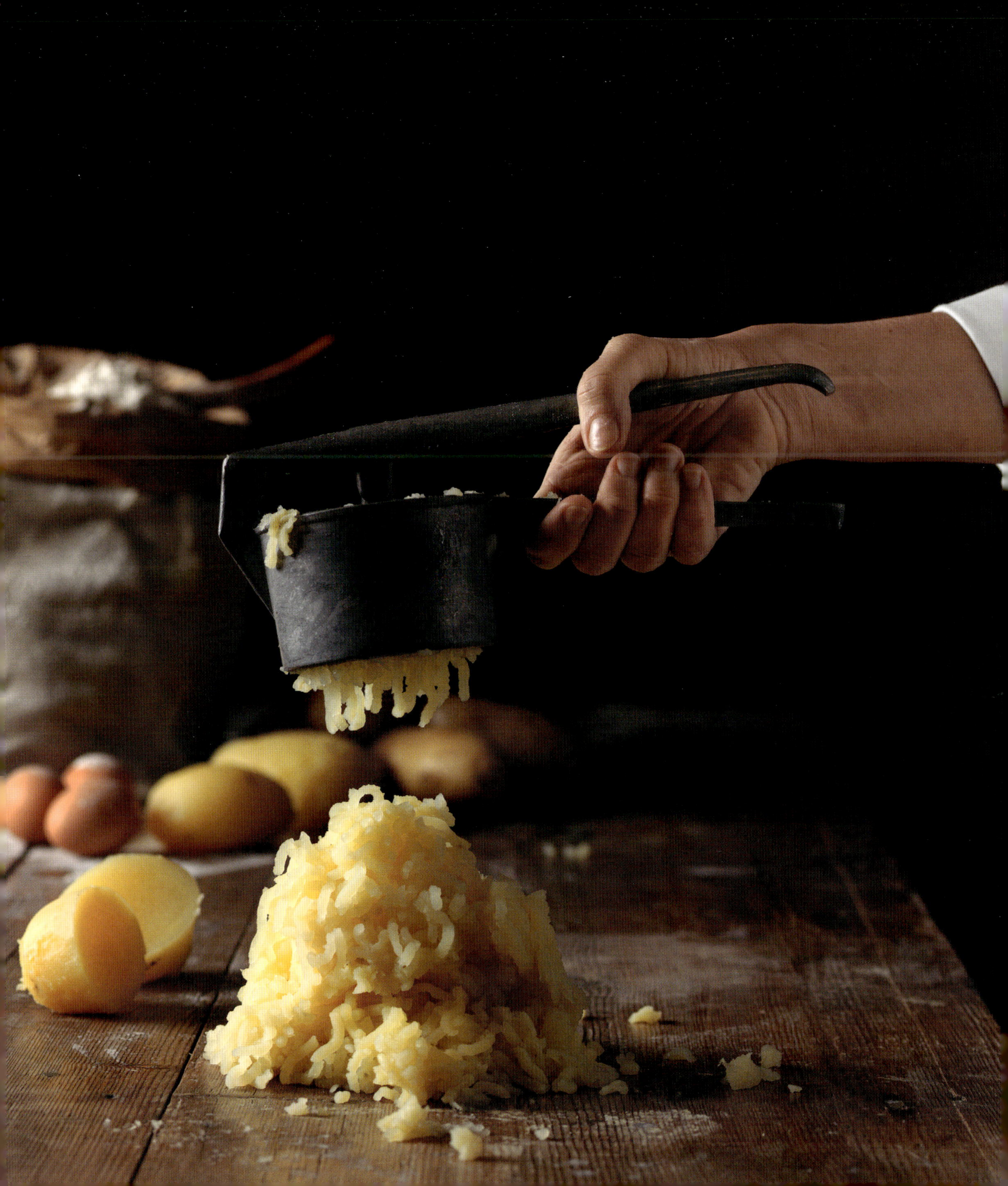

Gnocchi with Blu di Bufala and Spinach

Use the basic recipe for potato gnocchi. If you're feeling patient, roll the rope of dough very thin and cut the gnocchi very small to make tiny gnocchi the size of cannellini beans.

They'll disappear into this delicious sauce.

Serves 4 to 6

2 pounds spinach
Coarse sea salt to taste
7 ounces blu di bufala
1 cup mascarpone
¾ cup plus 2 tablespoons whole milk
½ cup grated Parmigiano Reggiano
8 fresh basil leaves
1 batch potato gnocchi (see page 148)
Black pepper to taste
2 tablespoons pine nuts, lightly toasted

Suggested Wine Pairing

Gewürztraminer
Producer:
Hofstatter
Grape:
Gewürztraminer
Region:
Trentino Alto Adige

Preparation

- Wash the spinach. Remove and discard any tough stems. Set aside 8 to 10 spinach leaves.
- Bring a large pot of water to a boil and season with coarse sea salt. Boil the spinach, then remove with a slotted spoon to a colander. Let the water return to a boil. Puree the cooked spinach with the blu di bufala, the mascarpone, the milk, about half of the grated Parmigiano, and 6 of the basil leaves. The mixture should be thick and smooth.
- Boil the gnocchi in the same water used to cook the spinach. A few minutes after they float to the surface, drain and transfer to a bowl. Toss the gnocchi with the spinach and cheese mixture. Arrange the reserved spinach in a serving bowl and sprinkle on the remaining Parmigiano. Arrange the gnocchi on top of the spinach.
- Season with pepper and garnish with the pine nuts and 2 reserved basil leaves.

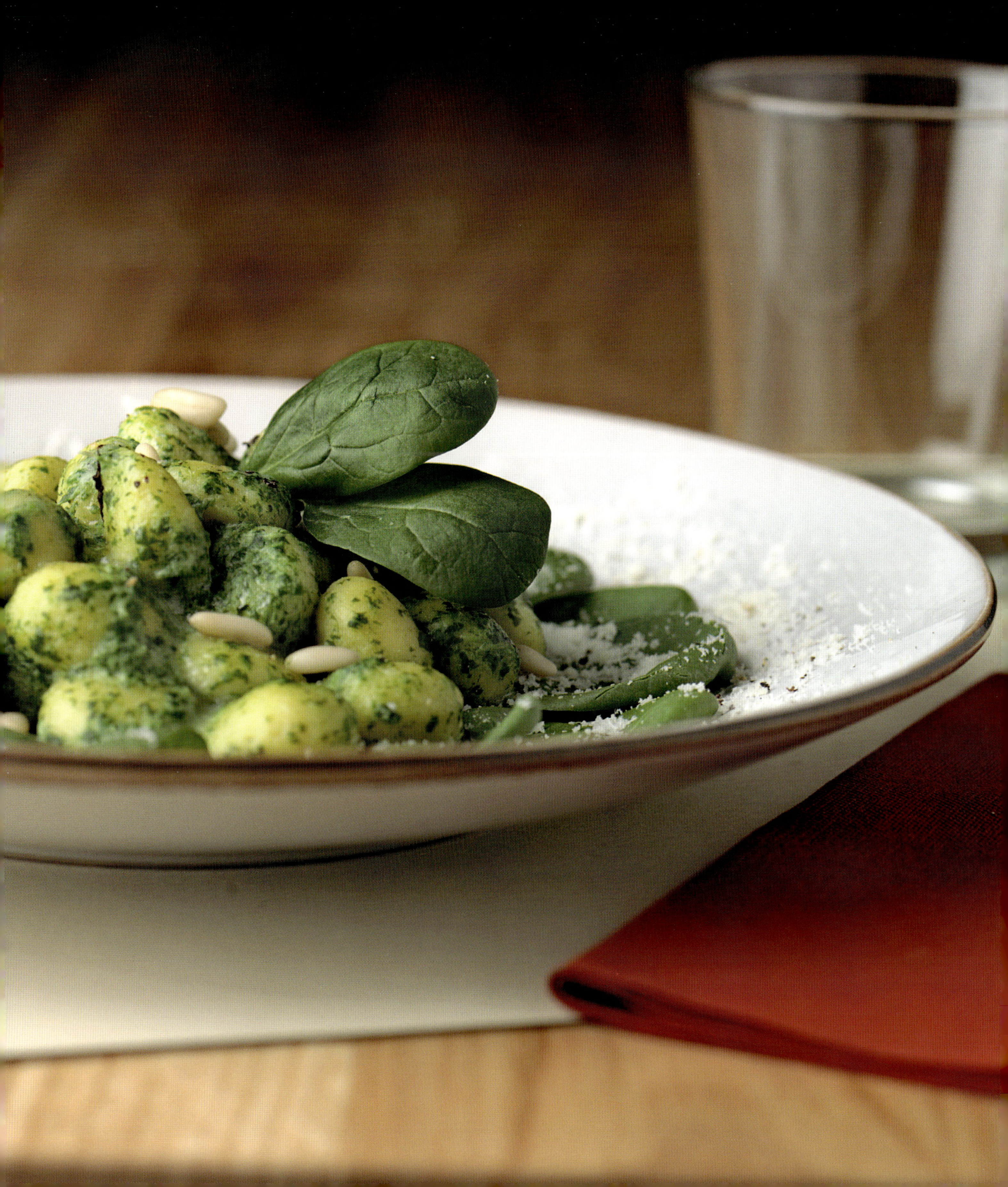

Gnocchi with N'duja and Tomatoes

This sauce made with Calabrian n'duja is strong and spicy. Keep in mind that soft n'duja salami contains a healthy dose of hot pepper—adjust the amount of salami to your own taste. If you're averse to tomato skins, cut a small X in the bottom of each of the grape tomatoes with a paring knife and dunk them in salted boiling water very briefly—about 30 seconds. The skins should slip right off.

Serves 4 to 6

3½ ounces n'duja
3 tablespoons extra-virgin olive oil
3½ cups grape tomatoes, quartered
7 ounces buffalo milk ricotta
⅔ cup whole milk
Coarse sea salt to taste
1 batch potato gnocchi (see page 148)
8 fresh basil leaves, cut into strips
⅓ cup grated Parmigiano Reggiano

Suggested Wine Pairing

Ronco dei Quattro Venti, Cirò classico
Producer:
Fattoria San Francesco
Grape:
Gaglioppo
Region:
Calabria

Preparation

- Remove the casing from the n'duja and cut it into small pieces. Place it in a large saucepan with the oil.
- Place the pan over high heat and cook for 3 minutes, then add the tomatoes.
- Cook the mixture over high heat for 10 minutes, stirring occasionally. Meanwhile, combine the ricotta and the milk in a bowl. When the tomato mixture is cooked, remove it from the heat and stir in the ricotta mixture.
- Bring a large pot of water to a boil. Season with coarse sea salt, add the gnocchi, and stir gently.
- When the gnocchi float to the surface, drain them and toss with the sauce. Add the basil leaves and grated Parmigiano and toss to combine. Serve warm.

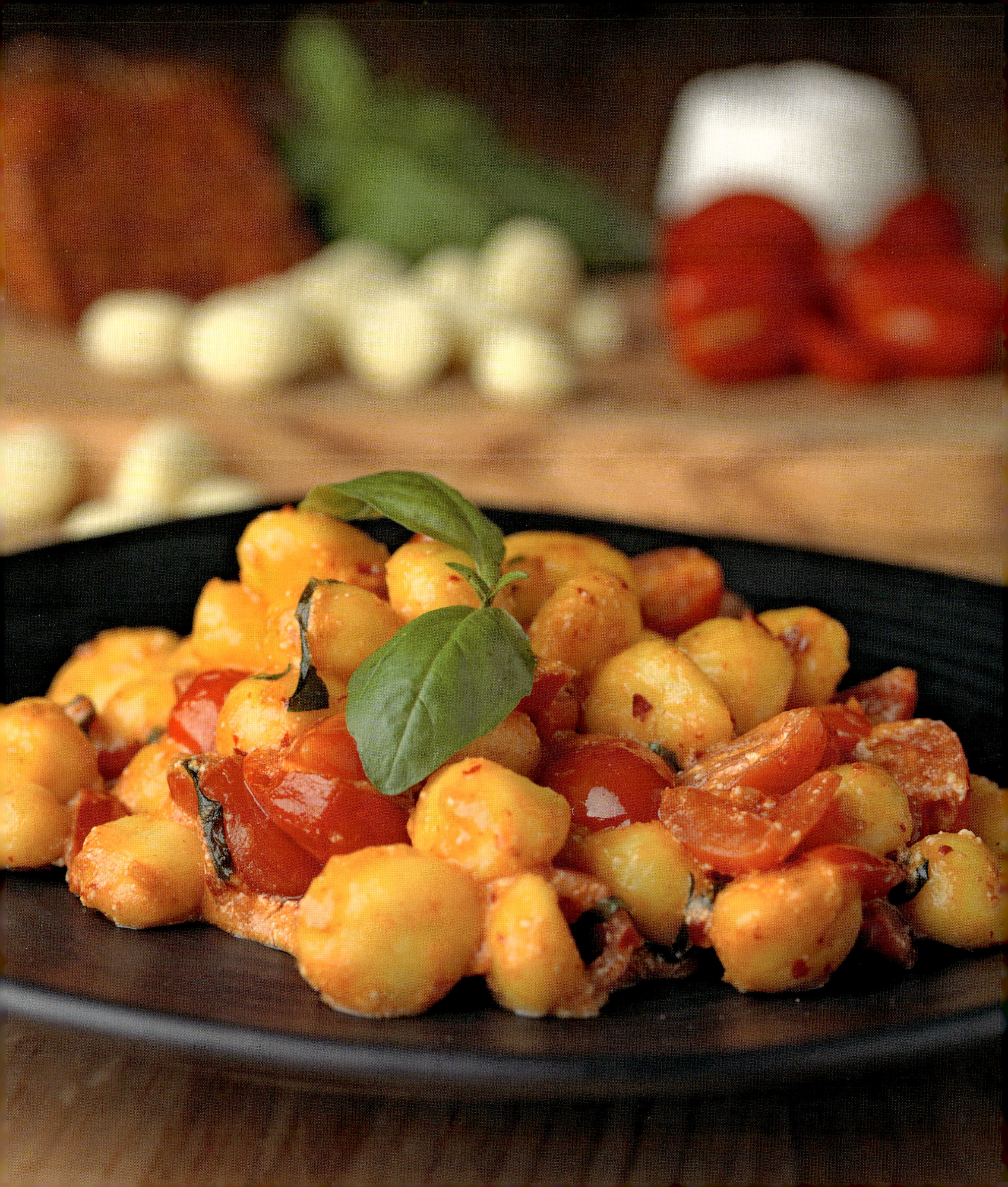

Orecchiette with Garden Peas and Sugar Snap Peas

Orecchiette is a durum wheat pasta from Puglia shaped like a concave disk with a smooth interior and a rough exterior. The word *orecchiette* means "little ears," and that's just what they resemble. This type of pasta goes well with all kinds of ingredients and sauces, as they adhere nicely to its rough surface. We like to pair it with guanciale (cured pork jowl), pecorino cheese, sugar snap peas, and garden peas.

Serves 4 to 6

1 cup shelled fresh garden peas
Salt and black pepper to taste
1 cup sugar snap peas, trimmed
7 ounces guanciale, plus thin slices for garnish
Coarse sea salt to taste
1 pound 2 ounces fresh orecchiette
1 cup grated pecorino Romano, plus shavings for garnish

Suggested Wine Pairing

Treiso Dolcetto d'Alba
Producer:
Fontanafredda
Grape:
Dolcetto
Region:
Piedmont

Preparation

- Bring a small pot of water to a boil, salt to taste, and boil the shelled garden peas until tender, about 4 minutes. Remove the peas with a slotted spoon to a blender or food processor fitted with a metal blade and puree them, then continue pureeing while drizzling in enough of the cooking water to make a thin, creamy mixture the consistency of sour cream. Season with salt and pepper and set aside.

- Blanche the sugar snap peas in salted water.

- Cut the guanciale into julienne and brown in a saucepan large enough to hold the pasta over medium heat. Add the sugar snap peas, then the garden pea mixture.

- Bring a large pot of water to a boil, salt, and cook the orecchiette until al dente. Reserve ½ cup pasta cooking water, then drain the orecchiette and transfer them to the pan. Add the pasta cooking water and the pecorino and toss over medium heat until the ingredients are combined and the liquid has been absorbed.

- Transfer the orecchiette to a serving bowl. Garnish with pecorino shavings and guanciale slices and season with additional pepper to taste.

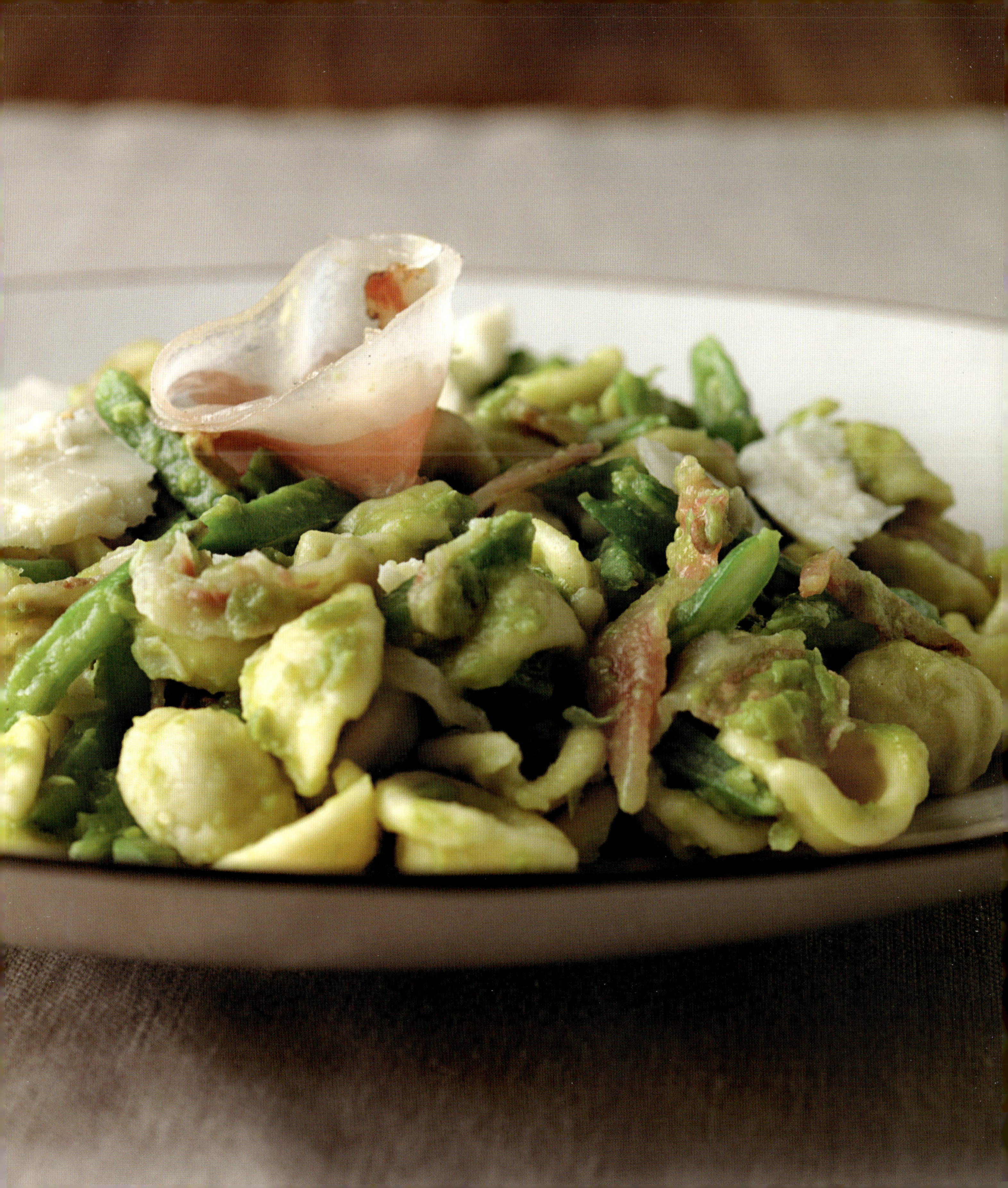

Orecchiette with Broccoli and Provolone

Orecchiette with broccoli rabe is a classic dish from Bari. This very tasty variation uses broccoli in place of the leafy greens. The secret to bringing out the full flavor in this dish is to cook the pasta in the same water used to cook the broccoli.

Serves 4 to 6

1 pound 9 ounces broccoli
Coarse sea salt to taste
⅓ cup plus 2 tablespoons extra-virgin olive oil
Red pepper flakes to taste
1 pound 2 ounces fresh orecchiette
½ cup grated spicy provolone
¼ cup Parmigiano Reggiano shavings

Suggested Wine Pairing

Tintilia del Molise
Producer:
Salvatore
Grape:
Tintilia
Region:
Molise

Preparation

- Chop the broccoli into small pieces. Bring a large pot of water to a boil, add salt to taste, and boil the broccoli until very tender, about 15 minutes.

- Remove the broccoli with a slotted spoon or skimmer and let the water return to a boil. Meanwhile, place ⅓ cup of the olive oil in a pan, add the red pepper flakes and the cooked broccoli and sauté, stirring frequently, over medium heat for 5 minutes. With a fork, crush the broccoli until it is broken down into fine pieces.

- Cook the orecchiette in the same water used to cook the broccoli. When the orecchiette are cooked al dente, reserve about ½ cup cooking water, then drain the pasta and add it to the pan with the broccoli. Sprinkle on the grated provolone and toss to combine. If the dish looks dry, add some of the pasta cooking water, a few tablespoons at a time, stirring to combine between additions.

- Transfer the pasta to a serving bowl. Drizzle on the remaining 2 tablespoons oil and sprinkle on the Parmigiano shavings.

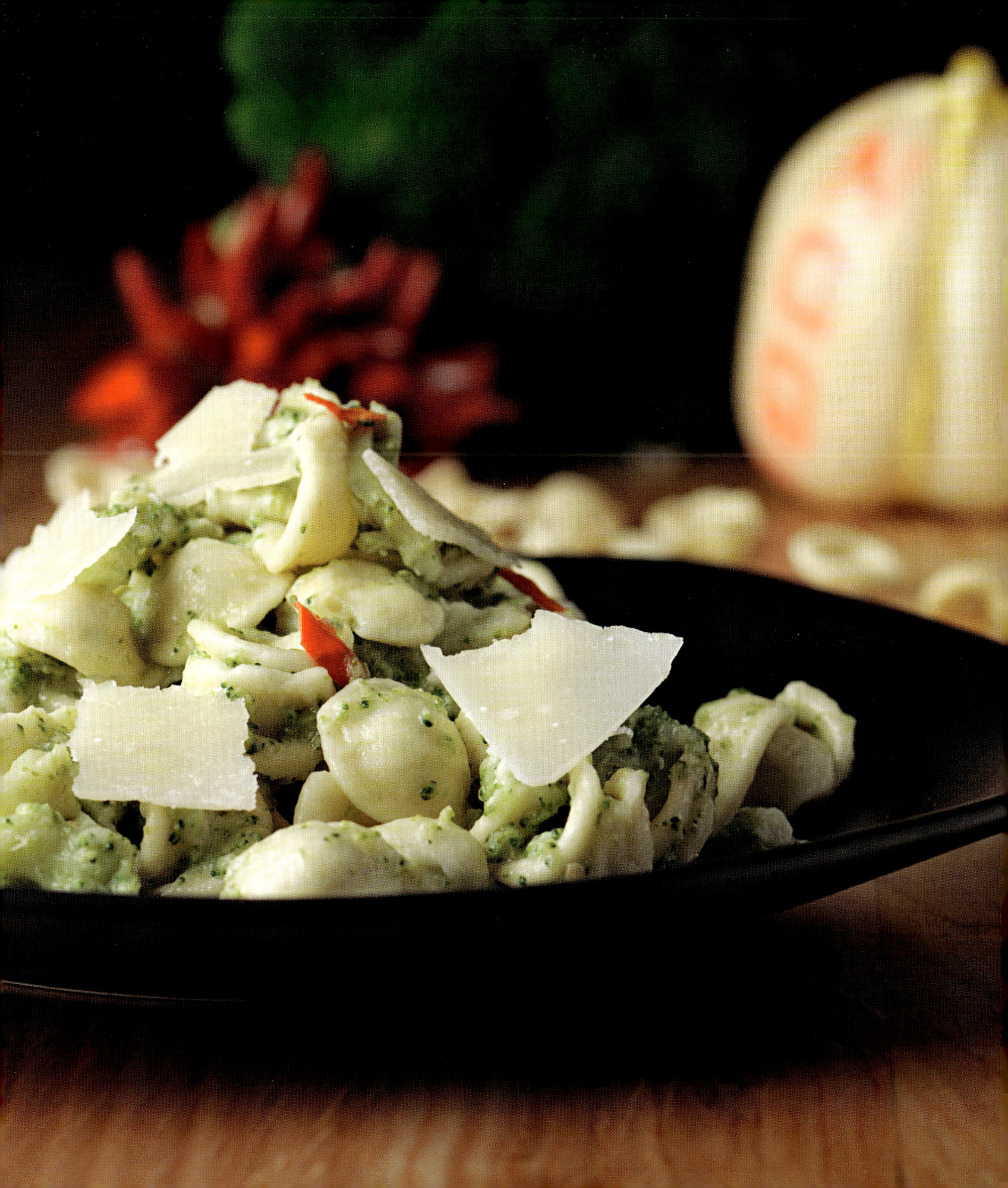

Fregola with Tuna and Tomatoes

Fregola, sometimes spelled fregula, is Sardinia's signature durum wheat pasta. It is somewhat similar to couscous. The dough is kneaded by hand in large earthenware bowls and then toasted in the oven.

Serves 4 to 6

Coarse sea salt to taste
1 pound 2 ounces fregola
¼ cup extra-virgin olive oil
9 ounces mozzarella di bufala Campana DOP
2½ cups grape tomatoes, halved
9 ounces canned tuna in oil, drained
1½ ounces (¼ cup) Cetara anchovy fillets, drained and minced
¼ cup Pantelleria salted capers, soaked and drained
10 fresh mint leaves

Preparation

- Bring a large pot of water to a boil, season with coarse sea salt, and cook the fregola. Drain the pasta and transfer to a large platter or jelly-roll pan. Drizzle with 1 tablespoon of the olive oil, toss to combine, then set aside to cool.
- Drain the mozzarella and cut into ¼-inch cubes.
- When the fregola has cooled, transfer it to a serving bowl and add the mozzarella cubes, the tomatoes, the tuna, the anchovy fillets, and the capers. Drizzle on the remaining 3 tablespoons olive oil and toss gently to combine. Fold in the mint leaves. Allow to rest 2 hours before serving.

Suggested Wine Pairing

Terre Bianche Cuvée 161
Producer:
Sella&Mosca
Grape:
Torbato
Region:
Sardinia

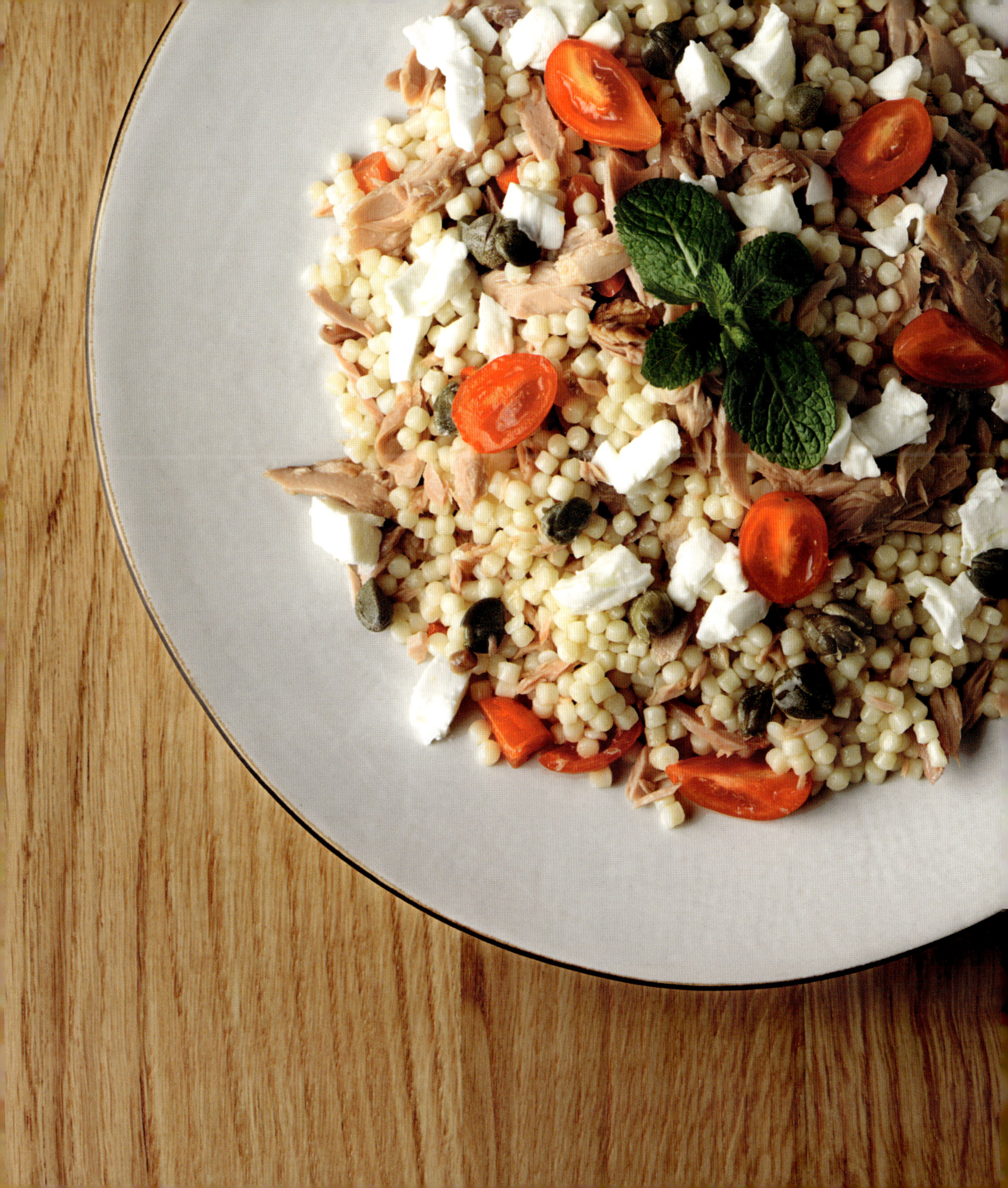

MILAN,
Piazza Duomo

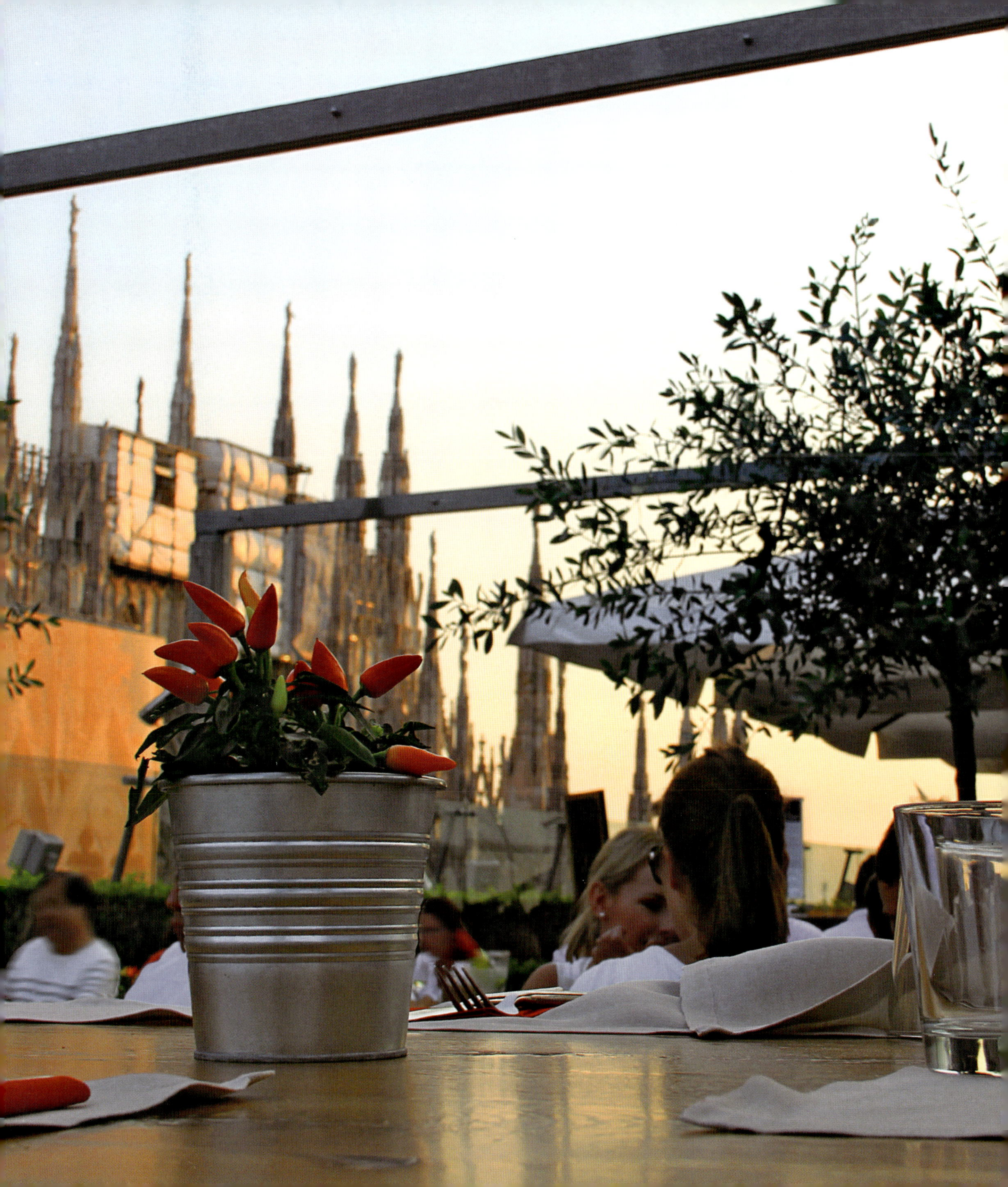

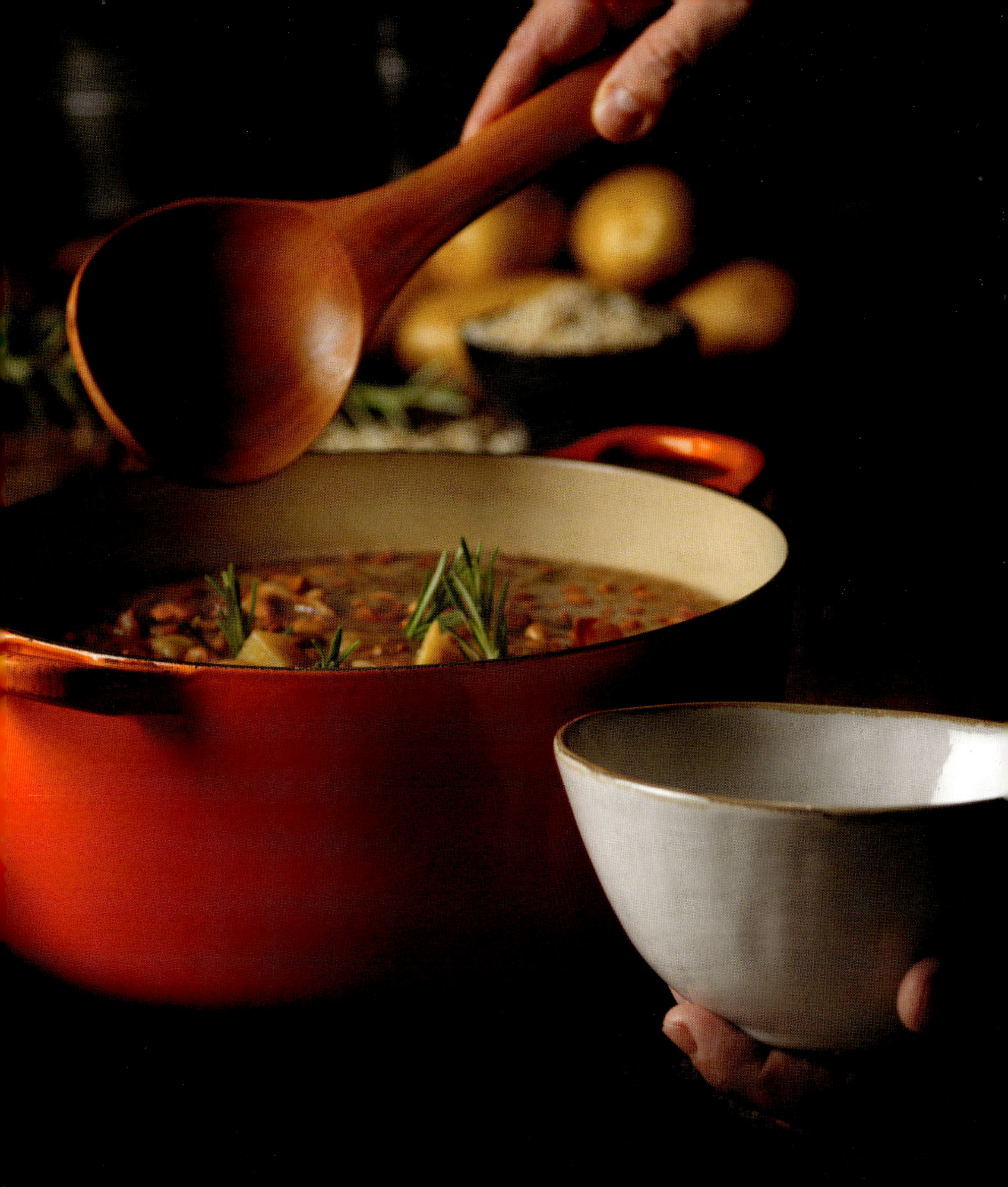

Zuppe

Tomato Soup

Squash with Bronte Pistachios

Zucchini with Mint

Lentil and Potato Soup

Farro and Spinach Soup

Zolfini Bean and Tuscan Kale Soup

Pasta e Ceci

Tomato Soup

This simple summertime recipe calls for fresh tomatoes, but you can also make tomato soup year-round with high-quality preserved tomatoes—we favor the La Motticella brand of peeled whole tomatoes.

Serves 4 to 6

¼ cup loosely packed fresh basil leaves

4 pounds tomatoes, roughly chopped

⅓ cup plus 2 tablespoons extra-virgin olive oil

Salt to taste

Black pepper to taste

9 ounces stracciatella di burrata

Croutons for serving

Suggested Wine Pairing

Franciacorta Brut
Producer:
Bellavista
Grapes:
Chardonnay, Pinot Nero, Pinot Bianco
Region:
Lombardy

Preparation

- Set aside a few basil leaves for garnish. Place the tomatoes, the remaining basil leaves, and the oil in a food processor fitted with a metal blade.
- Process into a smooth thick mixture. Season to taste with salt, then distribute among individual soup bowls.
- Garnish the soup with the reserved basil leaves and season with pepper.
- Serve with the cheese and croutons on the side.

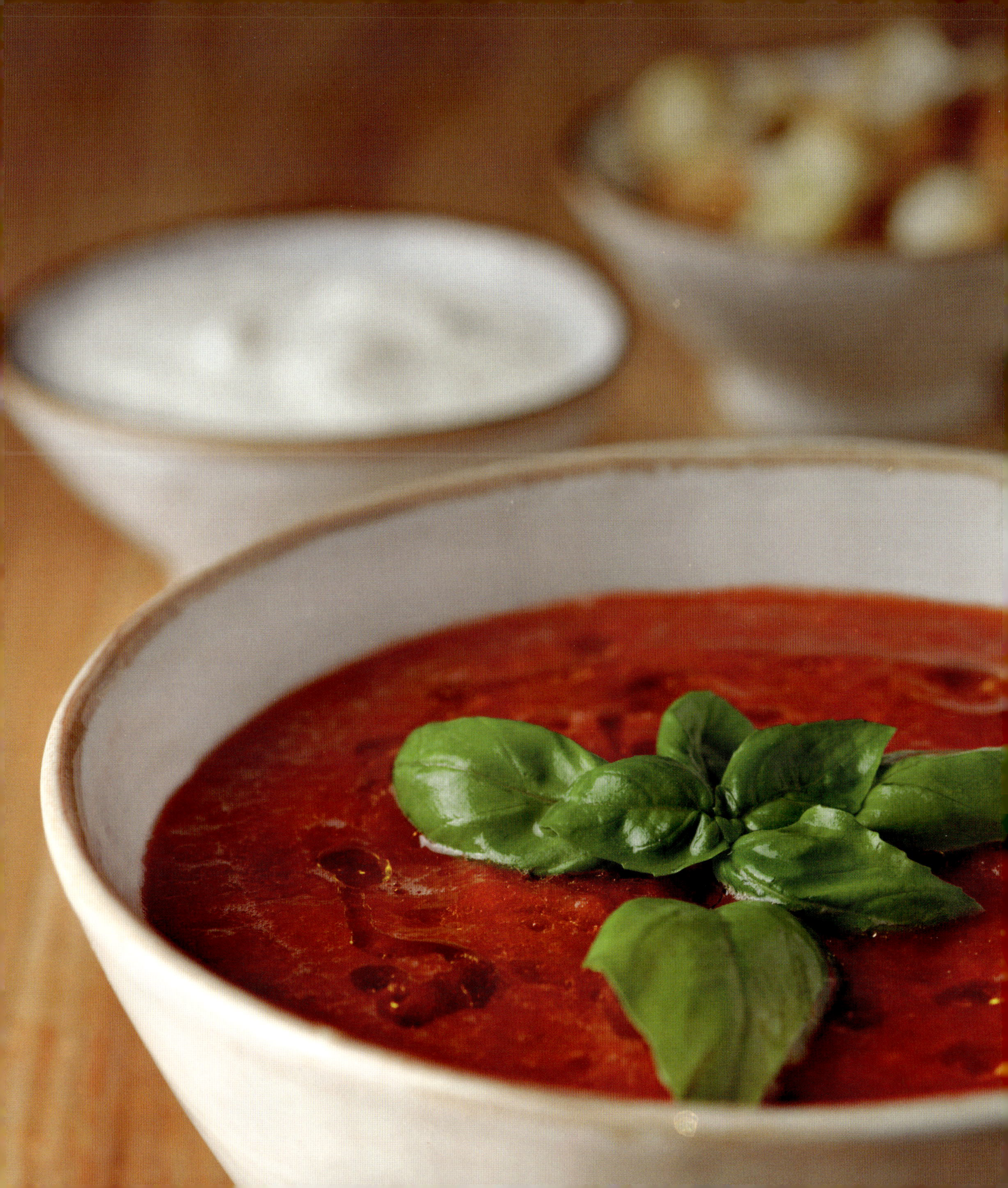

Squash with Bronte Pistachios

The appearance of squash in the market heralds the arrival of the fall season. Squash comes in a great variety of different shapes, sizes, and colors. For this soup we use Marina di Chioggia squash. It has a bumpy rind, and its firm flesh is an orange-yellow color. This soup is good both hot and cold. Add a few extra drops of lemon juice to the cold version right before serving.

Serves 4 to 6

3 pounds 9 ounces peeled and seeded Marina di Chioggia squash, chopped
3¼ cups vegetable stock
3 sprigs thyme, plus more for garnish
Salt to taste
Red pepper flakes to taste
⅓ cup plus 1 tablespoon extra-virgin olive oil
Freshly grated nutmeg to taste
½ teaspoon lemon juice
¼ cup shelled Bronte pistachios, chopped
Croutons for serving

Suggested Wine Pairing

Soave Classico
Producer:
Pieropan
Grape:
Garganega
Region:
Veneto

Preparation

- In a pot, combine the squash, stock, and 3 sprigs thyme. Season with salt and red pepper flakes.
- Bring to a boil, then simmer, covered, until the squash is very soft, about 40 minutes.
- Remove the squash from the heat and allow to cool.
- Remove and discard the thyme sprigs. Place the squash in a food processor fitted with a metal blade. Add about half of the oil, the nutmeg, and the lemon juice and puree until smooth.
- Divide the soup among individual soup bowls. Garnish with the chopped pistachios and thyme sprigs and drizzle on the remaining oil.
- Serve with croutons.

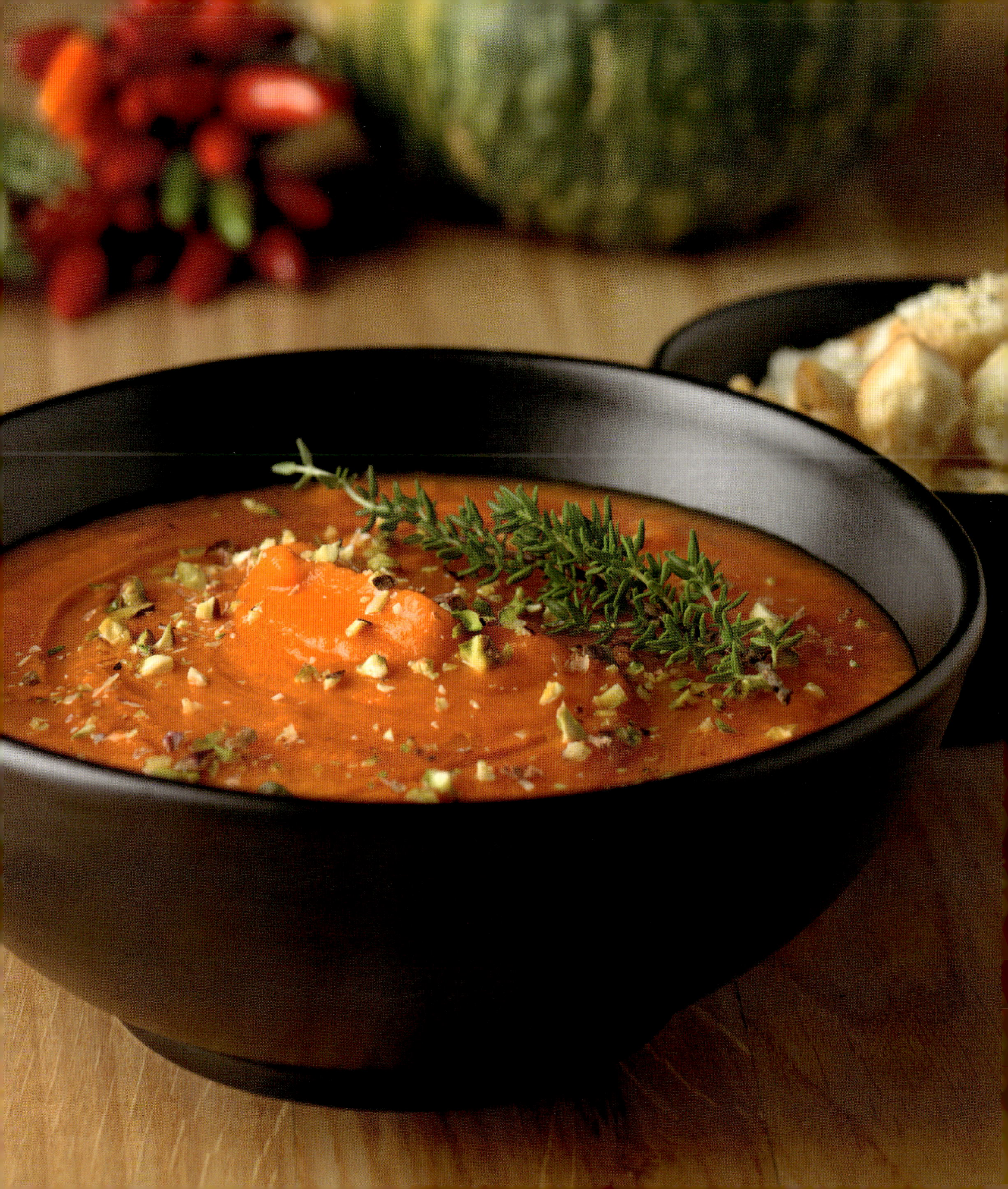

Zucchini with Mint

This easy summer recipe can be eaten hot or cold, accompanied by creamy stracciatella di burrata, a product from Puglia made with strands of mozzarella mixed with cream.

Look for small, light green Romanesco zucchini, which are not only tasty but also seedless.

Serves 4 to 6

4 pounds Romanesco zucchini, trimmed and chopped
5 cups vegetable stock
10 fresh mint leaves
⅓ cup extra-virgin olive oil, plus more for drizzling
9 ounces stracciatella di burrata
Croutons for serving

Suggested Wine Pairing

Antisa
Producer:
Tasca d'Almerita
Grape:
Catarratto
Region:
Sicily

Preparation

- Combine the zucchini and vegetable stock in a pot and place over high heat. Bring to a boil, then simmer, covered, until the zucchini are tender, about 20 minutes. Set aside to cool.

- In a food processor fitted with a metal blade, puree the zucchini and any liquid left in the pot with 6 of the mint leaves and the oil. Process until smooth.

- Divide the soup among individual soup bowls. Garnish with the reserved mint leaves and drizzle with oil.

- Place the cheese in a small bowl and serve on the side with the croutons.

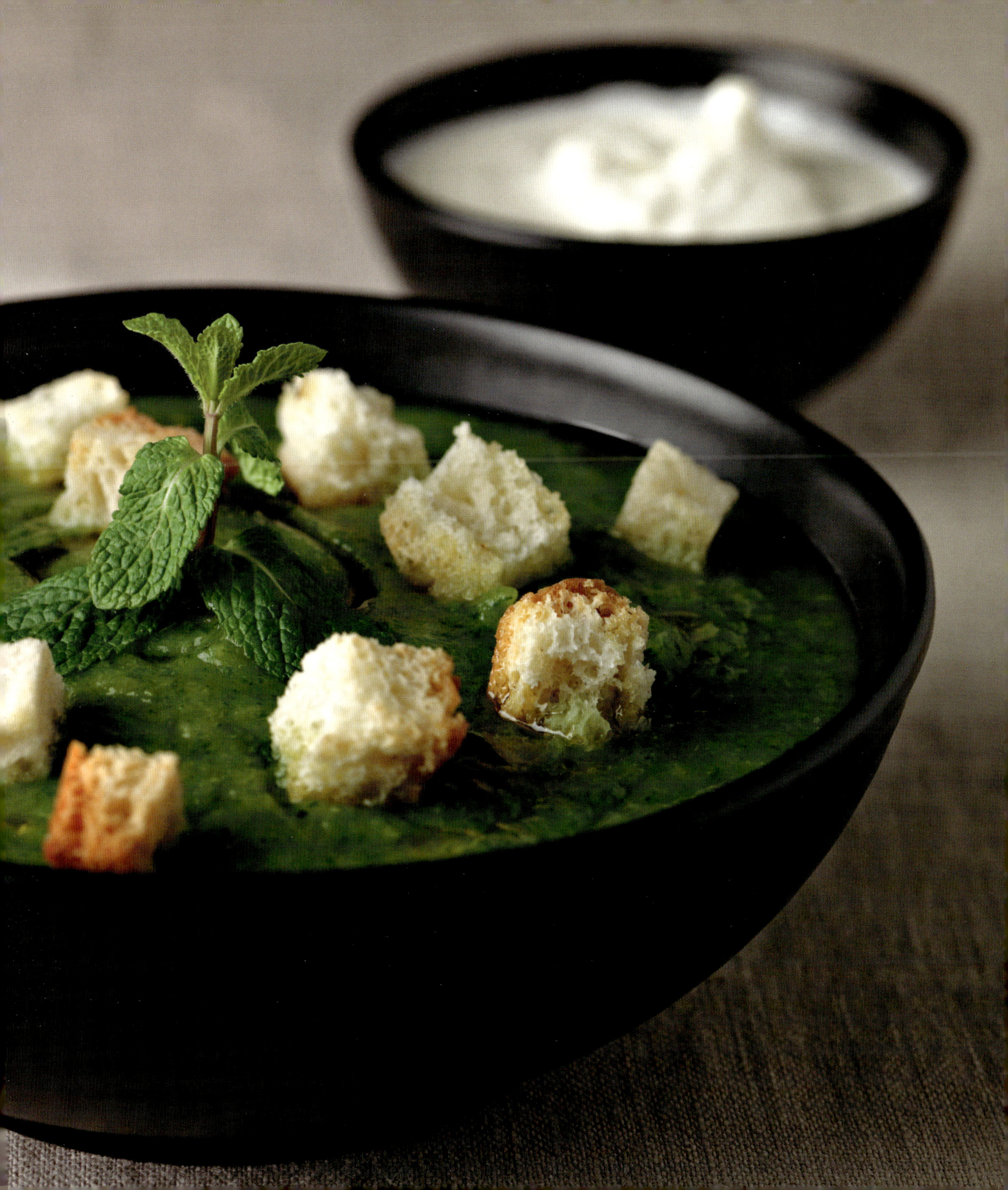

Tasca D'Almerita

The Tasca d'Almerita family has been in love with the land for two centuries, tending it and cultivating it with great passion. Sicily offers an array of flavors and aromas through its wines, foods, and traditions, and that experience can be shared on five estates: historic Regaleali, in the heart of Sicily; Tascante, on the slopes of Mount Etna; Capofaro Malvasia, a resort bathed in the sunlight of the island of Salina; Tenuta Whitaker on the Phoenician island of Mozia; and Sallier de La Tour, in the hills outside Palermo.

Tasca Experience includes a cooking school run by Anna Tasca Lanza and *NaturaInTasca.it*, a network of farmers and artisans selected to spotlight Sicily's finest products.

On the front lines of environmental protection, Tasca is the pilot company of SOStain, a project created to help companies develop winemaking with less environmental impact by using available resources as best as possible. Without respect for the place, nothing can endure, so Tasca is committed to treading lightly on the land.

OPPOSITE:
Lucio Tasca d'Almerita with his sons Giuseppe (left) and Alberto (right).

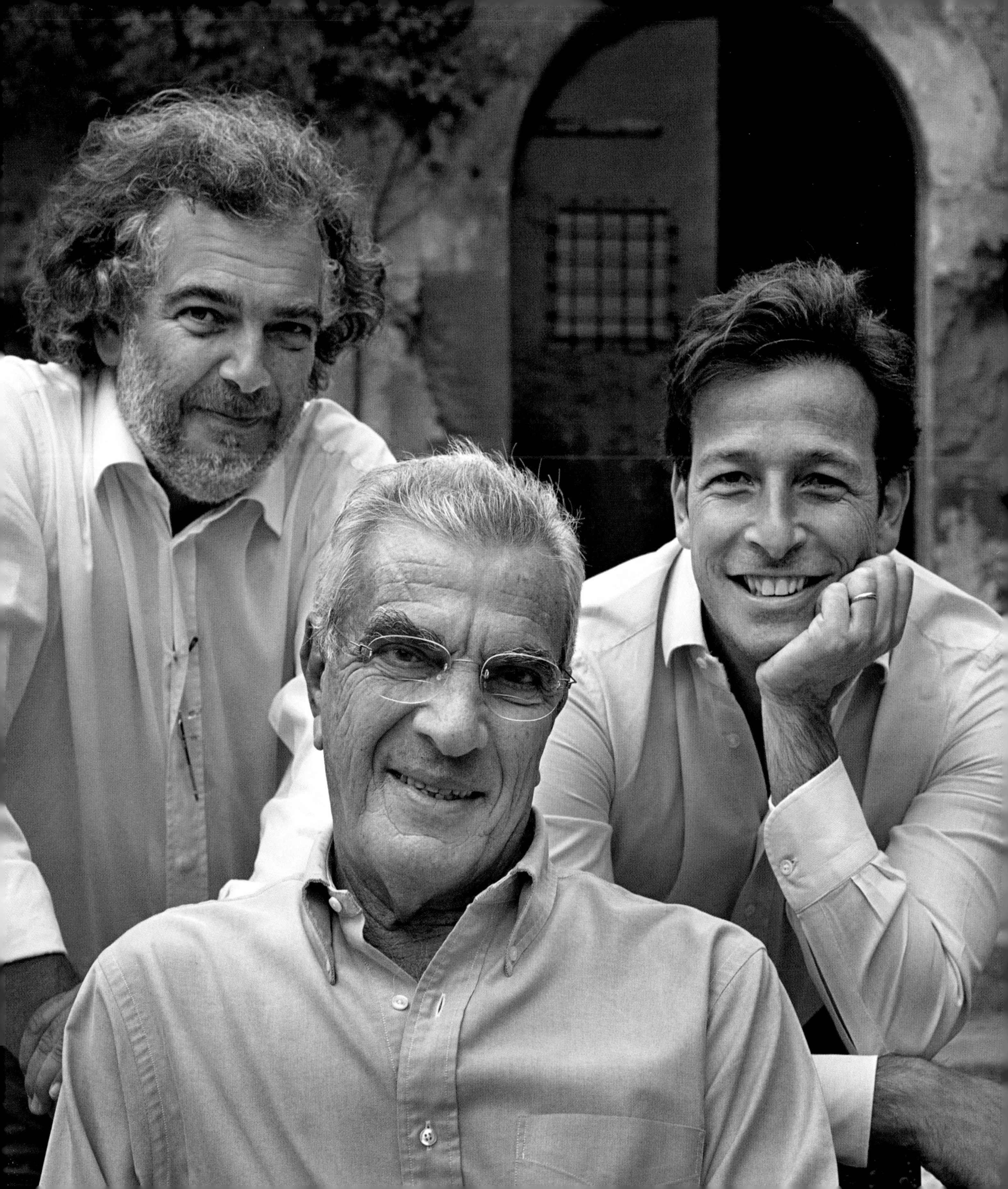

Lentil and Potato Soup

Lentils are grown throughout the Abruzzo, Campania, and Lazio regions. We use only the finest varieties of lentils, including those from Castelluccio di Norcia (DOP), green lentils from Altamura, Villalba lentils, and Colfiorito lentils. To shorten the cooking time, we recommend soaking the lentils 4 to 8 hours. Cooking time will vary depending on the variety of lentils and how long ago they were dried.

Serves 4 to 6

2¼ cups Castelluccio di Norcia lentils
2½ quarts vegetable stock
Parsley sprigs to taste
Bay leaves to taste
Rosemary sprigs to taste, plus more for garnish
¾ cup diced celery
¾ cup diced carrots
¾ cup diced peeled potatoes
¾ cup plus 2 tablespoons (7 ounces) La Motticella peeled tomatoes
Salt to taste
3 tablespoons extra-virgin olive oil
Croutons for serving

Suggested Wine Pairing

Conero Riserva
Producer:
Garofoli
Grape:
Montepulciano d'Abruzzo
Region:
Marche

Preparation

- Soak the lentils in cold water to cover for about 6 hours, then rinse them thoroughly under running water and drain.
- Place the vegetable stock in a large pot. Make a bouquet garni by tying the parsley, bay leaves, and rosemary together with kitchen twine and add it to the pot. Add the lentils.
- Bring the stock to a boil, then simmer for 30 minutes. Add the celery, carrots, and potatoes. Drain the tomatoes, cut them into strips, and add them to the pot.
- Continue to simmer for another 20 minutes.
- Remove and discard the bouquet garni and season with salt.
- Divide the soup among individual soup bowls. Drizzle on the oil and sprinkle on the croutons. Garnish with rosemary sprigs.

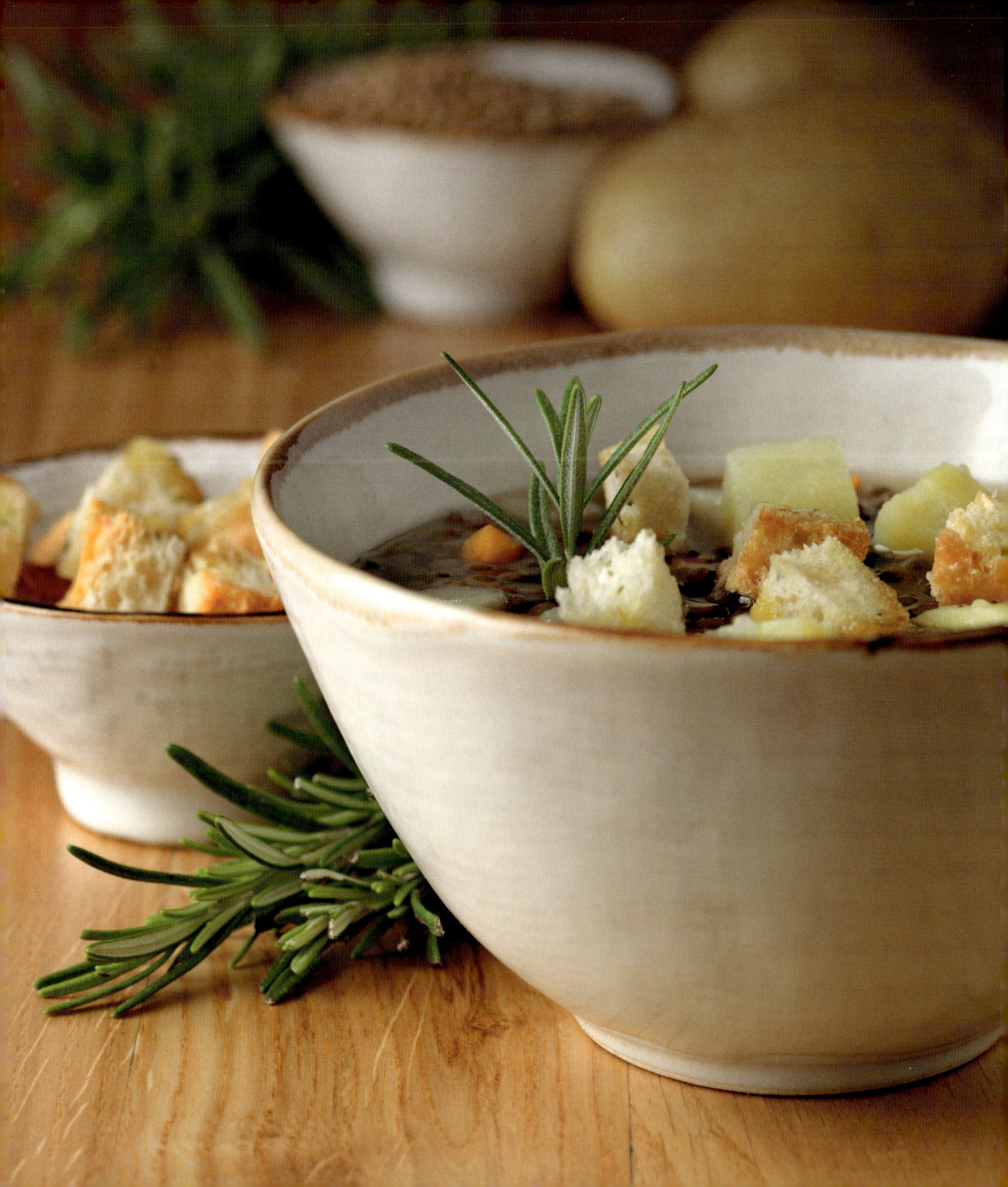

Farro and Spinach Soup

Farro soup is a genuine institution in Lucca. Farro, a grain, is the "daily bread" throughout the Garfagnana area, where it has long held IGP status. Our farro soup is lighter than the classic one, and we've replaced the traditional pancetta with additional vegetables, making it a truly wonderful vegetarian dish.

Serves 4 to 6

¾ cup diced celery
3 tablespoons extra-virgin olive oil
2¼ cups farro, rinsed and drained
1½ quarts vegetable stock
¾ cup diced peeled potatoes
3 pounds spinach, chopped
½ cup grated pecorino Romano
Croutons for serving

Suggested Wine Pairing

Poggio ai Ginepri
Producer:
Tenuta Argentiera
Grapes:
Cabernet Sauvignon, Merlot, Syrah
Region:
Tuscany

Preparation

- Place the celery and 1 tablespoon of the olive oil in a Dutch oven or other large pot. Cook over medium heat, covered, for 3 minutes.
- Add the farro and vegetable stock and simmer for 20 minutes.
- Add the potatoes. Simmer for 15 minutes more.
- Add the spinach and cook for 5 minutes more.
- To serve, distribute the soup among individual soup bowls. Drizzle with the remaining 2 tablespoons oil and sprinkle with pecorino.
- Serve with croutons on the side.

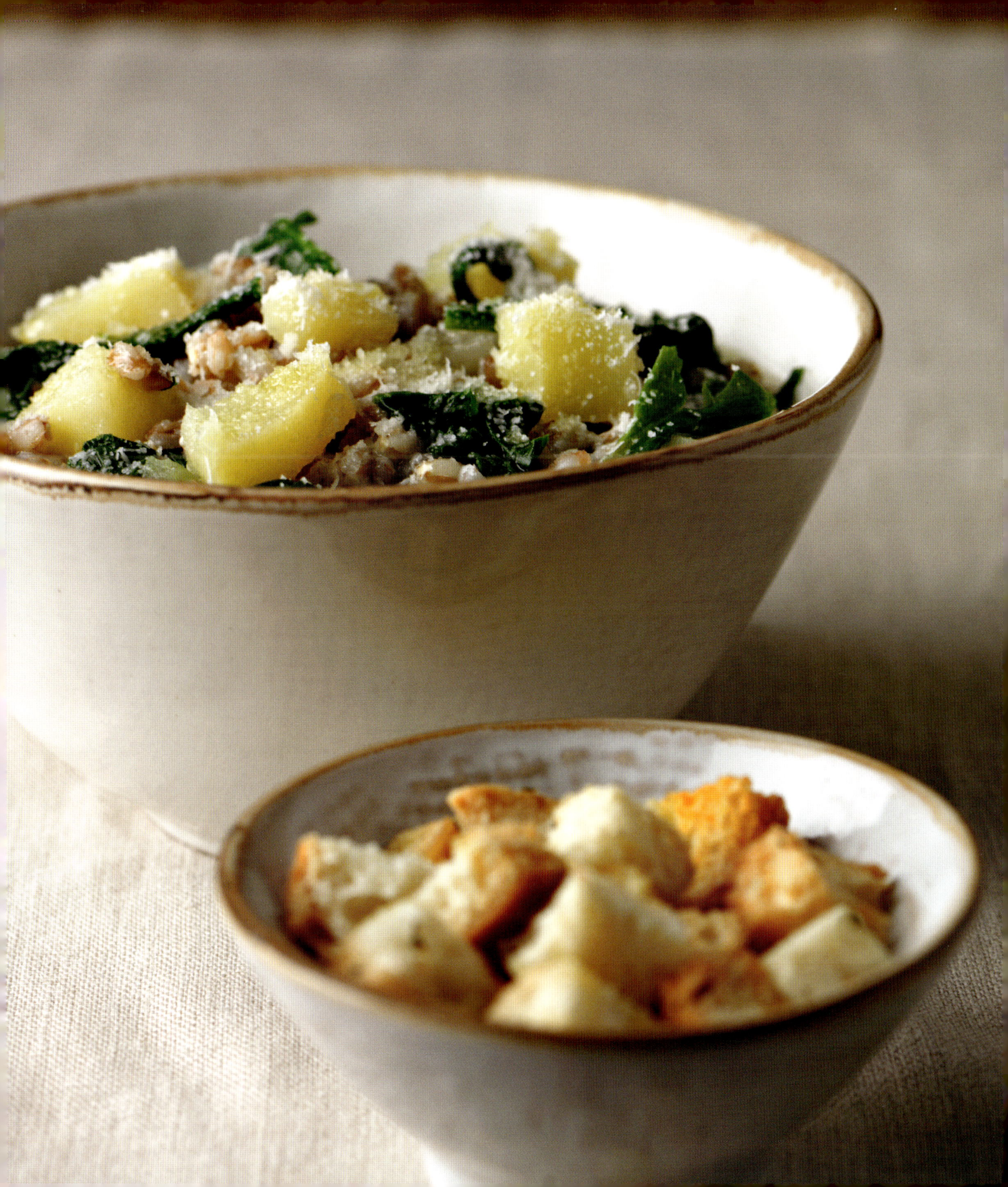

Zolfini Bean and Tuscan Kale Soup

Zolfini beans, a star of Tuscan cuisine, grow on the highlands of the Pratomagno mountain range between Reggello and San Giustino. These creamy, light beans are extremely thin skinned. They must be cooked as slowly and gently as possible, preferably in an earthenware pot. Another traditional dish calls for cooking the beans *al fiasco*, or in glass flasks that are buried in burning embers in a fireplace.

Serves 4 to 6

1½ cups dried zolfini beans
4 to 5 fresh sage leaves
2 pounds 2 ounces Tuscan kale
¼ cup extra-virgin olive oil
Red pepper flakes to taste
Salt to taste
¼ cup grated pecorino Romano
Croutons for serving

Suggested Wine Pairing

Chianti Classico Fonterutoli
Producer:
Mazzei
Grapes:
Sangiovese, Malvasia Nera, Colorino, Merlot
Region:
Tuscany

Preparation

- Soak the beans in cold water to cover for 12 hours.
- Rinse and drain the beans and place them in an earthenware pot with 1 quart cold water and the sage leaves. Simmer over low heat for 2 hours.
- With a slotted spoon, transfer about half of the cooked beans to a food processor fitted with a metal blade and puree. Add enough cooking water to make a thick, creamy mixture.
- Slice the Tuscan kale into ribbons. Heat 3 tablespoons of the oil in a large pot. Add the red pepper flakes and the kale and sauté briefly until the greens wilt, then add 1 cup water and braise over medium heat until the greens are soft.
- Add the pureed beans and the whole beans to the pot with the kale and simmer for 15 minutes.
- Season to taste with salt. Drizzle with the remaining 1 tablespoon oil and sprinkle on the pecorino. Serve with croutons.

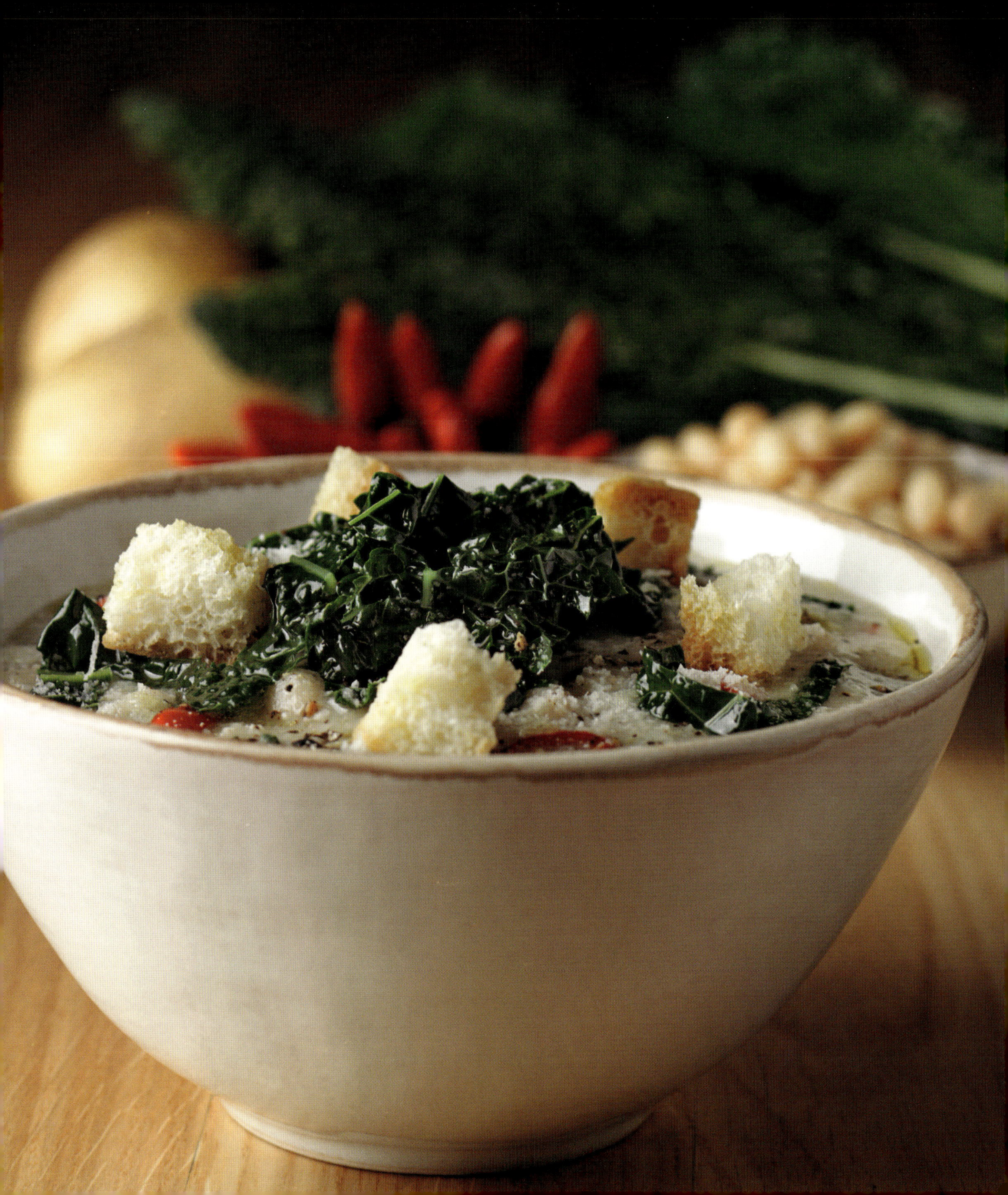

Pasta e Ceci

Many traditional Italian recipes call for chickpeas. They are excellent in thick soups with pasta, including Puglia's *ciceri e tria*, Campania's *laganelle e ceci*, and the recipe provided here, Rome's renowned *pasta e ceci*. When cooking legumes, never salt the cooking water, as it will cause their skins to harden and they will never be tender. One nice touch is to crisp strips of guanciale in a pan and garnish the finished soup with those and/or some rosemary sprigs.

Serves 4 to 6

1½ cups dried chickpeas
¼ cup extra-virgin olive oil
½ cup diced carrots
½ cup diced celery
3 ounces guanciale, diced
⅔ cup (5½ ounces) La Motticella peeled tomatoes
Parsley sprigs to taste
Bay leaves to taste
Rosemary sprigs to taste
About 5 cups vegetable stock
¾ cup Gentile short pasta

Suggested Wine Pairing

Montefalco Rosso
Producer:
Omero Moretti
Grapes:
Sangiovese, Sagrantino, Merlot
Region:
Tuscany

Preparation

- Soak the chickpeas in cold water to cover for 24 hours, then rinse and drain. Boil the chickpeas in unsalted water until tender. Drain and set aside.
- Place 3 tablespoons of the oil in a soup pot and add the carrots, celery, and guanciale. Cook over medium heat, stirring frequently, until browned, about 7 minutes.
- Add the cooked chickpeas. Drain the tomatoes, cut them into thin strips, and add them to the pot. Make a bouquet garni by tying the parsley sprigs, bay leaves, and rosemary sprigs with kitchen twine and add it to the pot.
- Add 5 cups stock and simmer for 45 minutes. The chickpeas should be very soft.
- If you would like a creamier soup, puree some of the mixture in the pot with an immersion blender, or remove some with a slotted spoon to a food processor fitted with a metal blade, puree, and return to the pot.
- Add the pasta and cook until tender.
- If the soup seems too thick, add a few additional tablespoons of stock.
- Drizzle the remaining tablespoon of oil onto the soup and serve.

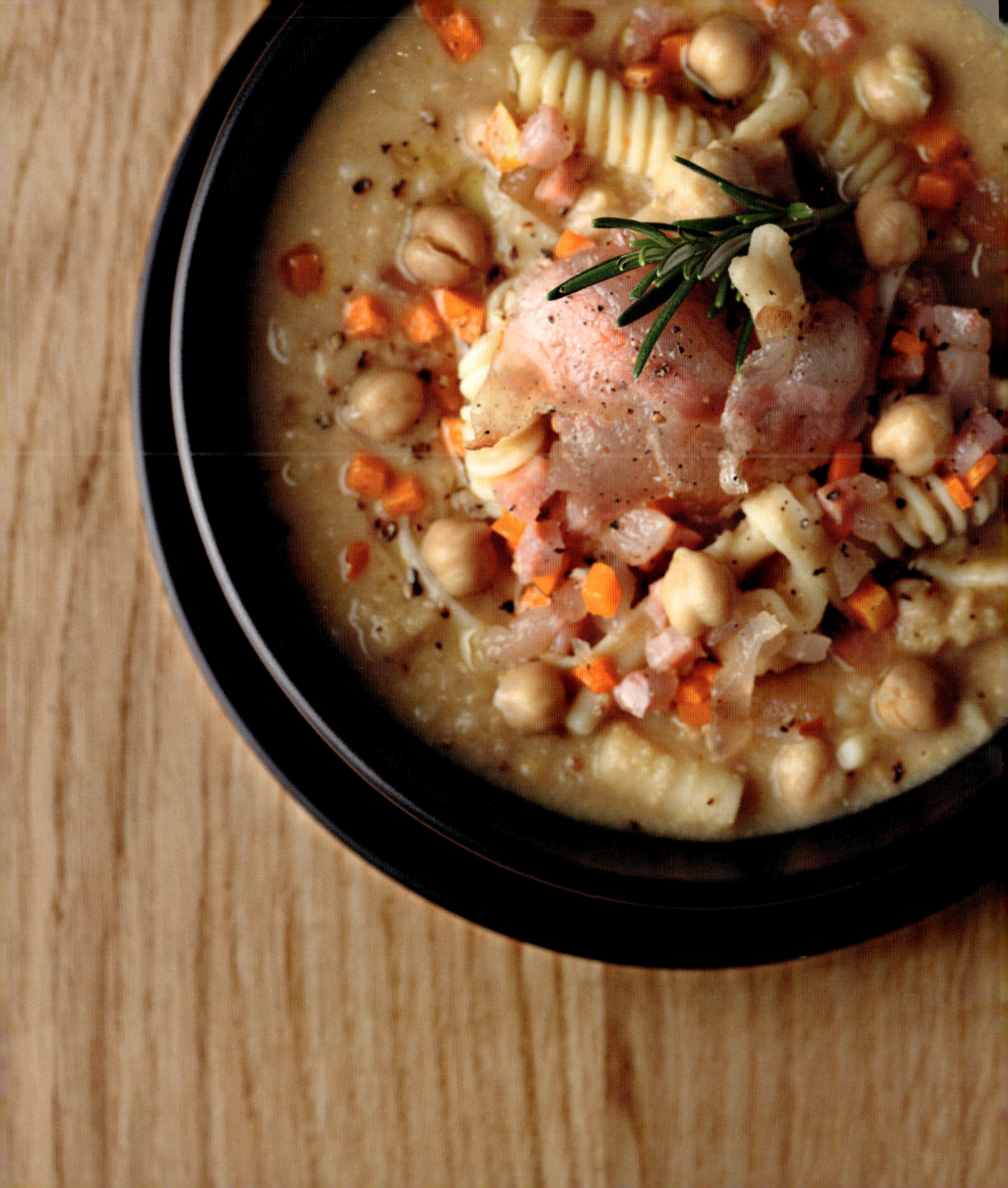

LONDON,
Charlotte Street

© Luke Hayes

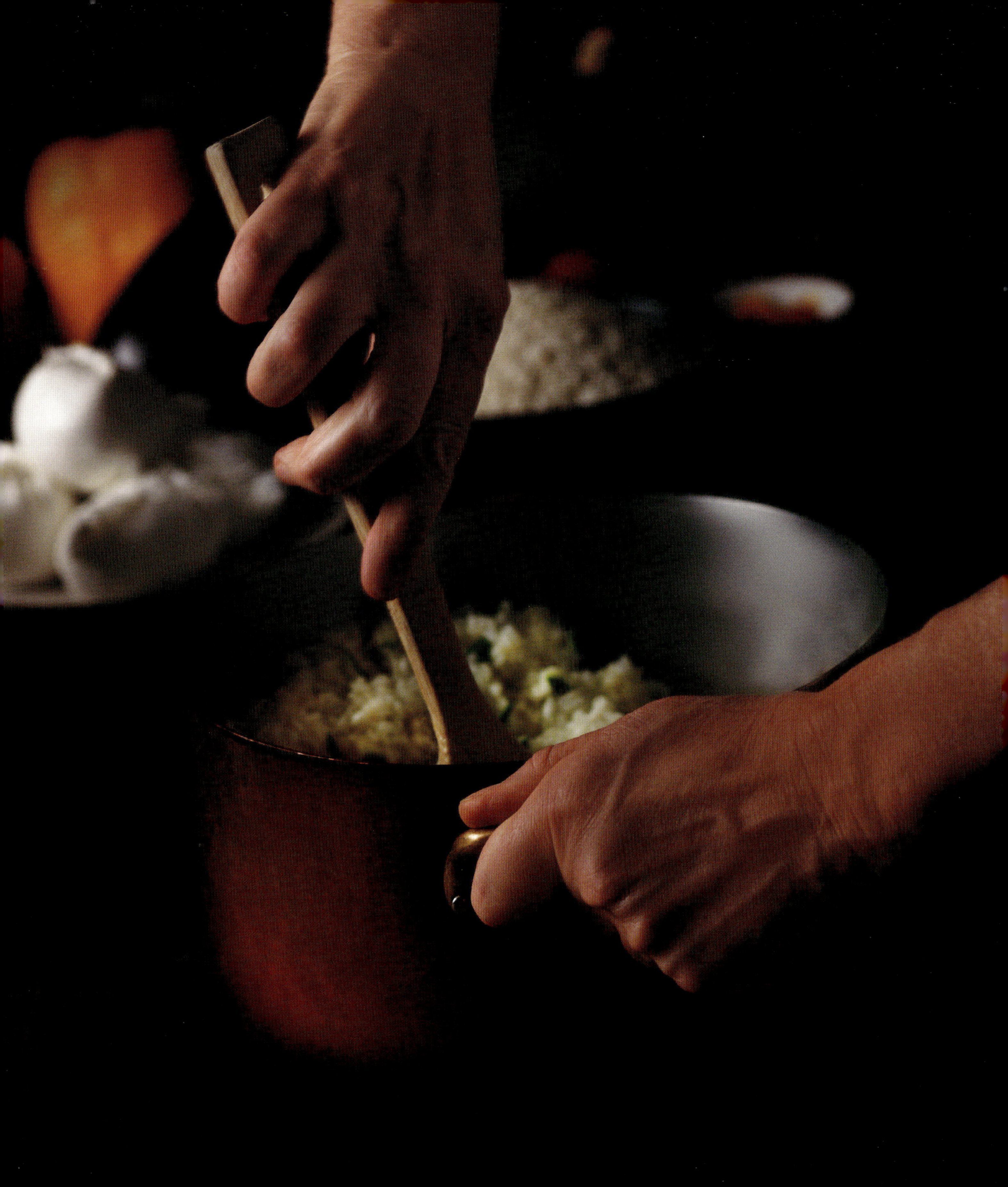

Risotti

Risotto with Porcini Mushrooms

Risotto with Shrimp and Asparagus

Risotto with Zucchini and Bottarga

Risotto with Black Truffle and Stracciatella

Risotto with Luganega Sausage and Radicchio

Risotto with Porcini Mushrooms

Fresh porcini mushrooms are available in October and November, when mushroom hunters pursue their quarry in oak, chestnut, and pine forests. They have a unique aroma and texture, ideal for risotto.

Serves 4 to 6

1 pound 12 ounces fresh porcini mushrooms
¼ cup extra-virgin olive oil
1 sprig rosemary, plus more for garnish
About 5 cups vegetable stock
2¼ cups carnaroli or vialone nano rice
⅔ cup dry white wine
3½ ounces blu di bufala
½ cup grated Parmigiano Reggiano, plus shavings for garnish
Black pepper to taste

Suggested Wine Pairing

Crognolo
Producer:
Tenuta Sette Ponti
Grapes:
Sangiovese, Merlot
Region:
Tuscany

Preparation

- Wipe the mushrooms clean with a damp cloth. Detach the stems and caps and slice both thinly.
- Place 1 tablespoon of the oil and the rosemary in a skillet over high heat. Add the mushrooms and sauté until they have given up all of their liquid, about 8 minutes. Add small amounts of vegetable stock to keep the mushrooms from sticking to the pan, if necessary. Set aside.
- Place the stock in a small pot and bring to a boil, then turn down the heat to a simmer. Heat the remaining 3 tablespoons oil in a wide, shallow pan. Add the rice and cook, stirring, until it becomes transparent. Add the white wine and cook until it has evaporated.
- Gradually add the simmering stock, about ½ cup at a time, to the rice, stirring constantly and waiting for the stock to be absorbed completely between additions. When the rice is cooked al dente but still firm in the middle, stir in the porcini mushrooms, the blu di bufala, and about half of the grated Parmigiano. Stir in 1 cup stock to combine and remove the pan from the heat.
- Let the risotto rest for 2 minutes without stirring. It will absorb the last addition of stock.
- Serve with pepper and garnish with rosemary sprigs and Parmigiano shavings.

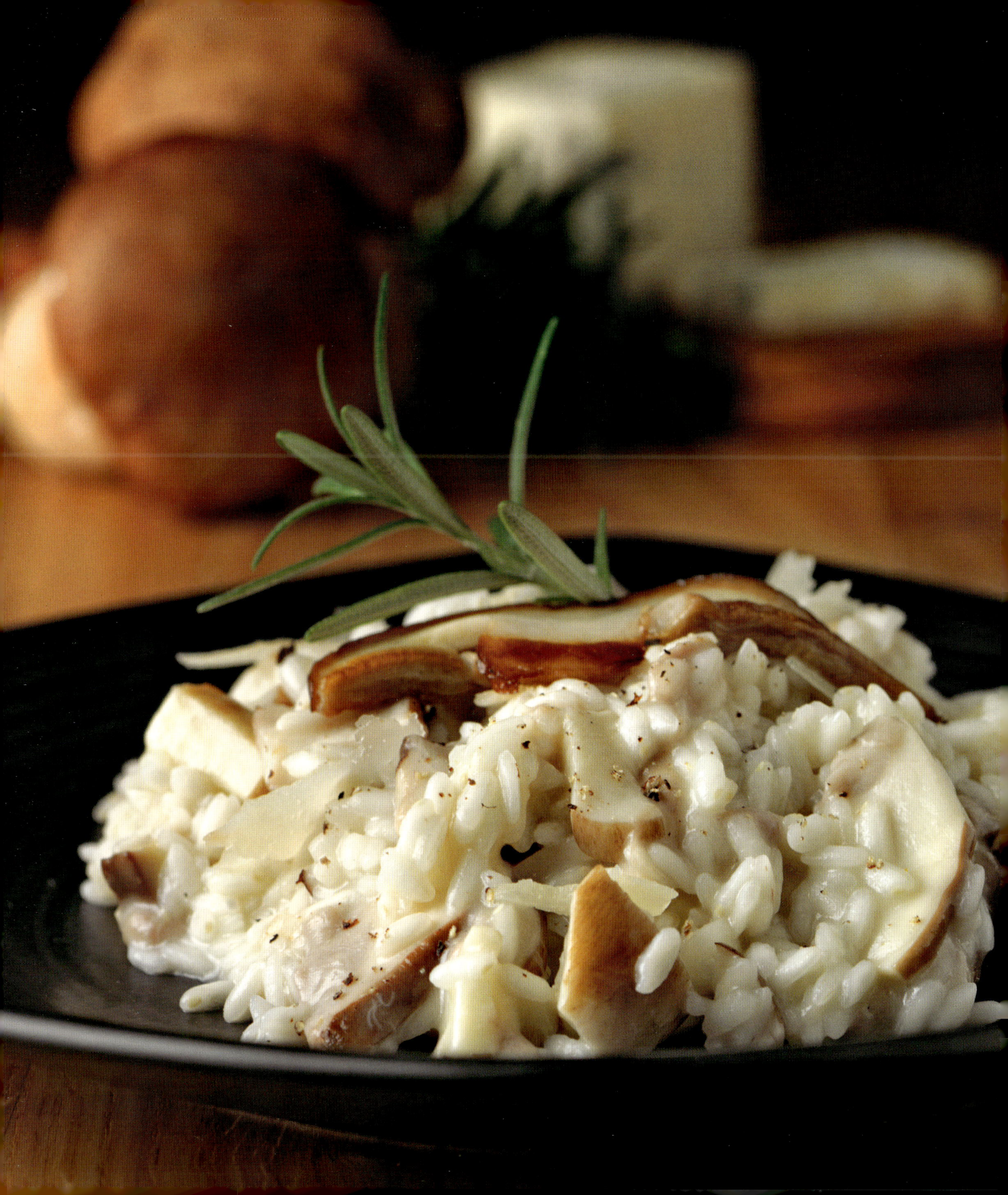

Risotto with Shrimp and Asparagus

The stock plays an essential role in the preparation of this risotto: the idea is to release the intense flavor of the sea that's preserved inside the shrimp heads, getting the most flavor out of them. This risotto should be served *all'onda,* or "wavy," meaning that it's fairly fluid, but not watery or soupy.

Serves 4 to 6

1 pound 12 ounces whole shrimp
½ cup chopped celery
½ cup chopped carrots
3 sprigs flat-leaf parsley
1 pound 6 ounces asparagus
¼ cup extra-virgin olive oil
2¼ cups carnaroli or vialone nano rice
1¼ cups prosecco
Parsley leaves for garnish

Suggested Wine Pairing

Nosiola
Producer:
Istituto Agrario San Michele
Grape:
Nosiola
Region:
Trentino Alto Adige

Preparation

- To make a shrimp stock, shell the shrimp and remove their heads. Place the shells and heads in a large pot with 3 quarts water, the celery, the carrots, and the parsley. Bring to a boil and then turn to low heat and simmer for 2 hours. Strain the stock through a fine-mesh sieve (a chinois works best) and place it in a pot over low heat, keeping it at a simmer.
- Trim the asparagus. Cut off the tips of the spears and reserve, then slice the stalks at an angle into 1-inch pieces.
- Put 3 tablespoons of the oil and the rice in a wide, shallow pan over medium heat. Cook, stirring frequently, until the rice is golden. Add the prosecco and allow it to evaporate.
- When the wine has evaporated, begin cooking the rice by adding the shrimp stock, about ½ cup at a time, stirring constantly and waiting for the liquid to be absorbed between additions.
- Add the asparagus stalks.
- When the rice is cooked al dente but still firm in the middle, stir in the asparagus tips and the shrimp. Stir in 1 cup stock to combine and remove the pan from the heat.
- Let the risotto rest for 2 minutes without stirring. It will absorb the last addition of stock.
- Garnish with parsley leaves and drizzle with the remaining 1 tablespoon oil.

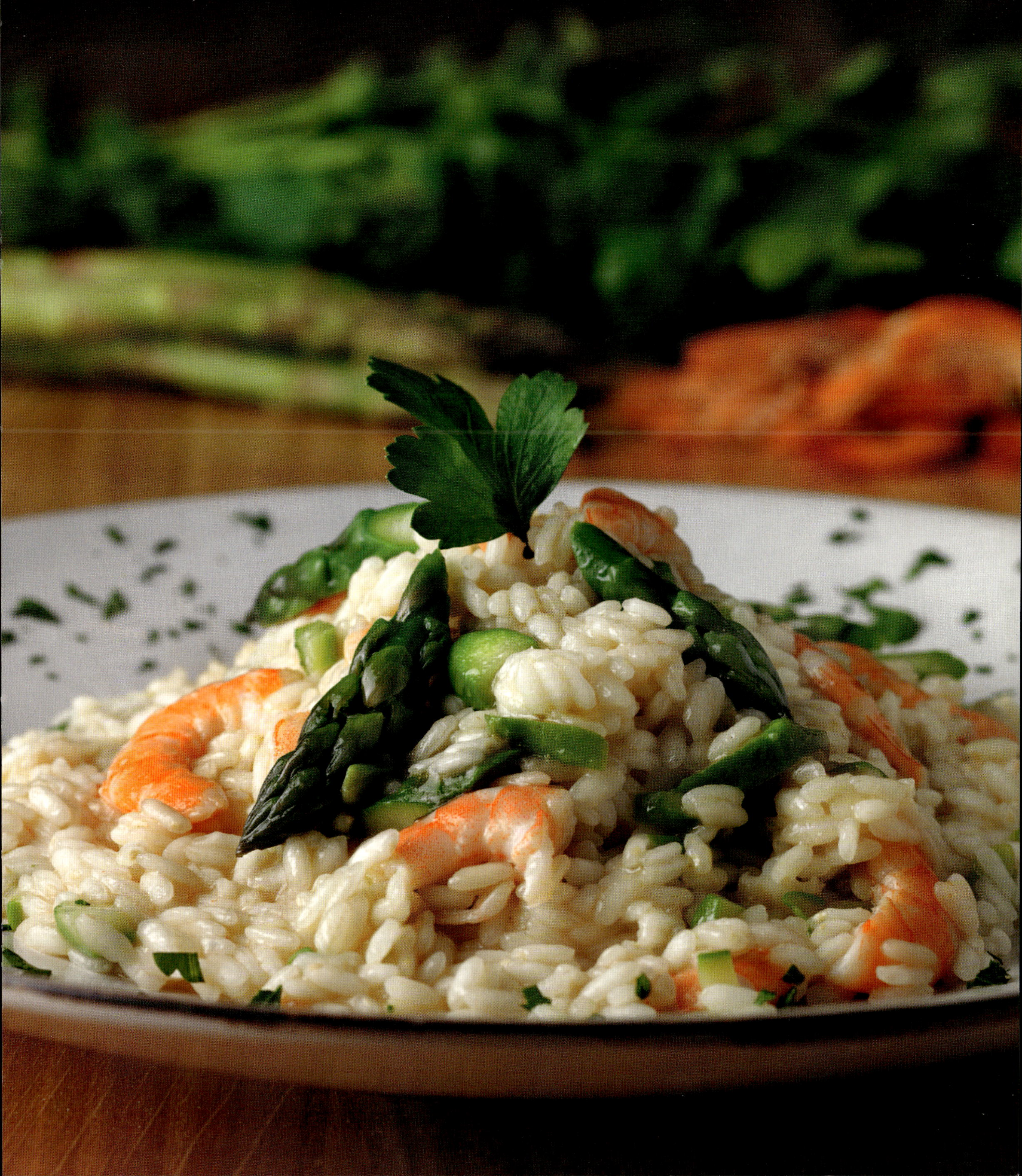

Risotto with Zucchini and Bottarga

We really love this summertime dish. The sweetness of the Romanesco zucchini and mozzarella di bufala Campana DOP are an ideal match for bottarga, which lends the briny flavor of the sea. Bottarga is pressed salted fish roe—this recipe uses mullet bottarga.

Serves 4 to 6

1 pound 6 ounces Romanesco zucchini, diced
Grated zest of ½ lemon
¼ cup plus 1 tablespoon extra-virgin olive oil
Salt and black pepper to taste
About 5 cups vegetable stock
2¼ cups carnaroli or vialone nano rice
⅔ cup dry white wine
1 cup grape tomatoes, quartered
5½ ounces mozzarella di bufala Campana DOP, diced
1½ ounces mullet bottarga
Fresh basil leaves for garnish

Suggested Wine Pairing

Vernaccia di Oristano Riserva
Producer:
Attilio Contini
Grape:
Vernaccia
Region:
Sardinia

Preparation

- Sauté the zucchini and the lemon zest in 1 tablespoon of the oil. When the zucchini is golden brown, season with salt and pepper and remove from the heat. Place the stock in a small pot and bring to a boil, then turn down the heat to a simmer.
- Heat 3 tablespoons of the oil in a wide, shallow pan. Add the rice and cook, stirring, until it becomes transparent. Add the white wine and cook until it has evaporated.
- Gradually add the stock, about ½ cup at a time, to the rice, stirring constantly and waiting for the stock to be absorbed completely between additions.
- After 10 minutes, add the tomatoes and the sautéed zucchini.
- When the risotto is cooked al dente but still firm in the center, stir in the mozzarella and 1 cup stock to combine and remove the pan from the heat.
- Place a lid on the pan and let it rest for 2 minutes.
- Shave the bottarga over the risotto. Drizzle on the remaining 1 tablespoon oil and garnish with basil leaves.

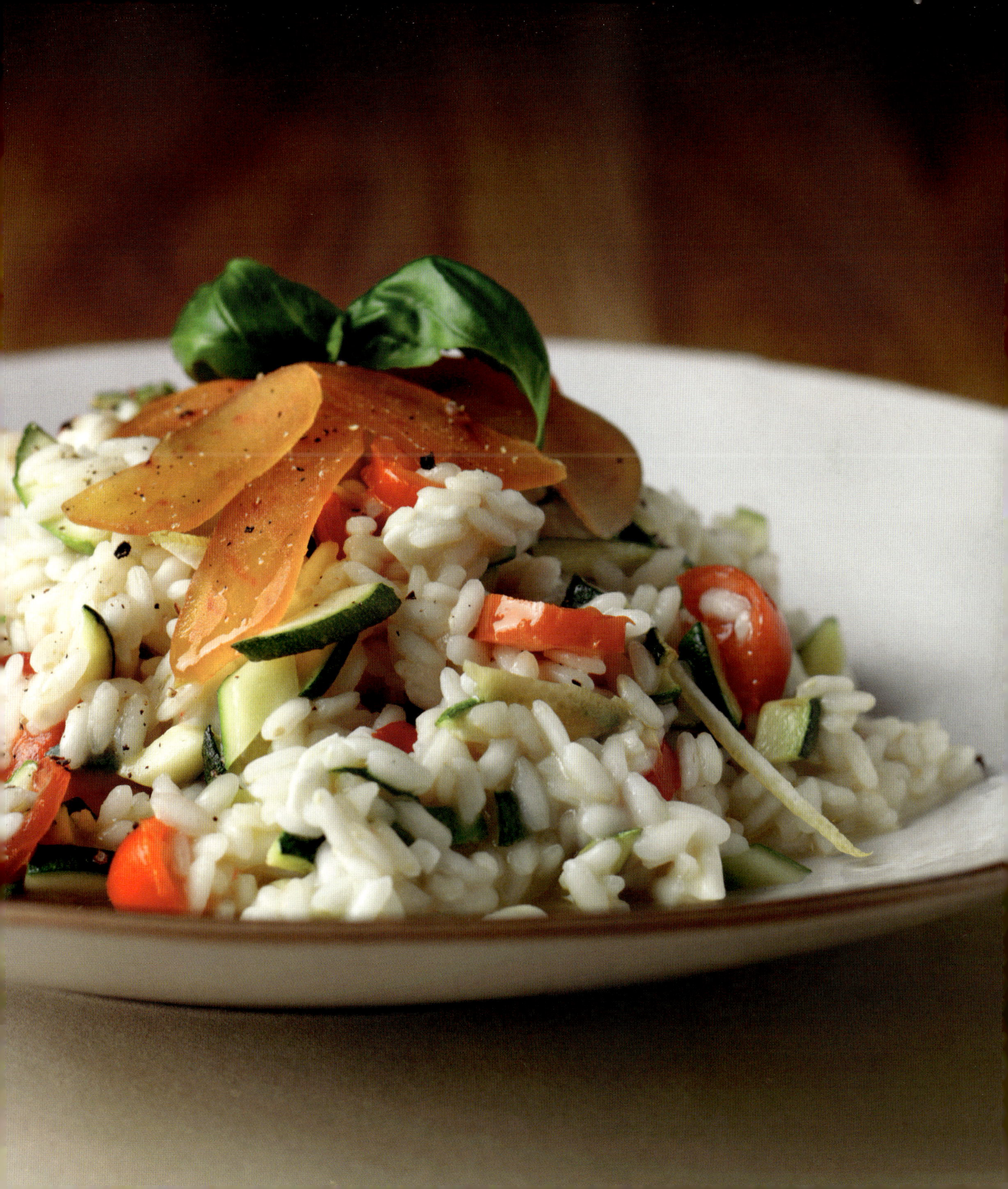

Risotto with Black Truffle and Stracciatella

This superb recipe for risotto comes from our restaurant in London, and it's a perfect use for creamy stracciatella di burrata and precious black truffle. To clean truffles, scrub them with a brush under cold running water, then dry them with a flat-weave cotton towel. Shave the truffle directly over the risotto with a truffle shaver.

Serves 4 to 6

About 5 cups vegetable stock
¼ cup extra-virgin olive oil
2¼ cups carnaroli or arborio rice
½ cup dry white wine
¼ cup grated Parmigiano Reggiano
7 ounces stracciatella di burrata, diced
3 ounces black truffle or black summer truffle
Black pepper to taste
¼ cup Parmigiano Reggiano shavings

Suggested Wine Pairing

Morellino di Scansano
Producer:
Bruni Marteto
Grapes:
85% Sangiovese; 15% nonaromatic autochthonous red grapes
Region:
Tuscany

Preparation

- Place the stock in a small pot and bring to a boil, then turn down the heat to a simmer.
- Heat 3 tablespoons of the oil in a wide, shallow pan. Add the rice and cook, stirring, for 2 minutes. Add the white wine and cook until it has evaporated.
- Gradually add the stock, about ½ cup at a time, to the rice, stirring constantly and waiting for the stock to be absorbed completely between additions.
- When the risotto is cooked al dente but still firm in the center, stir in the grated Parmigiano and about half of the stracciatella. Shave over about half of the truffle. Add 1 cup stock, stir to combine, and remove the pan from the heat.
- Cover the pan and set aside to rest for 2 minutes.
- Dot the risotto with the remaining burrata and season with pepper, then sprinkle on the Parmigiano shavings and shave the remaining truffle over the dish.

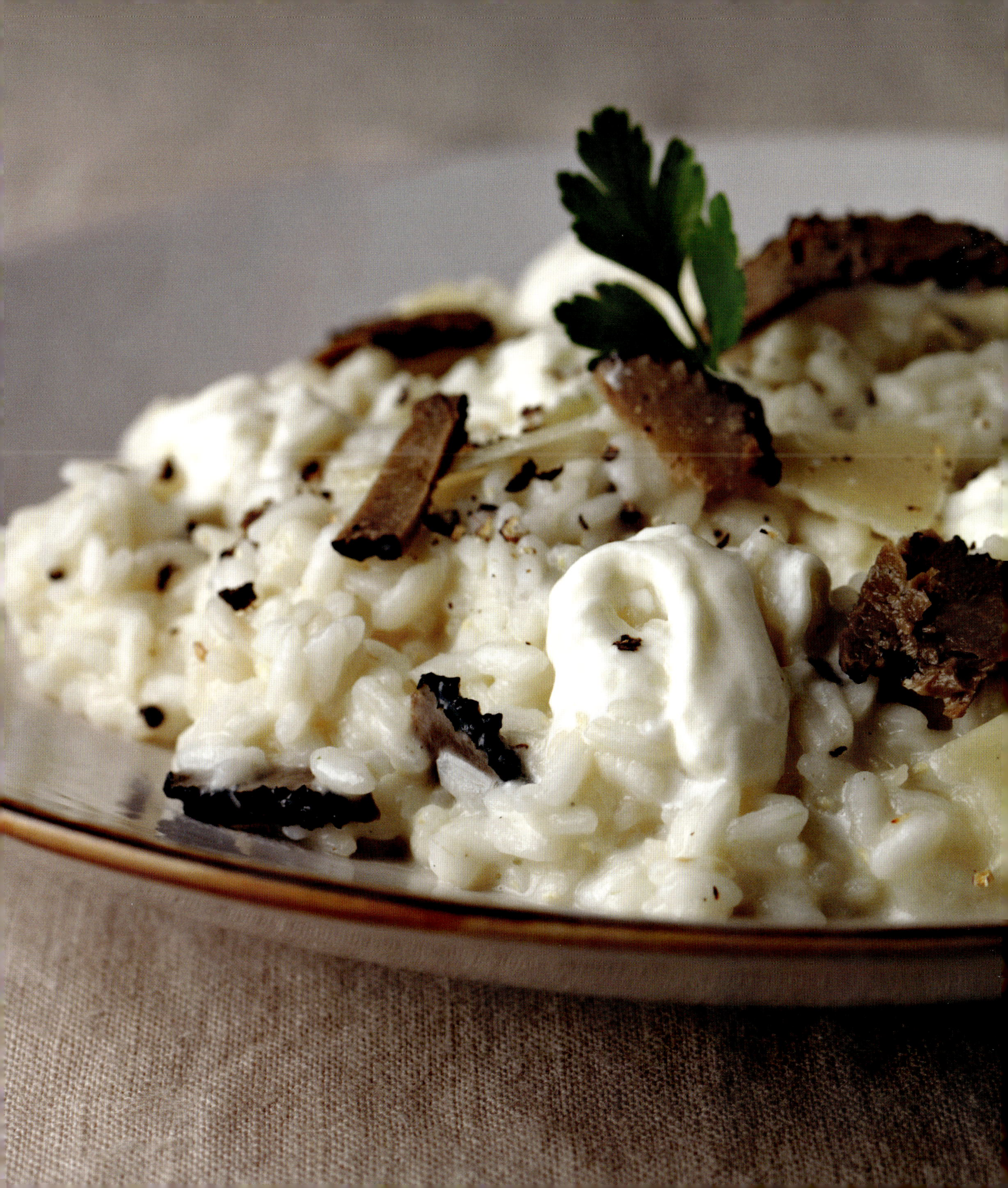

Risotto with Luganega Sausage and Radicchio

Valpollicella's ruby red color tints this strong-flavored risotto, and its notes of cherry and red currant are ideal with luganega sausage. Both of these ingredients hail from the Veneto region of Italy, as does Treviso radicchio, which has long, dark red and white leaves and a pleasantly bitter edge. If you want to serve this risotto in the form of little individual timbales, divide it among preheated single-serving silicone pans and unmold it onto individual serving dishes.

Serves 4 to 6

About 2¾ cups vegetable stock
1½ cups loosely packed Treviso radicchio
2 tablespoons extra-virgin olive oil
2¼ cups carnaroli or vialone nano rice
10 ounces luganega sausage, casing removed
3 cups Valpollicella red wine
4 tablespoons unsalted butter, cut into pieces
⅓ cup grated Parmigiano Reggiano, plus shavings for garnish
Black pepper to taste

Suggested Wine Pairing

Amarone
Producer:
Bertani Valpantena
Grapes:
Corvina, Rondinella, Molinara
Region:
Veneto

Preparation

- Place the stock in a small pot and bring to a boil, then turn down to a simmer. Cut the radicchio into julienne, reserving a few whole leaves for garnish.
- Heat the oil in a wide, shallow pan. Add the rice and cook, stirring, until transparent, about 2 minutes.
- Crumble the sausage into the pan with the rice. Add 1 cup of the wine and cook, stirring frequently, until evaporated. Add another 1 cup wine and cook, stirring frequently, until evaporated. Add the remaining 1 cup wine and cook, stirring frequently until evaporated.
- Gradually add the stock, about ½ cup at a time, to the rice, stirring constantly and waiting for the stock to be absorbed completely between additions.
- When the risotto is cooked al dente but still firm in the center, stir in the radicchio. Continue adding broth and stirring.
- When the risotto is cooked, scatter on the butter and about half of the grated Parmigiano. Season to taste with pepper.
- Garnish with the reserved whole radicchio leaves and Parmigiano shavings.

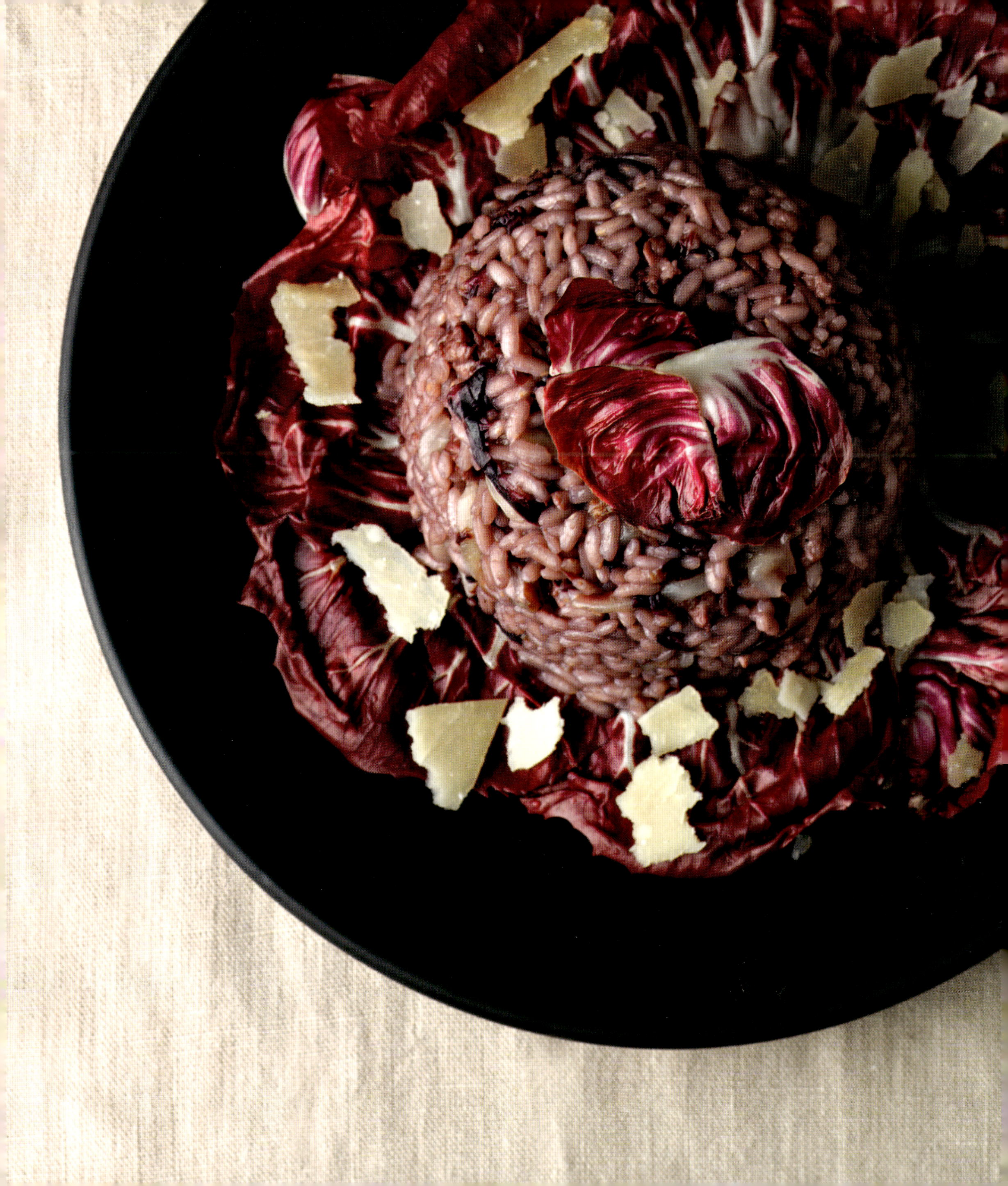

NEW YORK CITY,
Flatiron District

LOS ANGELES,
Santa Monica Boulevard

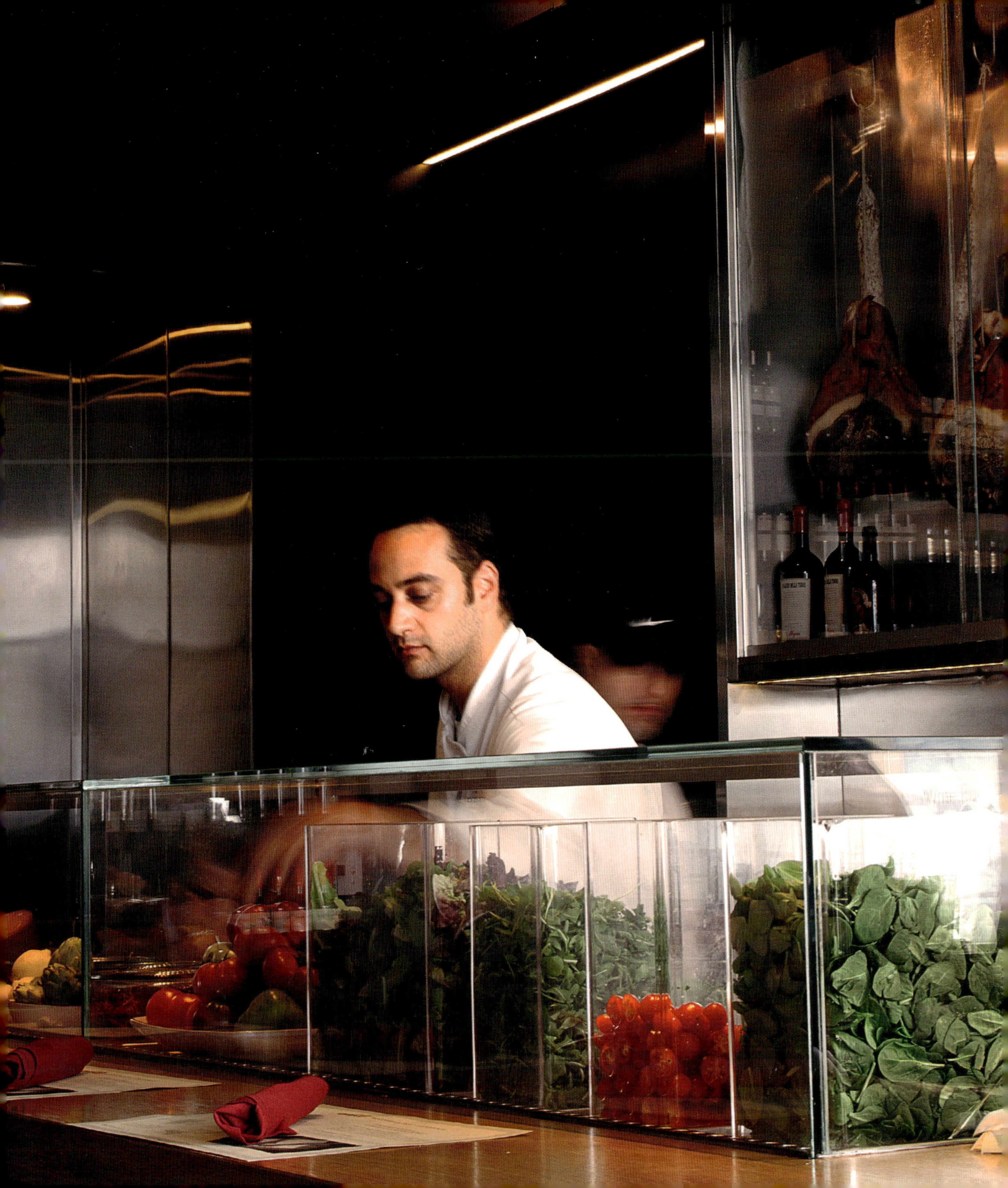

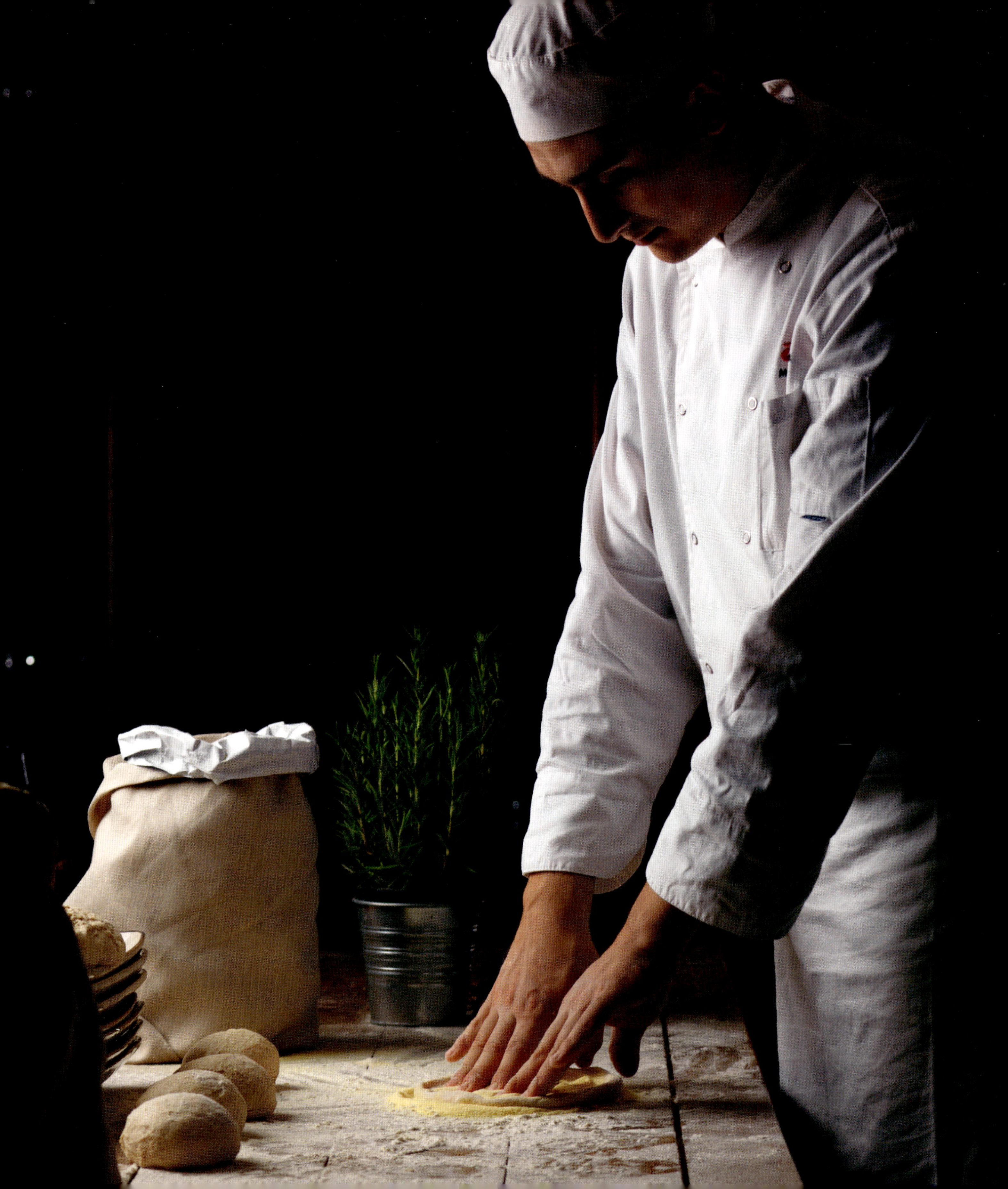

Pizze

Making Pizza Dough
Shaping and Baking

Organic Tomato and Stracciatella di Burrata

Grilled Vegetables and Smoked Buffalo Milk Mozzarella

Grilled Peppers and Tuna

Soft Buffalo Milk Cheese

Luganega sausage and Friarielli

N'duja and Stracciatella di Burrata

Anchovies and Capers

Bottarga and Grape Tomatoes

Open Calzone with Prosciutto Crudo di Parma

Prosciutto Cotto and Norcia Black Truffle

Soppressata Calabrese and Ricotta

Porcini Mushroom and Black Truffle

Making Pizza Dough

Dough and Rising

We use a slow-rise method to make our pizza. This results in a pizza that is soft in the middle with a crisp crust around the edges. It's also easier to digest. Don't be put off by the long amount of time required for the dough to rise. The yeast does all the work and you only have to handle the dough at brief intervals. The basic method is as follows:

For the first rise, you combine all of the water with the yeast and half of the flour. Then the rest of the flour and salt are added before the second rise, and in order to ensure that the dough will bake up soft yet crisp, some extra-virgin olive oil is added as well.

Next, the dough is shaped into a ball and allowed to rest. Then the dough is divided into portions for individual pizzas and rises for 24 hours in the refrigerator (35°F) and then sits for at least 3 hours at room temperature (1 to 2 hours in the summer). Finally, the dough is stretched, topped, and baked.

You can adjust the amount of yeast used depending on how long you want that first rise to last and the temperature of the room where you are working. With a room temperature of about 68°F, the amount of yeast should be as follows:

1 tablespoon plus 1 teaspoon for a first rise lasting 2 to 3 hours
2 teaspoons for a first rise lasting 5 to 7 hours
1 teaspoon for a first rise lasting 8 to 10 hours
½ teaspoon for a first rise lasting 12 to 24 hours

During the warm summer season, the amount of yeast should be decreased slightly, or the dough should be allowed to rise for less time. A small additional amount of yeast can be added during the second rise if absolutely necessary when working in a cold room.

Pizza and Temperature

Temperature is very important when making pizza dough.

The ideal situation is for the temperatures in Celsius of the air, the flour, and the water to add up to 60°C. (Please note that while 60°C is equivalent to 140°F, this formula will not work with Fahrenheit temperatures.) Example:
WATER 15°C (59°F) + FLOUR 20°C (68°F) + AIR 25°C (77°F) = 60°C (140°F)

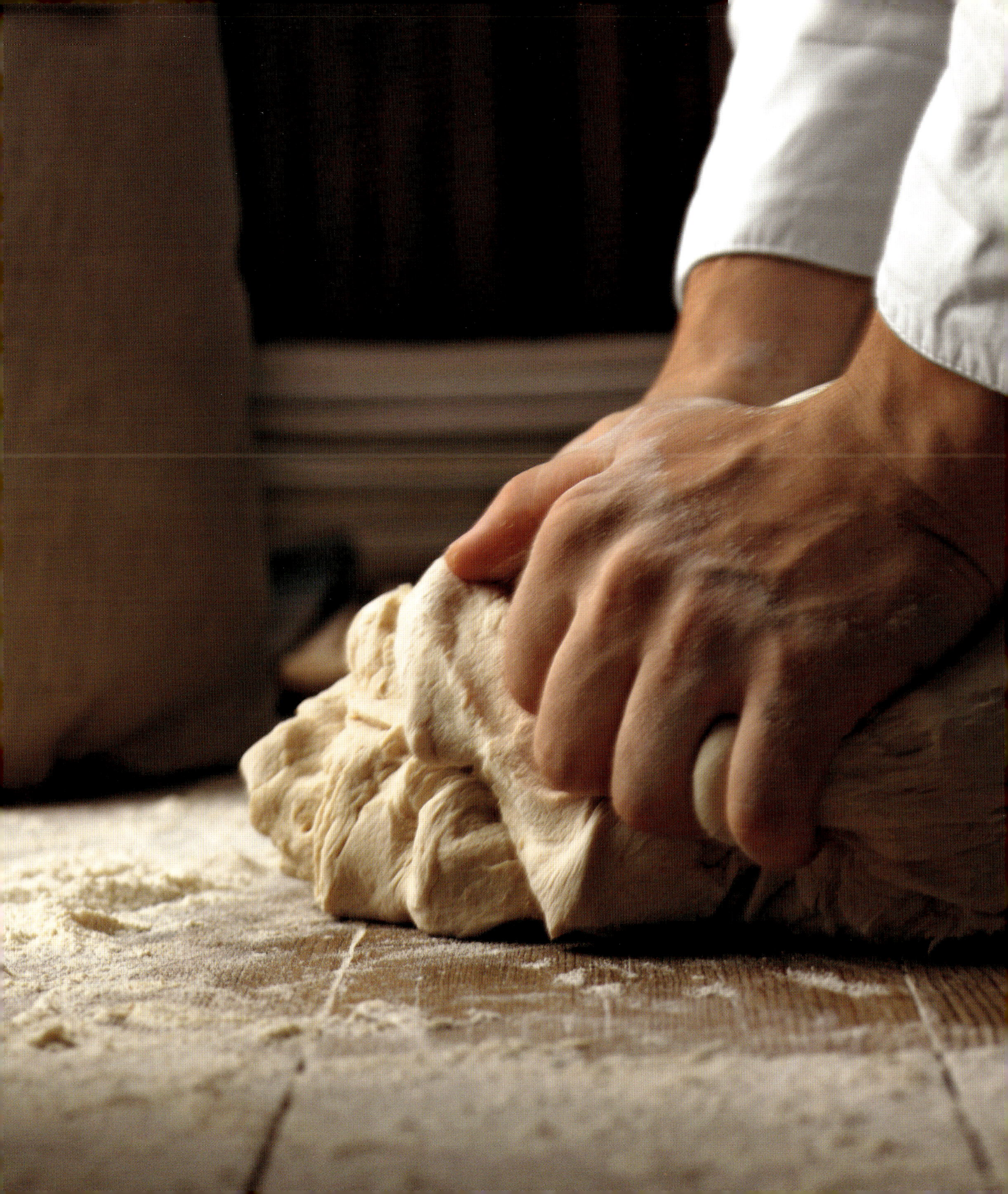

The water temperature is the easiest variable to control. We recommend using mineral water, but make sure it is not straight out of the refrigerator and cold.

The "air" temperature is the room temperature. The dough shouldn't be made in a place that's too warm; somewhere between 68°F and 77°F is ideal.

Be careful not to store flour in an overly damp or warm spot.

Preparation

Makes enough dough for 6 individual pizzas

½ teaspoon yeast
2 cups still mineral water, at about 59°F
4 cups unbleached all-purpose flour
1 tablespoon plus 1½ teaspoons salt
1 tablespoon plus 1½ teaspoons extra-virgin olive oil

- For the first rise, whisk the yeast into the water in the bowl of a stand mixer for 30 seconds. Add 2 cups of the flour and mix on low speed, using a spatula to clean the sides of the bowl.

- Transfer the mixture to a large container and cover with plastic wrap. Let rest for 1 hour at room temperature, then transfer to the coldest spot in the refrigerator for 24 hours.

- Transfer the dough (which will have tripled in size and will be very bubbly) to the bowl of a stand mixer and let stand at room temperature for 20 minutes. Add the remaining 2 cups flour and the salt. Mix on low speed for 10 minutes, then add the oil and mix until combined.

- Transfer the dough to a container and cover with plastic wrap. Let the dough rest for 15 minutes, then divide into 6 equal portions, about 8 ounces each. (It may be easiest to use a kitchen scale to do this.) Shape each portion into a ball. Arrange the balls of dough on a jelly-roll pan or rectangular plastic container, leaving some room between them.

- Cover the dough and place it in the coldest part of the refrigerator for 24 hours.

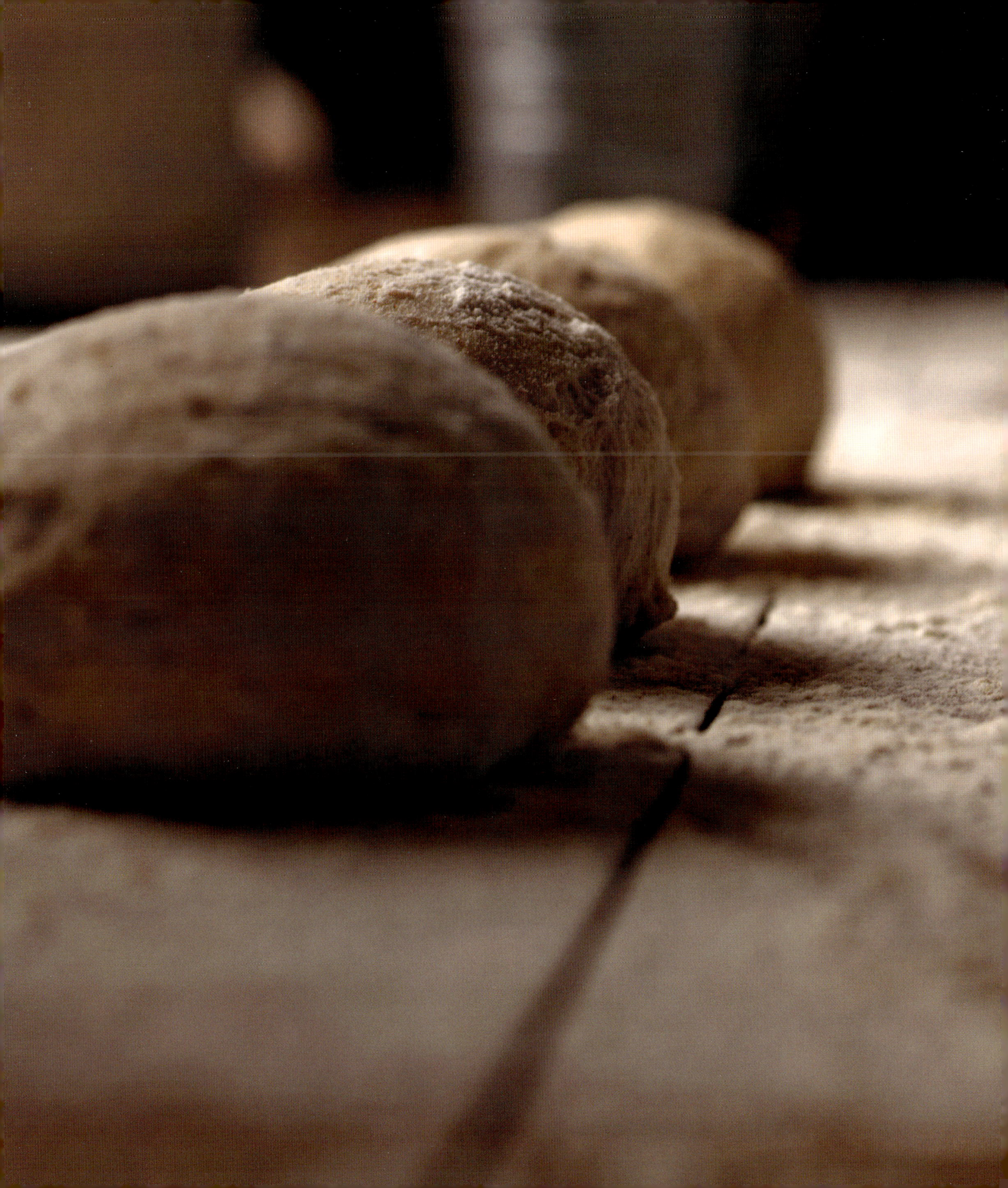

Shaping and Baking

Shaping

- Remove the dough from the refrigerator and let stand at room temperature for about 1 hour.
- In a bowl, prepare a mixture of equal parts semolina flour and unbleached all-purpose flour.
- Roll a ball of proofed dough in the flour mixture. Flatten it into a disk, then place it on a floured marble work surface. Place your hands in the center of the dough and gently stretch outward. The perimeter should remain a little thicker than the rest of the dough.
- Continue stretching the dough until it is a thin oval or circle. Remove the stretched dough, clean the work surface, and begin with the next piece of dough. When the dough has all been stretched, add the toppings, then place each pizza on a pizza peel and slide it into the oven.

Baking

- The key to making a good pizza is to bake it in a very hot (570°F to 750°F) preheated oven for only a few minutes. The wood-fired oven in a pizzeria is so hot that it cooks a pizza in just 2 to 3 minutes, which keeps the toppings from drying out. A home oven can't reach such high temperatures, but if you preheat it properly and use a baking stone, you can still achieve excellent results.
- Preheat the oven to its maximum temperature. Place the baking stone in the upper part of the oven. Heat for 15 minutes. Turn on the broiler and continue to heat the baking stone for another 15 minutes. The oven is now ready to cook the pizza.
- Use a wooden pizza peel to pick up the pizza (with the toppings from one of the recipes that follow) and slide it onto the baking stone. Jerk the peel away sharply so as not to dislodge any of the toppings.
- Bake the pizza for 3 to 4 minutes.
- Before proceeding to baking another pizza, wait 10 minutes with the oven door closed to return the baking stone to the proper temperature. If you don't have a baking stone, you can bake the pizza in an electric oven. Preheat to the maximum temperature and place the pizza on a lightly oiled jelly-roll pan.

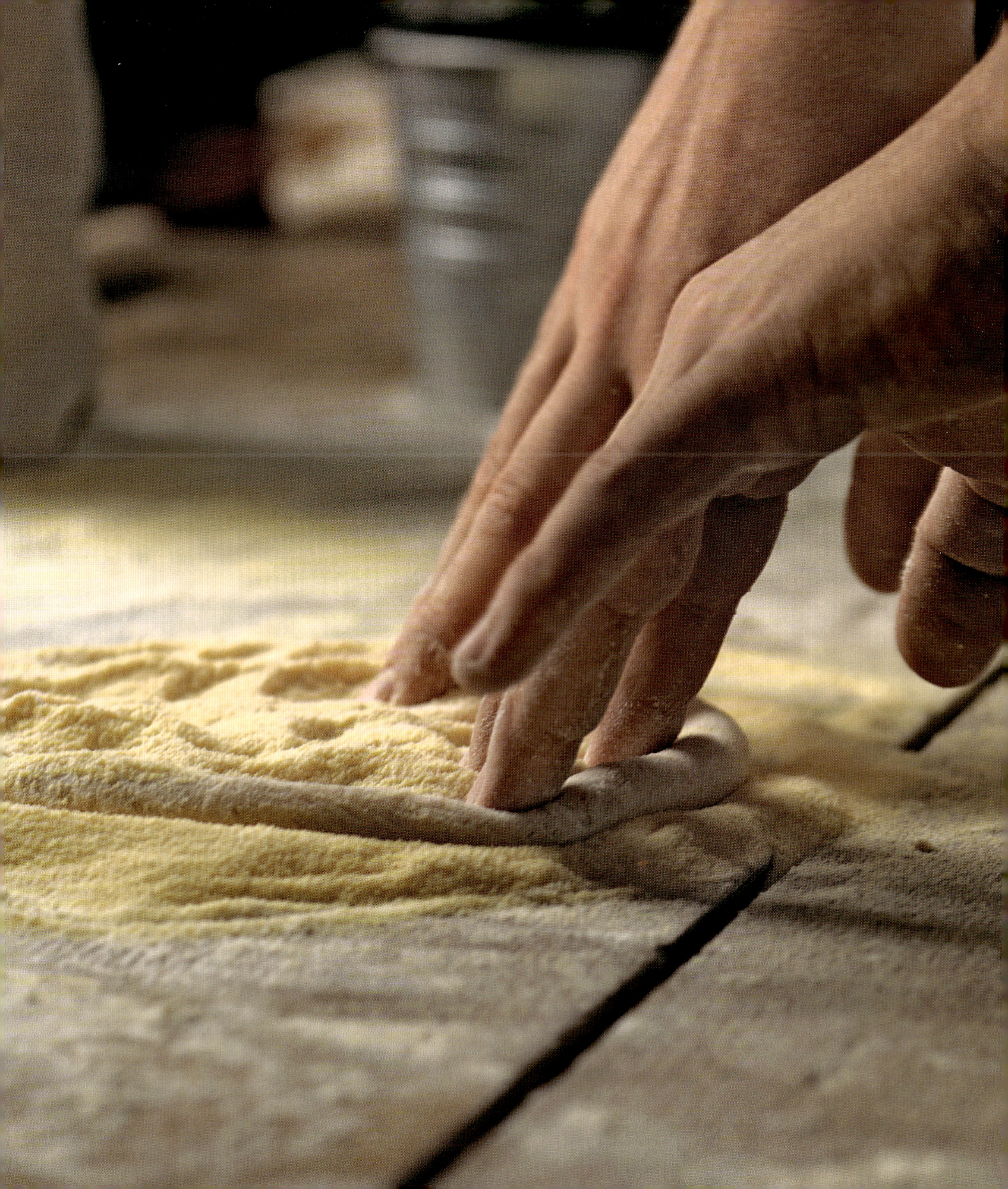

Organic Tomato and Stracciatella di Burrata

Be sure to drain the tomatoes and the mozzarella thoroughly so excess liquid won't collect on the pizza and make it soggy.

The stracciatella di burrata should be added after the pizza is cooked. The heat of the pizza will melt the cheese, but it will stay creamy.

Makes 1 individual pizza

1 (8-ounce) ball pizza dough (page 200)
¾ cup (6½ ounces) La Motticella peeled tomatoes, drained and cut into strips
3 ounces mozzarella di bufala Campana DOP
¾ ounces granbù di bufala, grated
2 ounces stracciatella di burrata
Fresh basil leaves to taste
Extra-virgin olive oil to taste

Suggested Beer Pairing

Bionda
Producer:
Menabrea
Description:
Hops and barley
Region:
Piedmont

Preparation

- Preheat the oven. (See page 202.)
- Stretch the dough into an oval. (See page 202.)
- With your hands, distribute the drained tomato strips on the surface of the pizza, leaving a ½-inch border around the perimeter.
- Squeeze the excess liquid from the mozzarella by hand, cut it into small dice, and scatter the mozzarella over the tomatoes.
- Scatter the grated cheese over the mozzarella.
- Use a pizza peel to pick up the pizza and slide it onto the preheated baking stone. Bake as described on page 202.
- Transfer the cooked pizza to a serving plate and tear the stracciatella di burrata over the top. Garnish with basil and drizzle with oil.

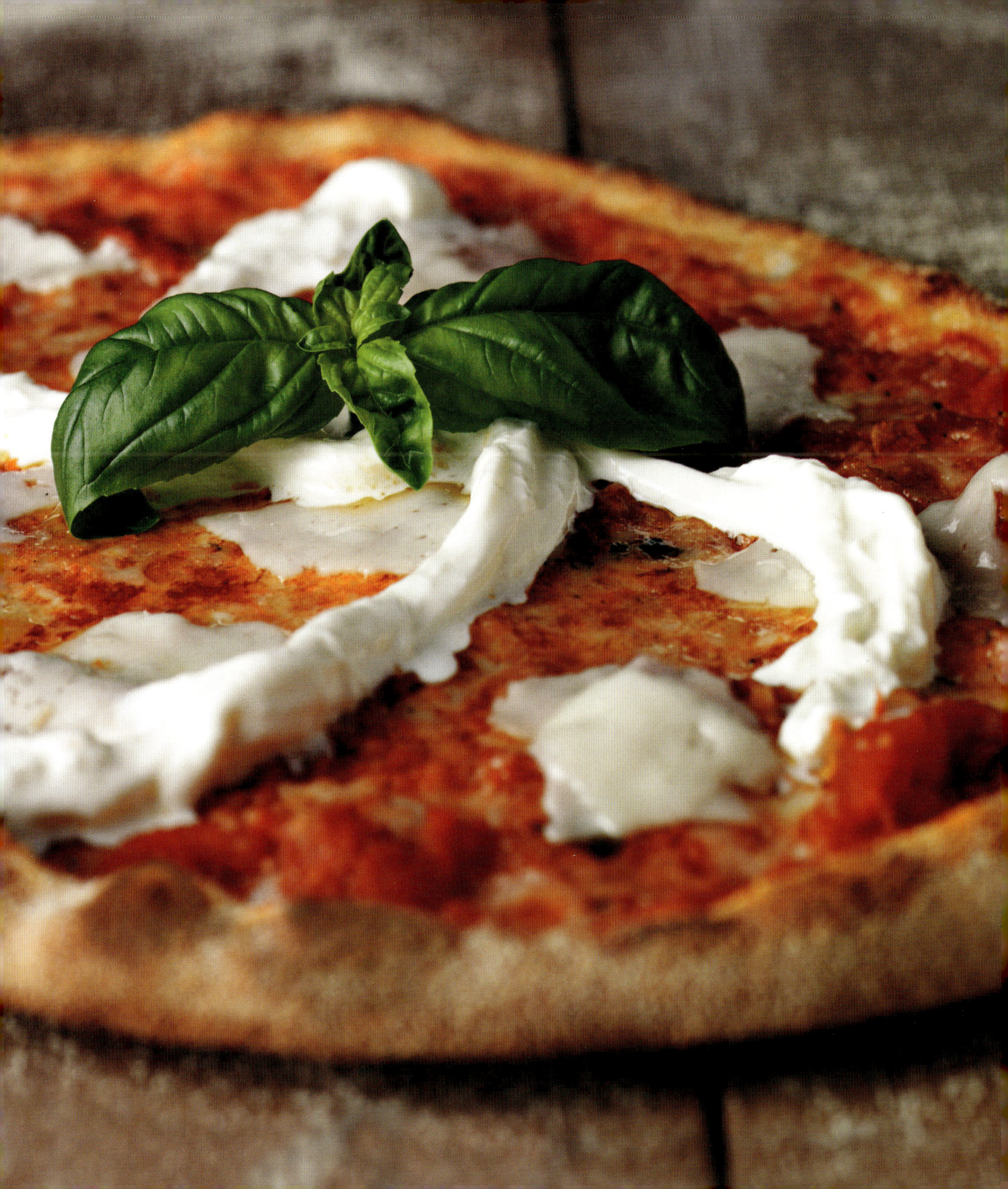

Grilled Vegetables and Smoked Buffalo Milk Mozzarella

The flavor of our smoked mozzarella di bufala Campana DOP goes perfectly with grilled vegetables, making this a truly delicious pizza.

This recipe calls for sautéing the fresh tomatoes briefly so they won't exude too much liquid on top of the pizza.

Makes 1 individual pizza

1 (8-ounce) ball pizza dough (page 200)
1 small zucchini
1 small eggplant
Extra-virgin olive oil to taste
½ cup grape tomatoes
3 ounces smoked mozzarella di bufala Campana DOP
Minced fresh parsley to taste

Suggested Wine Pairing

Langhe Bianco Tre Uve
Producer:
Malvirà
Grapes:
Chardonnay, Sauvignon, Arneis
Region:
Piedmont

Preparation

- Preheat the oven. (See page 202.)
- Stretch the dough into an oval. (See page 202.)
- Slice the zucchini and eggplant ½ inch thick and grill.
- Heat a small amount of olive oil in a pan. Cut the tomatoes in half and toss them very briefly in the pan over high heat until they have exuded their liquid. Set aside.
- Squeeze the liquid from the smoked mozzarella, cut about half of the cheese into cubes, and cut the other half into 2 to 3 slices and set aside. Place about half of the cubed cheese on the dough, leaving a ½-inch border around the perimeter. Arrange the grilled vegetables and tomatoes on top of the cheese.
- Top the vegetables with the remaining cubed smoked mozzarella.
- Use a pizza peel to pick up the pizza and slide it onto the preheated baking stone. Bake as described on page 202.
- Transfer the cooked pizza to a serving plate and sprinkle on the minced parsley. Arrange the reserved slices of smoked mozzarella on top and drizzle with olive oil.

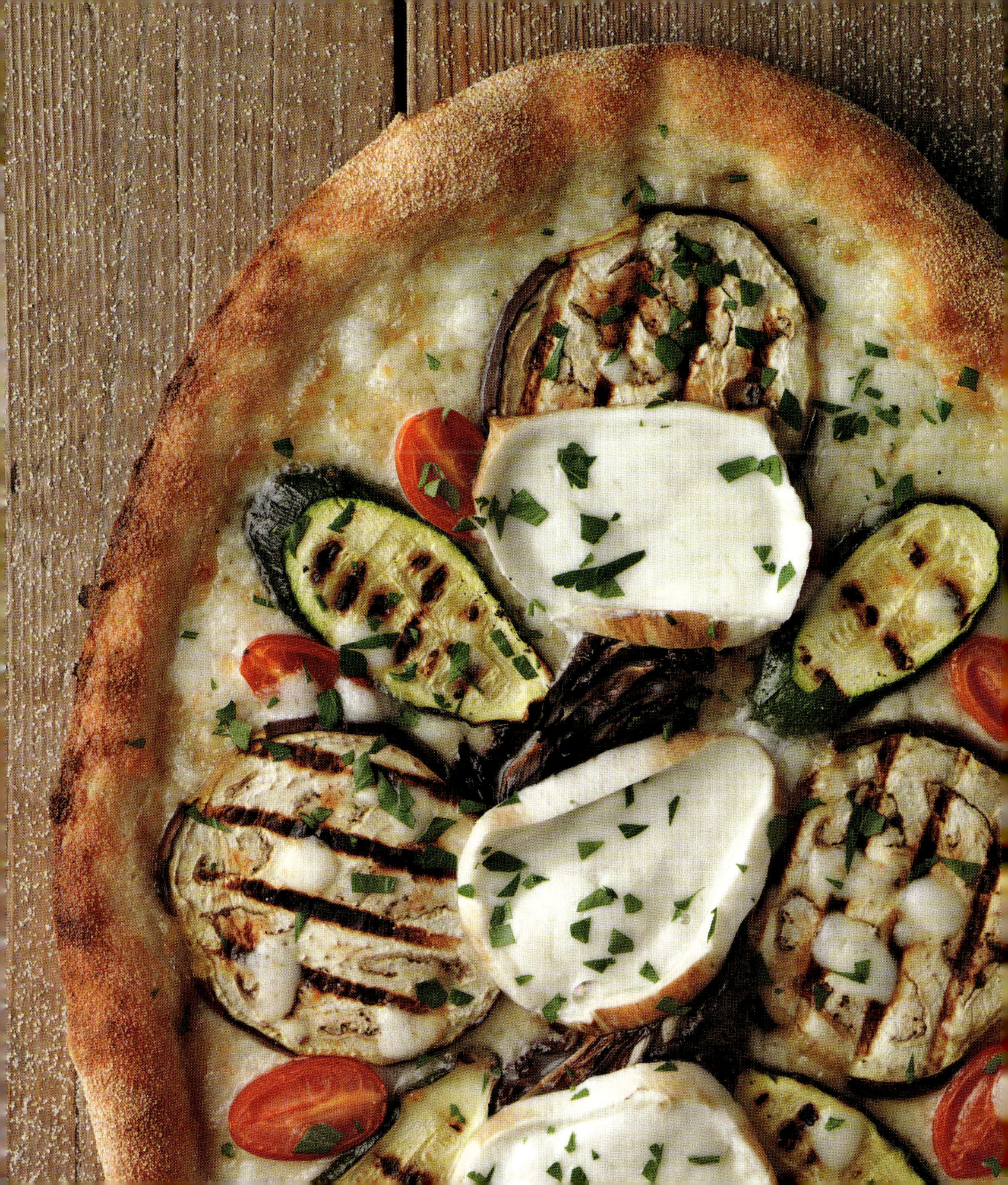

Grilled Peppers and Tuna

For this pizza we suggest using the tasty, spicy, and colorful Neapolitan papaccella peppers that you can purchase grilled and preserved in oil. These peppers are very meaty and go well with delicious Cetara anchovies.

Makes 1 individual pizza

1 (8-ounce) ball pizza dough (page 200)
¾ cup (6½ ounces) La Motticella peeled tomatoes, drained and cut into strips
3½ ounces mozzarella di bufala Campana DOP
1 tablespoon salted capers, soaked and drained
¼ cup black olives, pitted
¼ cup grilled peppers preserved in oil, drained
1 tablespoon Cetara anchovy fillets, drained and minced
3 ounces (⅓ cup) canned tuna in oil
Minced fresh thyme to taste
Extra-virgin olive oil to taste

Preparation

- Preheat the oven. (See page 202.)
- Stretch the dough into an oval. (See page 202.)
- With your hands, distribute the drained tomato strips on top of the pizza, leaving a ½-inch border around the perimeter.
- Squeeze the excess liquid from the mozzarella by hand, cut it into small dice, and scatter the mozzarella over the tomatoes. Add the capers, olives, grilled peppers, and anchovies.
- Use a pizza peel to pick up the pizza and slide it onto the preheated baking stone. Bake as described on page 202.
- Transfer the cooked pizza to a serving plate and flake on the tuna, sprinkle on the thyme, and drizzle with oil.

Suggested Beer Pairing

Marruca
Producer:
Birra Amiata
Description:
Saaz hops
Region:
Tuscany

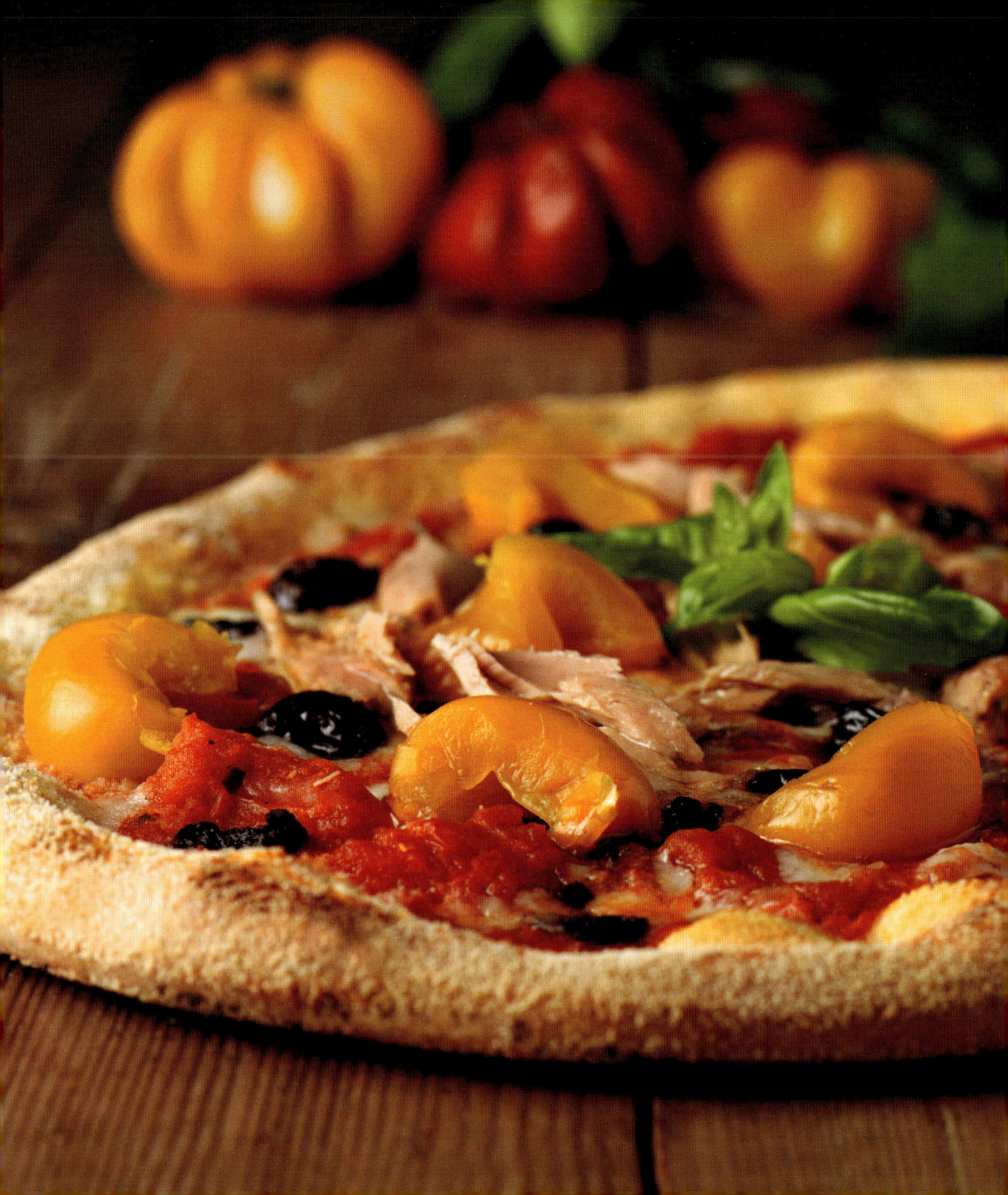

Soft Buffalo Milk Cheese

This pizza is made with four of our finest buffalo milk cheeses: mozzarella di bufala Campana DOP; casatica, a semi-aged soft white cheese with a delicate flavor; herb-laced and blue-veined blu di bufala, with intense flavor that gets better as it ages; and, last but not least, soft fresh buffalo milk stracchino. These cheeses make this pizza a true gem.

Makes 1 individual pizza

1 (8-ounce) ball pizza dough (page 200)
3½ ounces mozzarella di bufala Campana DOP, drained and diced
1½ ounces buffalo milk casatica, sliced with rind
1½ ounces blu di bufala, crumbled
1½ ounces buffalo milk stracchino
Fresh basil leaves to taste
Extra-virgin olive oil to taste

Suggested Wine Pairing

Ronco delle Mele
Producer:
Venica
Grape:
Sauvignon Blanc
Region:
Friuli

Preparation

- Preheat the oven. (See page 202.)
- Stretch the dough into an oval. (See page 202.)
- With your hands, distribute the mozzarella, casatica, and blu di bufala on top of the pizza, leaving a ½-inch border around the perimeter.
- Use a pizza peel to pick up the pizza and slide it onto the preheated baking stone. Bake as described on page 202.
- Transfer the cooked pizza to a serving plate and drop small pieces of stracchino on top. (Stracchino is too soft to cut.) Garnish with basil and drizzle with oil.

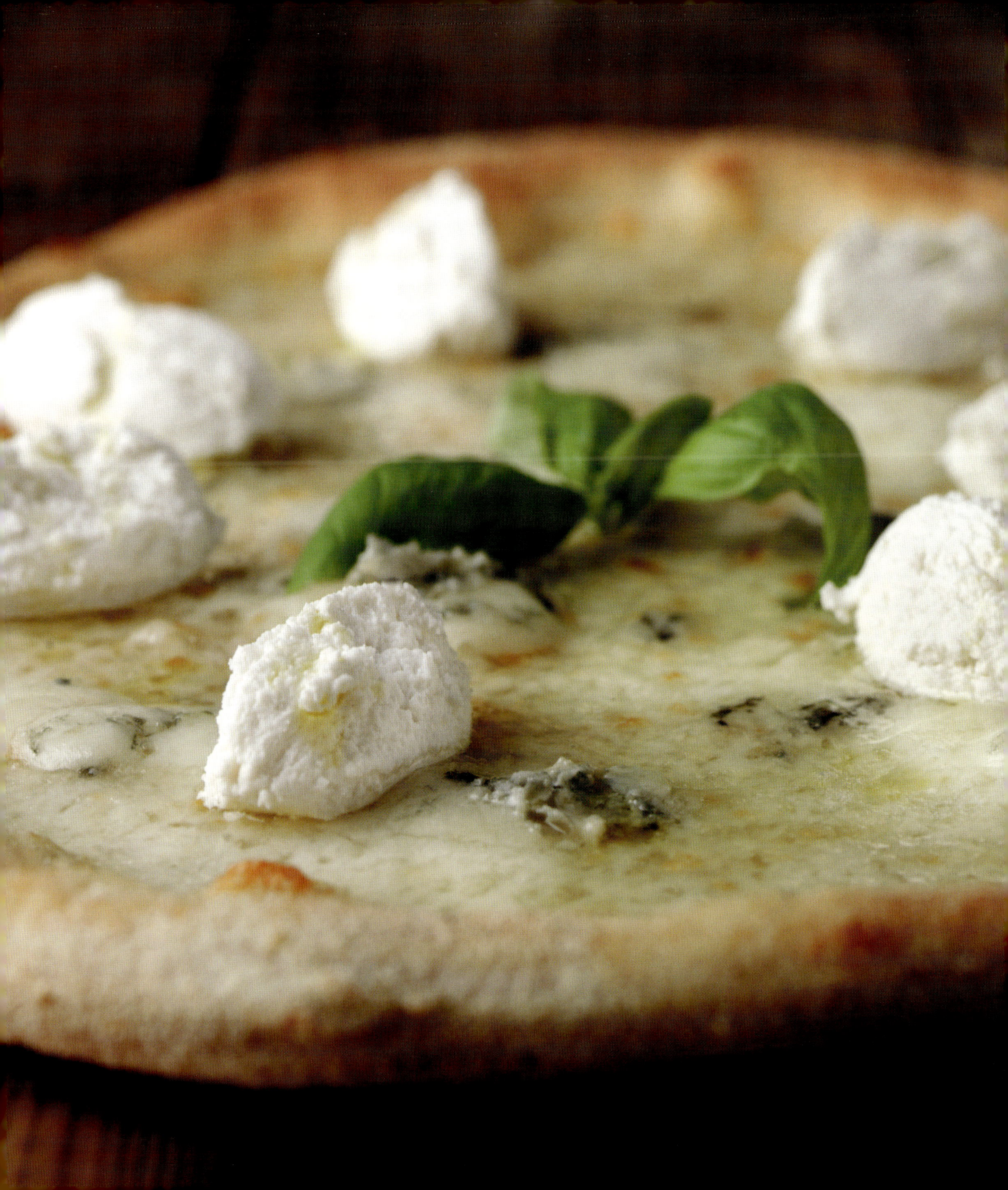

Luganega Sausage and Friarielli

This recipe from our pizza makers in the United States combines the delicious taste of luganega sausage and friarielli.

Luganega is a lean pork sausage from Monza in the Lombardy region, though its name hints that it has its roots in the Lucania area. Friarielli is broccoli rabe that has just barely begun to bud. It has a bracingly bitter flavor. Standard broccoli rabe makes a fine substitute.

Makes 1 individual pizza

1 (8-ounce) ball pizza dough (page 200)
½ cup tightly packed friarielli or broccoli rabe
Salt to taste
Extra-virgin olive oil to taste
Red pepper flakes to taste
3½ ounces luganega sausage, casing removed
3 ounces mozzarella di bufala Campana DOP, drained and diced
Chopped fresh fennel fronds for garnish

Suggested Wine Pairing

Taurasi DOCG
Producer:
Feudi di San Gregorio
Grape:
Aglianico
Region:
Campania

Preparation

- Preheat the oven. (See page 202.)
- Stretch the dough into an oval. (See page 202.)
- Trim any hard stalks from the friarielli. Chop the tender parts of the stalks and keep the leaves and buds whole.
- Bring a large pot of salted water to a boil and blanch the friarielli. Squeeze it dry and sauté in a pan with a small amount of oil and red pepper flakes.
- With your hands, distribute the mozzarella on top of the pizza, leaving a ½-inch border around the perimeter. Top with the friarielli. Crumble the sausage over the friarielli.
- Use a pizza peel to pick up the pizza and slide it onto the preheated baking stone. Bake as described on page 202 until the sausage is cooked but not too dark and the crust is golden.
- Transfer the cooked pizza to a serving plate and garnish with the fennel. Drizzle with olive oil and serve.

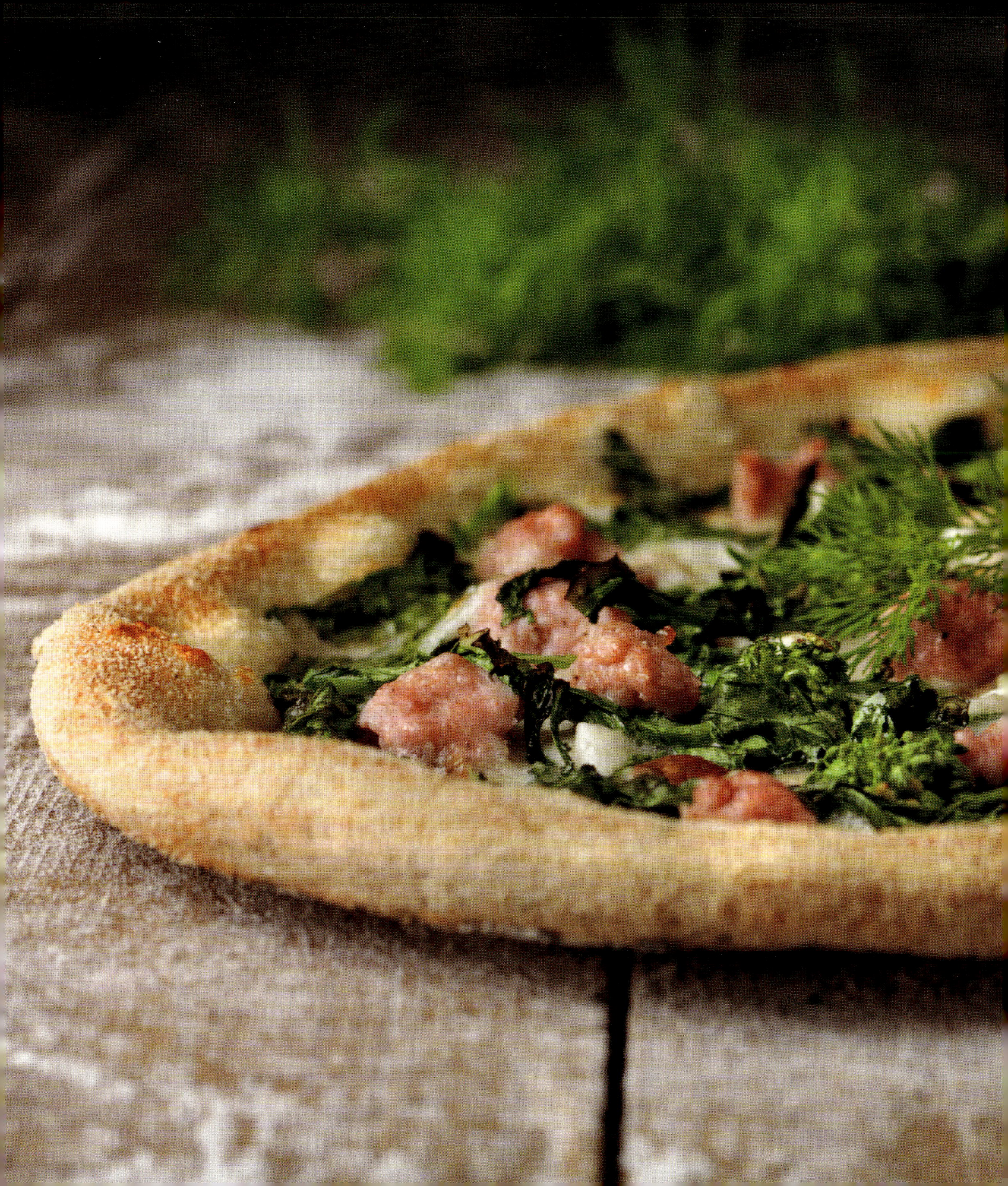

Feudi di San Gregorio

During the era of Pope Gregory the Great (590–604 B.C.), the Sannio and Irpinia areas, which had long been home to vineyards, became part of the Patrimony of Saint Peter. Today, this area in and around the hill town of Sorbo Serpico is still known as "San Gregorio" in memory of that time. Feudi di San Gregorio's vineyards are located here, and the company name reflects these historical roots.

Today, Feudi di San Gregorio is a leading winemaker in southern Italy and a leader in rediscovering true Mediterranean flavors.

The company implements a modern interpretation of the enduring tradition of its autochthonous grapes—Falanghina, Fiano, Greco, and Aglianico.

OPPOSITE:
Antonio Capaldo, president of Feudi di San Gregorio, in the wine cellars with Silvio Ursini.

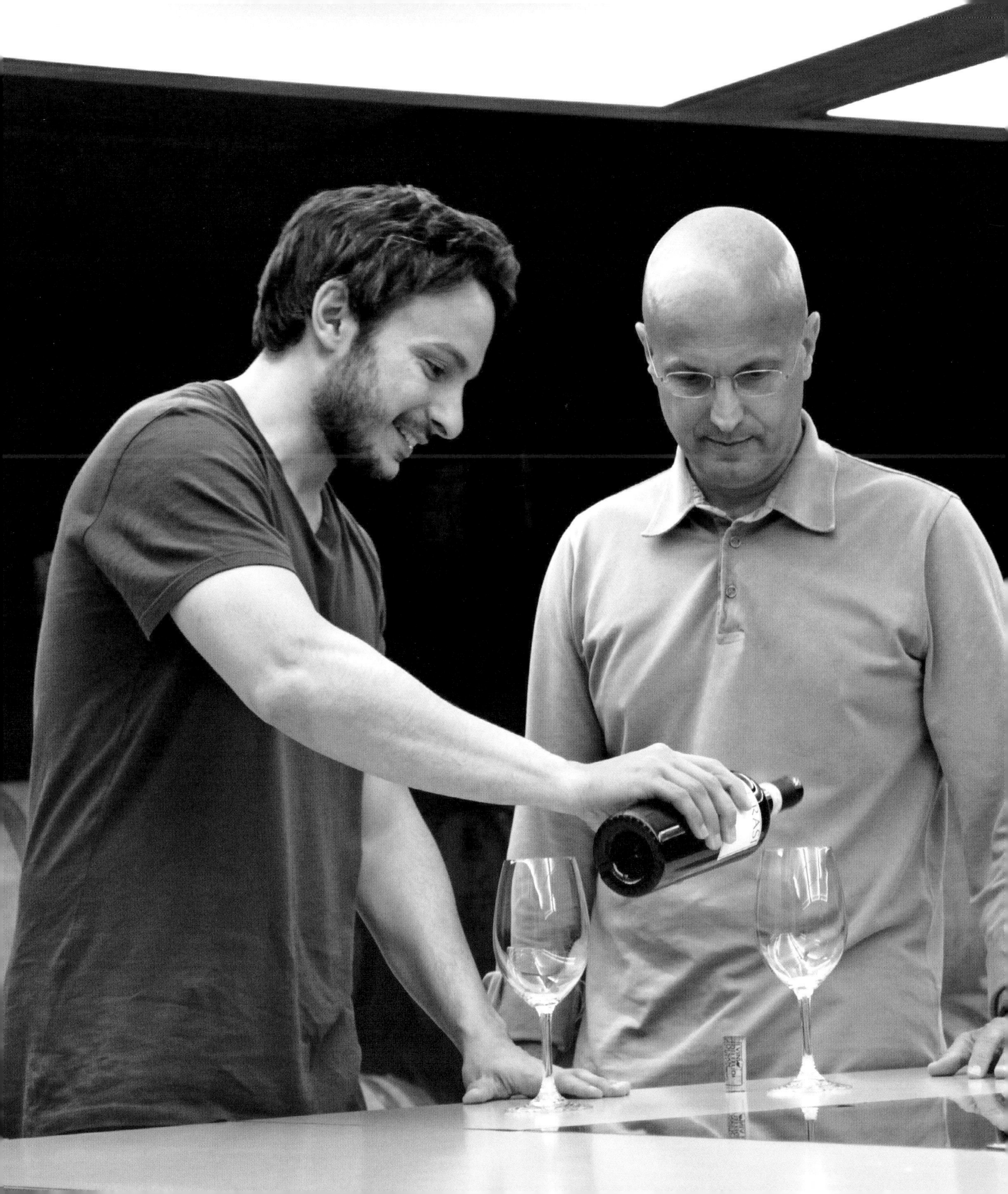

N'duja and Stracciatella di Burrata

N'duja is a soft Calabrian salami with an especially spicy flavor that marries well with sweet creamy stracciatella. If n'duja is a little too spicy for your taste, knead a few tablespoons of fresh tomato juice into it before placing it on the pizza to mellow the flavor.

Makes 1 individual pizza

1 (8-ounce) ball pizza dough (page 200)
¾ cup (6½ ounces) La Motticella peeled tomatoes, drained and cut into strips
2 ounces n'duja, casing removed
3½ ounces stracciatella di burrata
Fresh basil leaves to taste
Extra-virgin olive oil to taste

Suggested Wine Pairing

Doi Raps
Producer:
Russolo
Grapes:
Sauvignon Blanc, Pinot Bianco, Pinot Grigio
Region:
Friuli

Preparation

- Preheat the oven. (See page 202.)
- Stretch the dough into an oval. (See page 202.)
- With your hands, distribute the drained tomato strips on top of the pizza, leaving a ½-inch border around the perimeter. Crumble the n'duja over the tomatoes.
- Use a pizza peel to pick up the pizza and slide it onto the preheated baking stone. Bake as described on page 202.
- Transfer the cooked pizza to a serving plate and dot the top with pieces of stracciatella. Garnish with basil and drizzle with oil.

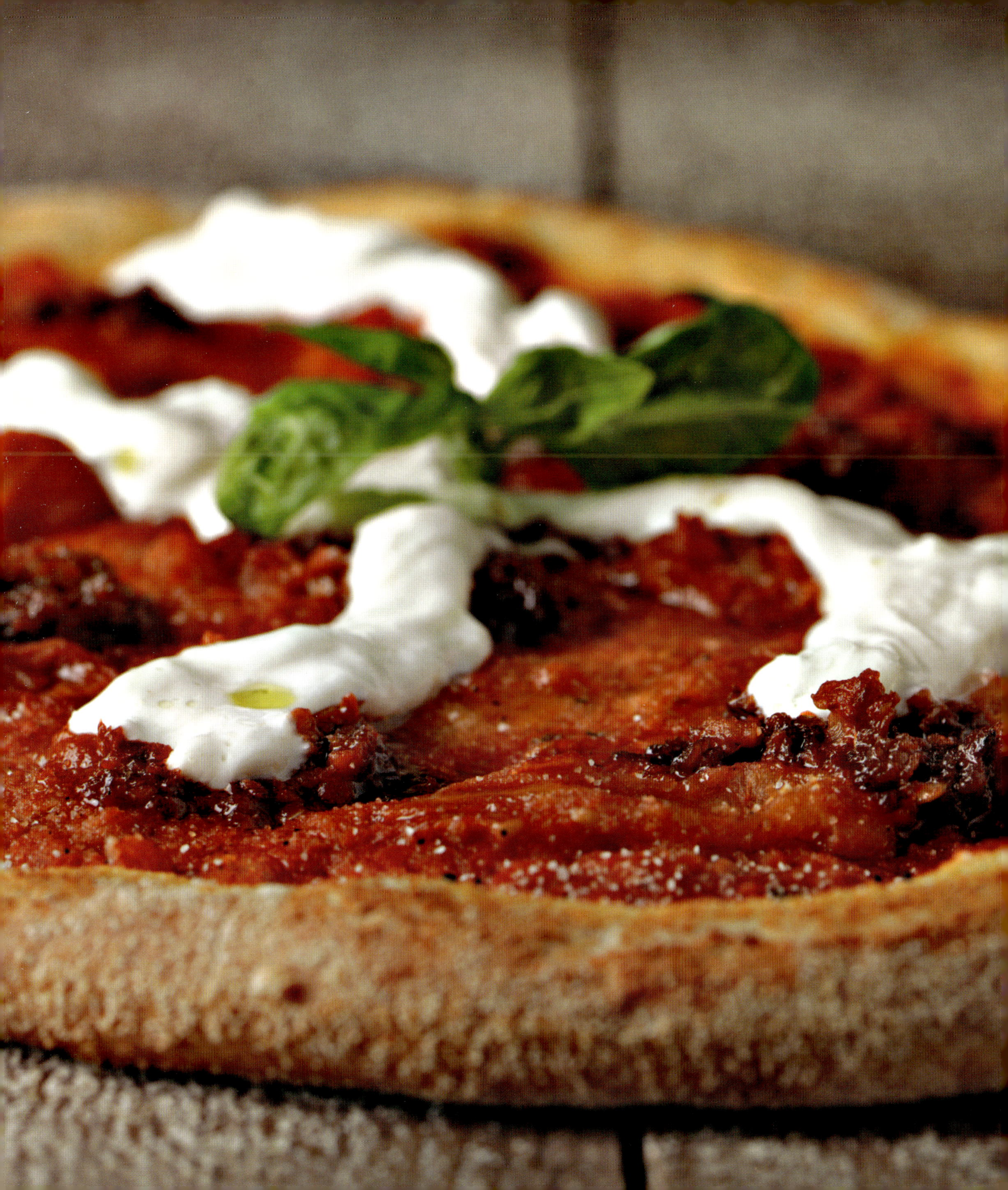

Anchovies and Capers

Cetara, a small seaside town on the Amalfi Coast, has one product that is closely connected to the history and traditions of this ancient land of fishermen and sailors: anchovies. The fish is skillfully preserved in salt inside chestnut wood barrels, and then jarred in oil. Drain the anchovies of excess oil before using them, and always place whole anchovies on pizza after it is cooked—they will dry out if cooked in the oven.

Makes 1 individual pizza

1 (8-ounce) ball pizza dough (page 200)
¾ cup (6½ ounces) La Motticella peeled tomatoes, drained and cut into strips
3 ounces mozzarella di bufala Campana DOP, drained and diced
1 tablespoon salted capers, soaked and drained
4 Cetara anchovy fillets, rinsed
Dried oregano to taste
Extra-virgin olive oil to taste

Suggested Wine Pairing

Trebbiano d'Abruzzo
Producer:
Valentini
Grape:
Trebbiano
Region:
Abruzzo

Preparation

- Preheat the oven. (See page 202.)
- Stretch the dough into an oval. (See page 202.)
- With your hands, distribute the drained tomato strips on top of the pizza, leaving a ½-inch border around the perimeter. Scatter the mozzarella over the tomatoes. Scatter on the capers.
- Use a pizza peel to pick up the pizza and slide it onto the preheated baking stone. Bake as described on page 202.
- Transfer the cooked pizza to a serving plate and arrange the anchovy fillets on top. Garnish with oregano and drizzle with oil.

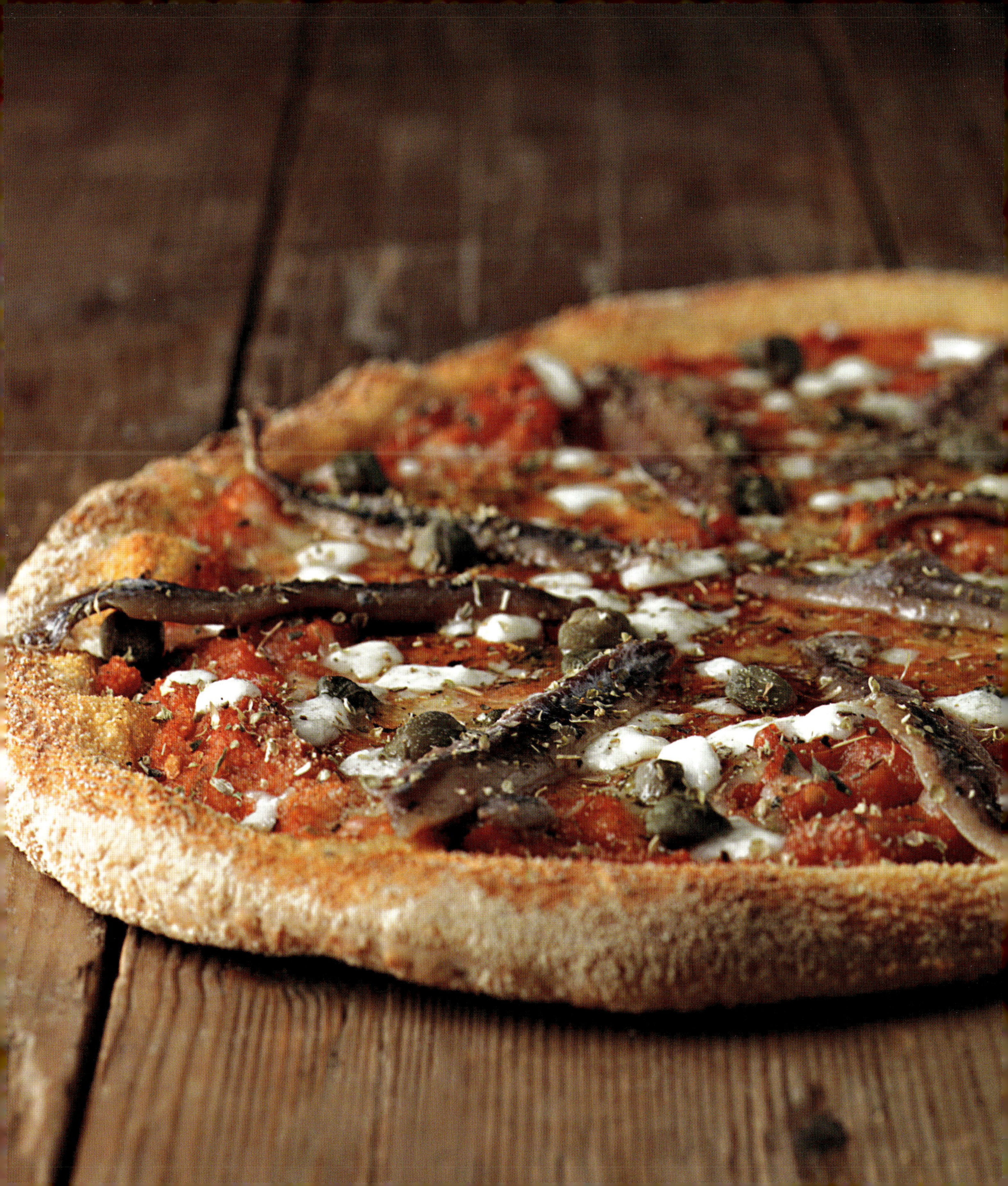

Bottarga and Grape Tomatoes

Orbetello bottarga is protected by Slow Food. To make it, mullet roe is cured in salt for a few hours and then dried. Unlike Sardinian bottarga, which can be aged for up to six months, amber-colored Orbetello bottarga is aged fifteen days at most, so it's softer. Its nutty flavor is especially delicious paired with the sweetness of buffalo milk mozzarella.

Makes 1 individual pizza

1 (8-ounce) ball pizza dough (page 200)
4½ ounces mozzarella di bufala Campana DOP, drained and diced
⅓ cup grape tomatoes, halved
1½ ounces buffalo milk ricotta
1 tablespoon Bronte pistachios
¾ ounce Orbetello bottarga
Fresh basil leaves to taste
Extra-virgin olive oil to taste

Suggested Wine Pairing

Verdicchio di Matelica Mirum Riserva
Producer:
La Monacesca
Grape:
Verdicchio
Region:
Marche

Preparation

- Preheat the oven. (See page 202.)
- Stretch the dough into an oval. (See page 202.)
- With your hands, distribute the mozzarella and tomatoes on top of the pizza, leaving a ½-inch border around the perimeter.
- Use a pizza peel to pick up the pizza and slide it onto the preheated baking stone. Bake as described on page 202.
- Transfer the cooked pizza to a serving plate. Dot with the ricotta. Scatter on the pistachios and shave the bottarga over the pizza. Garnish with basil and drizzle with oil.

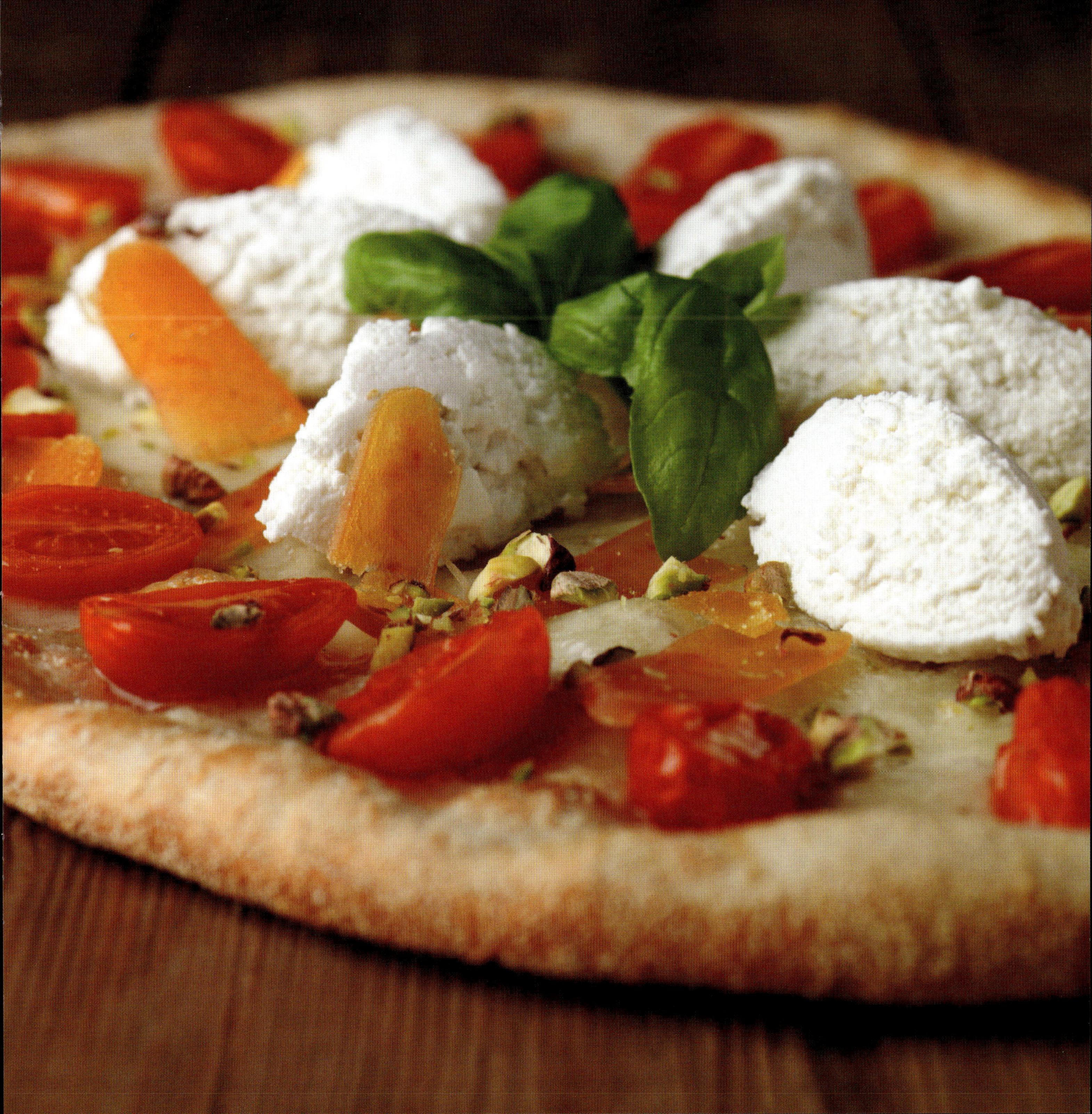

Open Calzone with Prosciutto Crudo di Parma

Our pizza makers in the United States came up with this fun and delicious alternative to a traditional calzone. It's actually a kind of pizza sandwich with excellent aged prosciutto di Parma, creamy buffalo milk ricotta, and pleasantly bitter arugula. We like to serve this with an arugula and tomato salad on the side.

Makes 1 individual pizza

1 (8-ounce) ball pizza dough (page 200)
3½ ounces buffalo milk ricotta
2 tablespoons whole milk
¾ cup loosely packed arugula
Extra-virgin olive oil to taste
2 ounces thinly sliced prosciutto crudo di Parma
⅓ cup grape tomatoes, quartered
Salt to taste

Suggested Wine Pairing

Rosè Belguardo
Producer:
Mazzei
Grapes:
Sangiovese, Shiraz
Region:
Tuscany

Preparation

- Preheat the oven. (See page 202.)
- Stretch the dough into an oval. (See page 202.)
- Mix the ricotta and milk together in a bowl and set aside.
- Use a pizza peel to pick up the pizza dough and slide it onto the preheated baking stone.
- Bake for 20 seconds, then with a fork poke a few holes in the dough to prevent it from getting too puffy. Return to the oven and bake until golden, about 1 minute.
- Spread the ricotta mixture over one half of the pizza crust. Scatter about half of the arugula over the ricotta mixture, drizzle on a little oil, and arrange the prosciutto slices on top.
- Fold the empty half of the crust over the filling, then cut into 4 wedges. Toss the remaining arugula with the tomatoes, dress with a little extra-virgin olive oil and salt, and serve on the side.

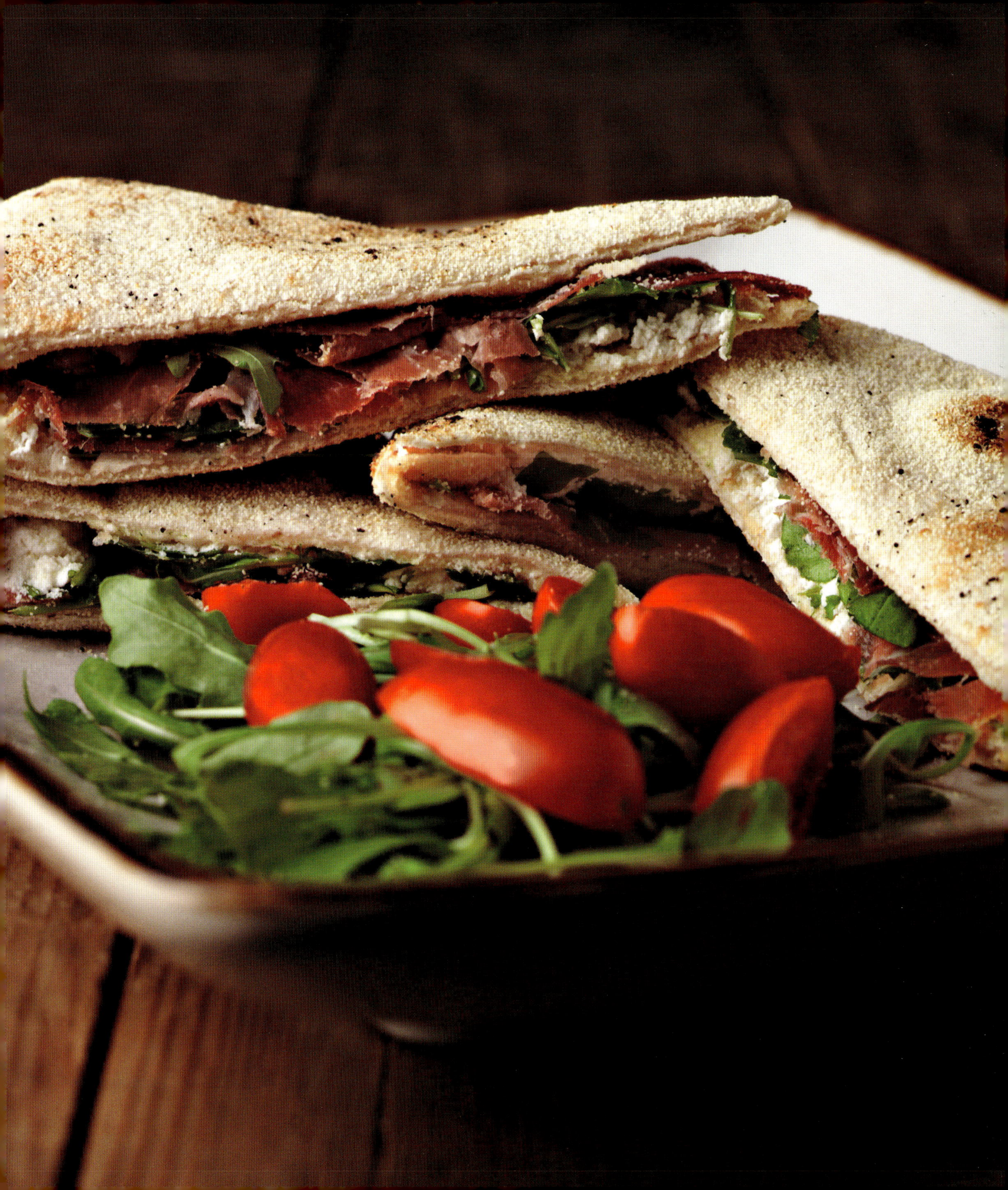

Marchesi Mazzei

The Mazzei family is linked not only to winemaking in Tuscany, but to the political and cultural life of that region as well. The earliest mention of the Mazzei family—originally from the winemaking area of Carmignano—appears in documents that date to the early eleventh century. Ser Lapo Mazzei is believed to have coined the name "Chianti," as it appeared for the first time in a business contract he signed in 1398.

The members of the Mazzei family who lead the company today aim to keep the values of this family's history and tradition alive, expressing them in ways that can meet market demand and make use of the opportunities offered by modern technology.

OPPOSITE:
Francesco and Filippo Mazzei run the family company with their father, Lapo.

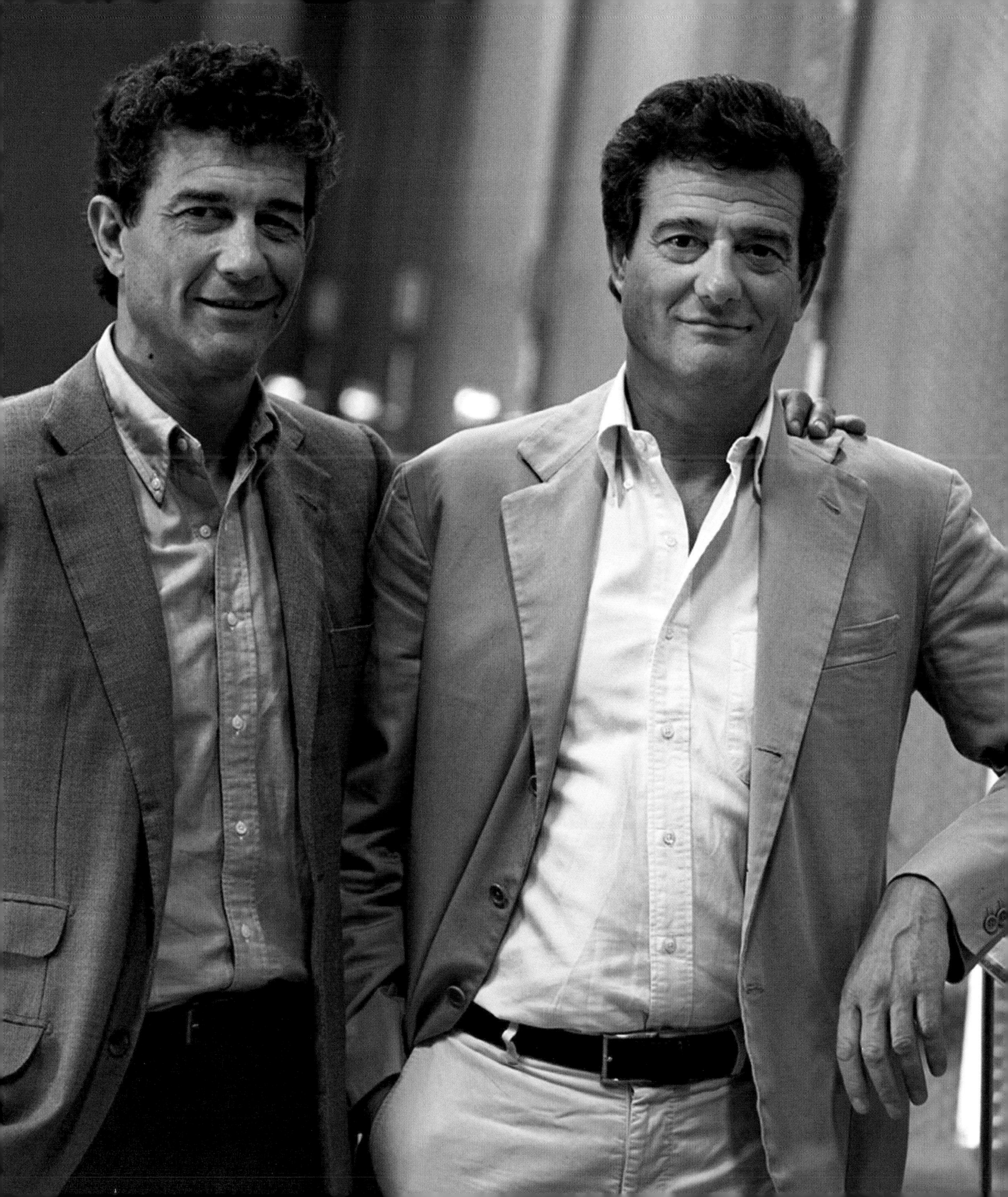

Prosciutto Cotto and Norcia Black Truffle

Two of the finest products are used as toppings for this pizza: tender prosciutto cotto, or baked ham, which is trussed by hand and steamed, and delicious black truffle from Norcia with its intense aroma.

Makes 1 individual pizza

1 (8-ounce) ball pizza dough (page 200)
2 ounces buffalo milk ricotta
1 tablespoon whole milk
3 ½ ounces mozzarella di bufala Campana DOP, drained and diced
1 ½ ounces thinly sliced prosciutto cotto
¾ ounce Norcia black truffle
Extra-virgin olive oil to taste

Suggested Wine Pairing

Petit Arvine
Producer:
Elio Ottin
Grape:
Petite Arvine
Region:
Valle d'Aosta

Preparation

- Preheat the oven. (See page 202.)
- Stretch the dough into an oval. (See page 202.)
- Mix the ricotta and milk together in a bowl and set aside. Scatter the mozzarella on top of the pizza, leaving a ½-inch border around the perimeter.
- Use a pizza peel to pick up the pizza and slide it onto the preheated baking stone. Bake as described on page 202.
- Transfer the cooked pizza to a serving plate and arrange the sliced prosciutto cotto on top. Dot with the ricotta mixture. Shave on the truffle and drizzle with oil.

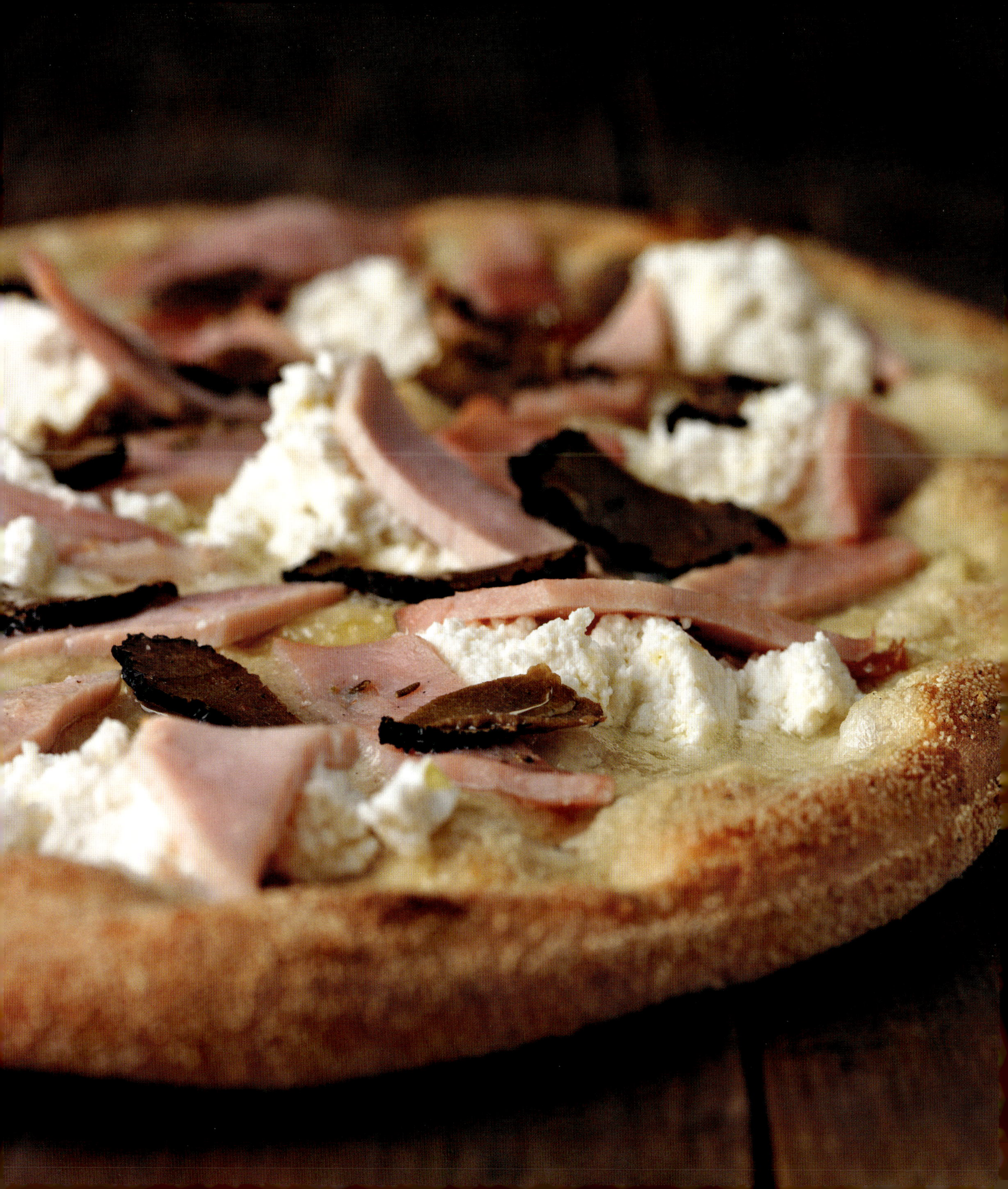

Soppressata Calabrese and Ricotta

Calabrian soppressata is a raw-pressed salami that is still made according to traditional methods handed down from generation to generation. The exact amount and selection of salt, sweet and spicy peppers, and pork cuts (haunch, shoulder, belly, and so on) used to make it are very important, and each producer jealously guards its own recipe. We pair soppressata with sweet buffalo milk ricotta, a handful of grape tomatoes, and some fresh arugula.

Makes 1 individual pizza

1 (8-ounce) ball pizza dough (page 200)
2 ounces buffalo milk ricotta
1 tablespoon whole milk
3½ ounces mozzarella di bufala Campana DOP, drained and diced
⅓ cup grape tomatoes, halved
½ cup loosely packed arugula
2 tablespoons pitted Taggiasche olives
2 ounces thinly sliced Calabrian soppressata
Extra-virgin olive oil to taste

Suggested Wine Pairing

Montepulciano Podere
Producer:
Umani Ronchi
Grape:
Montepulciano d'Abruzzo
Region:
Abruzzo

Preparation

- Preheat the oven. (See page 202.)
- Stretch the dough into an oval. (See page 202.)
- Mix the ricotta and milk together in a bowl and set aside. Scatter the mozzarella and the tomatoes on top of the pizza, leaving a ½-inch border around the perimeter.
- Use a pizza peel to pick up the pizza and slide it onto the preheated baking stone. Bake as described on page 202.
- Transfer the cooked pizza to a serving plate. Dot with the ricotta mixture. Scatter on the arugula and olives and top with the soppressata. Drizzle with oil and serve.

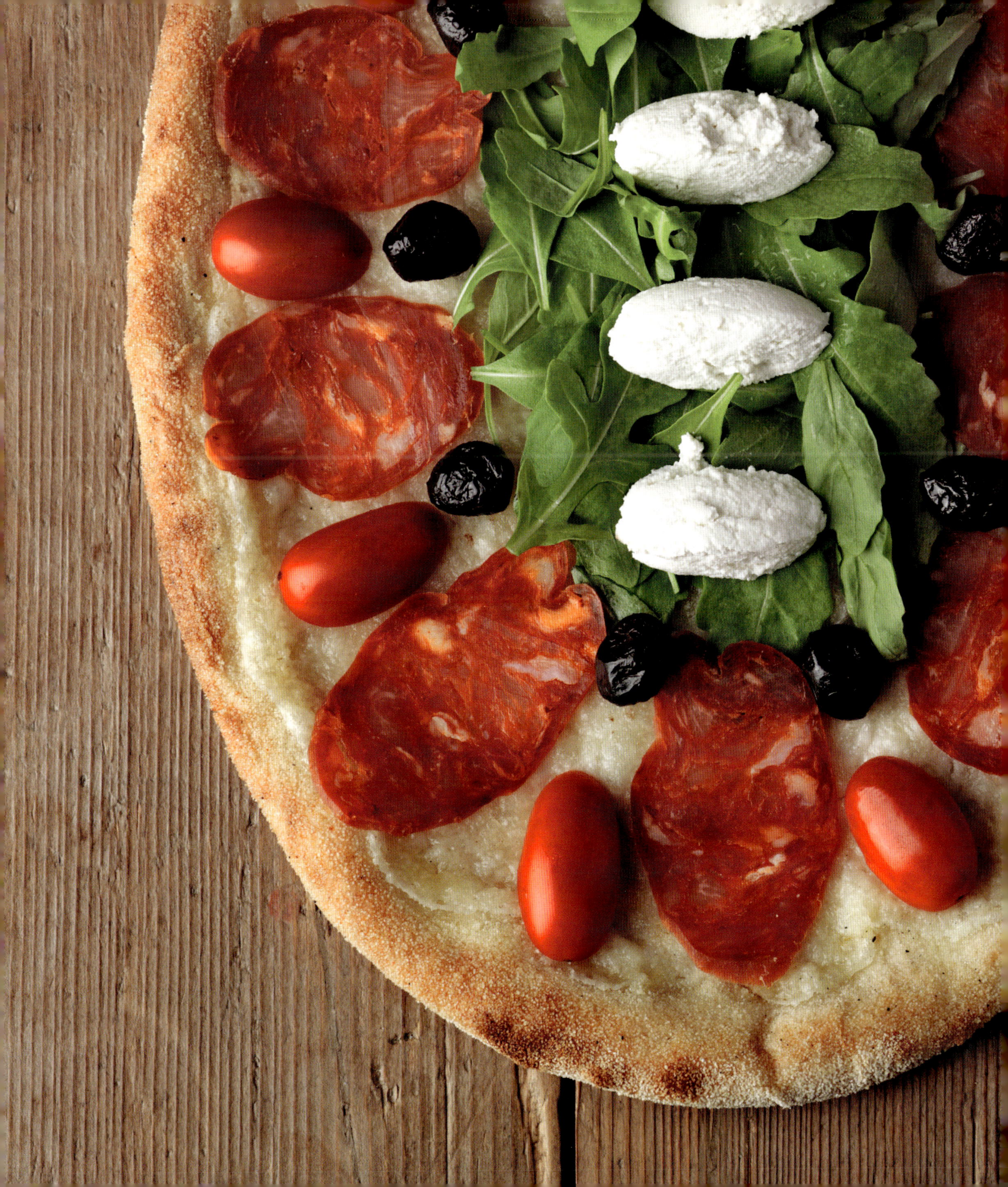

Porcini Mushroom and Black Truffle

Every year we eagerly await fall, when we can make this fantastic seasonal pizza using porcini mushrooms, truffles, and smoked mozzarella di bufala Campana DOP.

Makes 1 individual pizza

1 (8-ounce) ball pizza dough (page 200)
4 ounces fresh porcini mushrooms
4 ounces smoked mozzarella di bufala Campana DOP, drained and diced
¾ ounce black truffle
Minced parsley to taste
Salt and black pepper to taste
Extra-virgin olive oil to taste

Suggested Wine Pairing

Torrette superiore
Producer:
Feudo San Maurizio
Grapes:
Petit Rouge, Syrah
Region:
Valle d'Aosta

Preparation

- Preheat the oven. (See page 202.)
- Stretch the dough into an oval. (See page 202.)
- Scrape the mushrooms clean with the blunt side of a knife blade, then wipe with a damp cloth. Detach the stems and caps and slice both thinly.
- Scatter the mozzarella and mushrooms on top of the pizza, leaving a ½-inch border around the perimeter.
- Use a pizza peel to pick up the pizza and slide it onto the preheated baking stone. Bake as described on page 202.
- Transfer the cooked pizza to a serving plate and shave on the truffle. Sprinkle on parsley, season with salt and pepper, drizzle with oil, and serve.

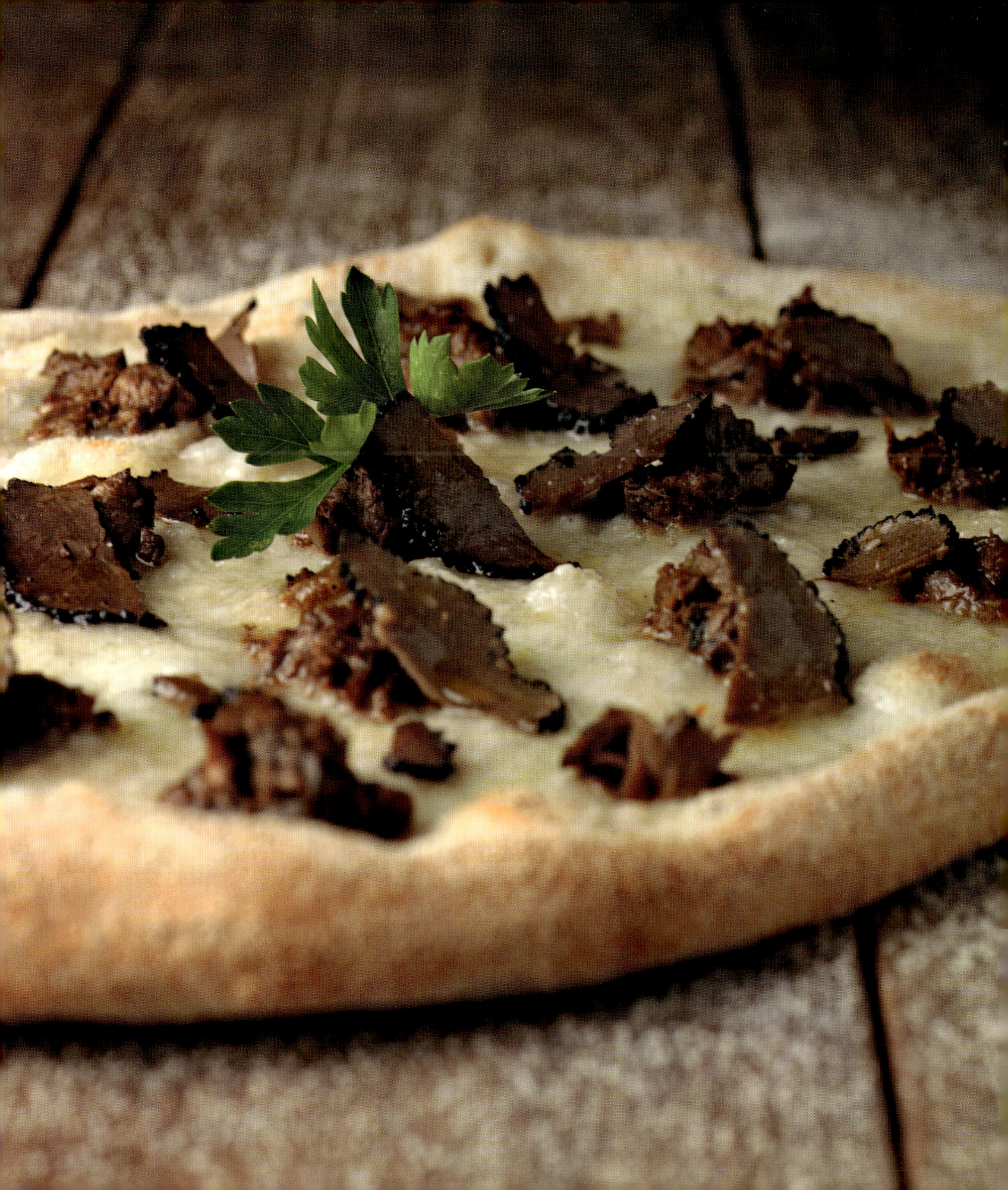

© Luke Hayes

LONDON,
Poland Street

©Luke Hayes

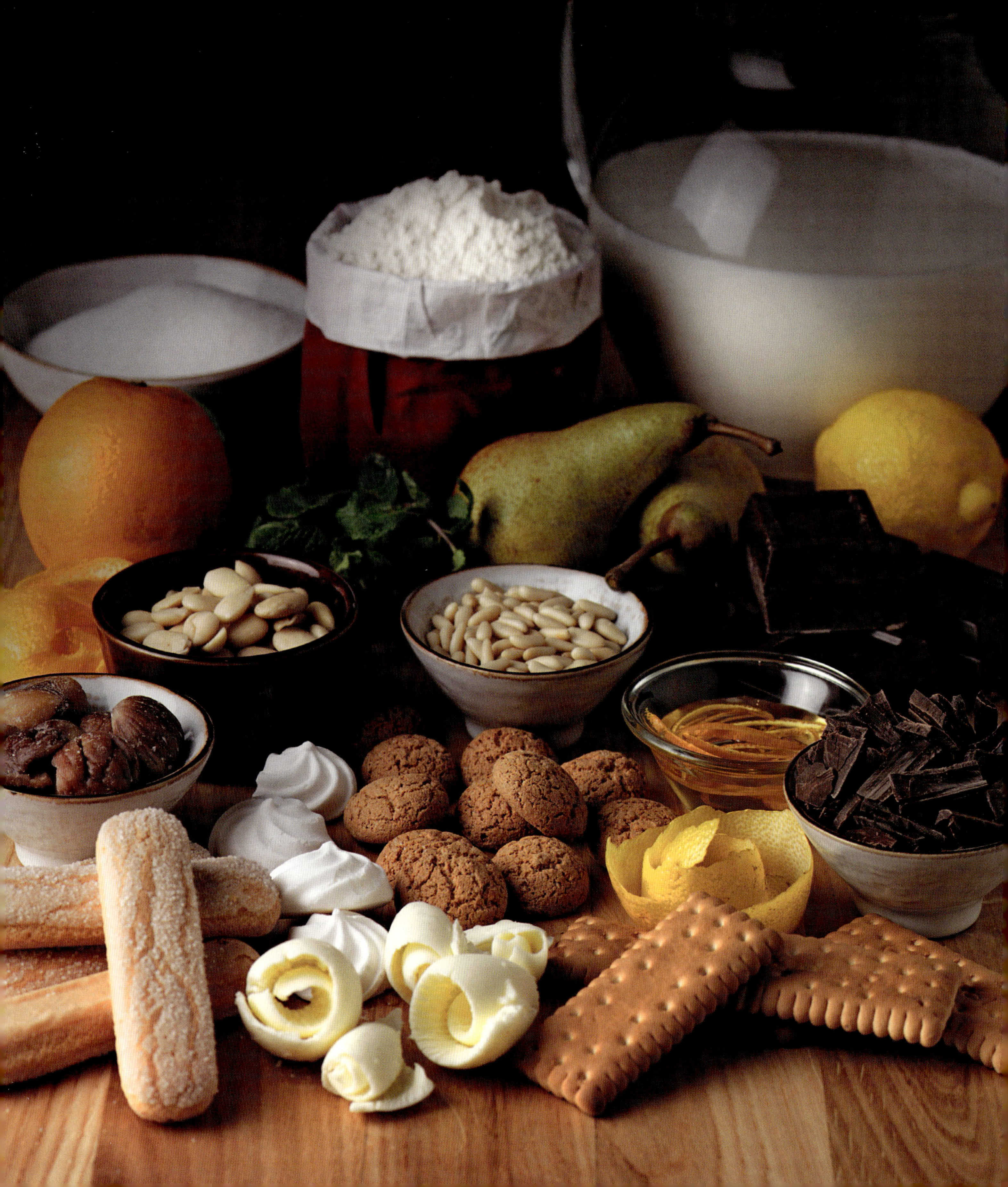

Dolci

Ricotta with Honey and Pine Nuts

Torta di Capri

Ricotta and Pear Tart

Tiramisù

Crema with Bronte Pistachios

Monte Bianco with Candied Chestnuts

Zuccotto with Dark Chocolate

Limoncello Babà with Vanilla Custard

Ricotta with Honey and Pine Nuts

This delicate spoon dessert is very easy to make. The orange blossom honey and toasted pine nuts harmonize beautifully with the buffalo milk ricotta.

Serves 4

⅓ cup plus 2 tablespoons whipping cream
⅓ cup sugar
14 ounces buffalo milk ricotta
2 tablespoons pine nuts, lightly toasted
¼ cup orange blossom honey
Zest of ½ orange

Suggested Wine Pairing

Dindarello
Producer:
Maculan
Grape:
Moscato
Region:
Veneto

Preparation

- Place the beaters and bowl of an electric mixer in the freezer for a few minutes to chill, then combine the cream and sugar in the bowl and whip to soft peaks.
- Fold the whipped cream into the ricotta.
- Transfer the ricotta mixture to a pastry bag and pipe into four small individual bowls. Sprinkle on the pine nuts. Heat the honey very gently over low heat, then drizzle it on.
- Use a zester to create thin strips of orange zest. Scatter them onto the dessert and serve.

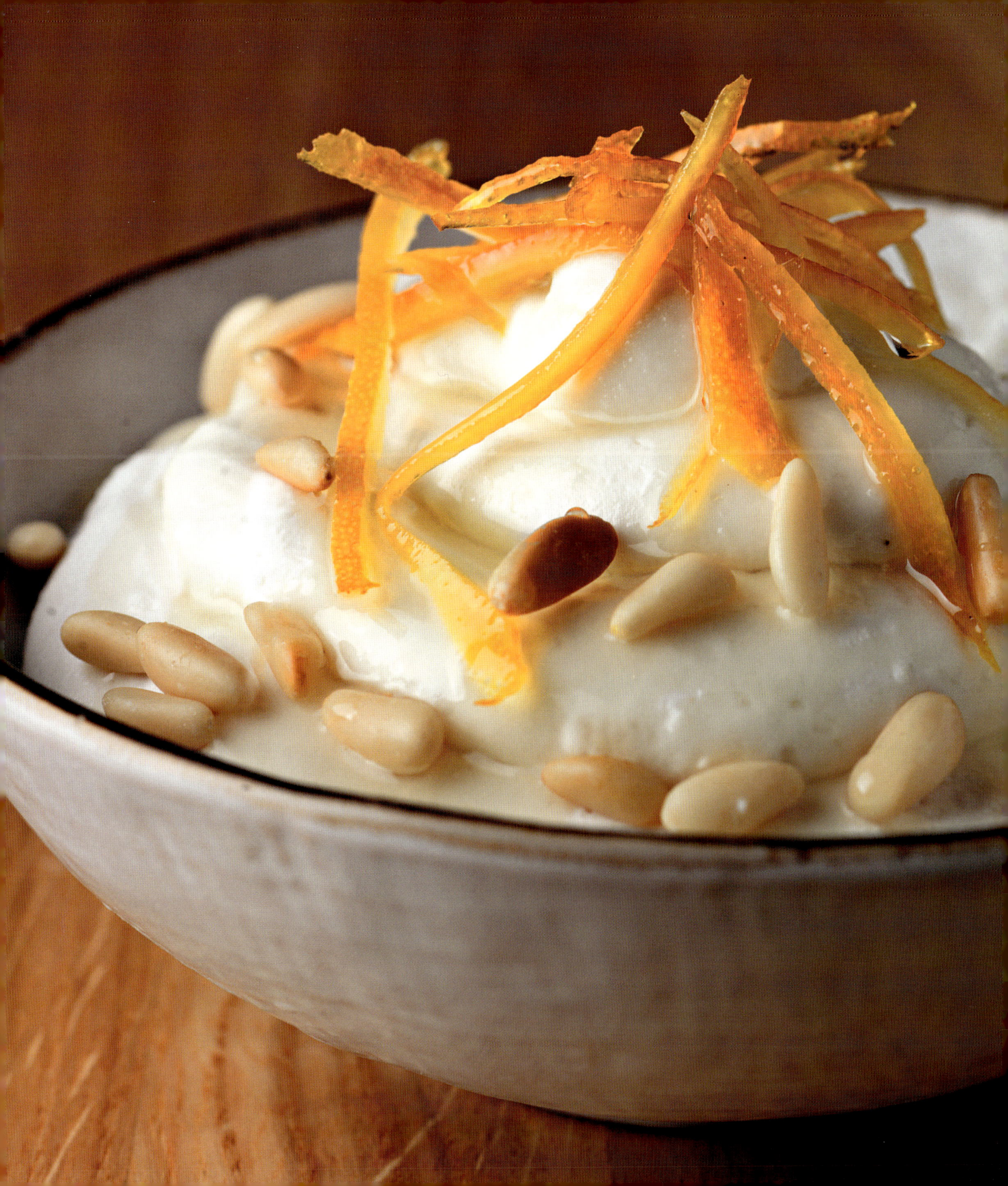

Torta di Capri

This dessert from the island of Capri was invented in the 1920s. Legend has it that Carmine di Fiore, a baker, forgot to add flour to his chocolate cake and serendipitously invented a delicious cake that would soon be famous throughout the Sorrento Peninsula. We make it the traditional way, so that it's not very thick, crunchy on the outside, soft on the inside, and packed with dark chocolate and almonds.

Makes one 10-inch round cake, about 8 servings

2 sticks unsalted butter, softened, plus more for buttering pan
9 ounces dark chocolate
¾ cup sugar
5 medium eggs, separated
1½ cups blanched almonds, lightly toasted and ground
1 pinch salt
Confectioners' sugar for garnish
Fresh mint leaves for garnish

Suggested Wine Pairing

Passito di Malvasia Rossa
Producer:
Tenuta Montemagno
Grape:
Malvasia di Casorzo
Region:
Piedmont

Preparation

- Preheat the oven to 320°F. Butter a 10-inch round cake pan and set aside.
- Melt the chocolate, whisking frequently, in the top of a bain-marie until perfectly smooth. Allow to cool slightly.
- Place the butter, about ¼ cup plus 2 tablespoons of the sugar, and the egg yolks in the bowl of an electric mixer and beat until smooth and well-combined.
- Add the melted chocolate and the ground almonds and mix to combine.
- In a clean bowl, beat the egg whites with the salt and the remaining ¼ cup plus 2 tablespoons sugar until they form stiff peaks, then fold the egg whites into the chocolate and almond mixture with a spatula, working gently from bottom to top to deflate the mixture as little as possible.
- Transfer the batter to the prepared cake pan.
- Bake in the preheated oven until a tester inserted in the center emerges clean and the top of the cake springs back when pressed with a finger, about 40 minutes.
- Let the cake cool completely, then unmold to a cake plate.
- Dust with confectioners' sugar and garnish with mint leaves.

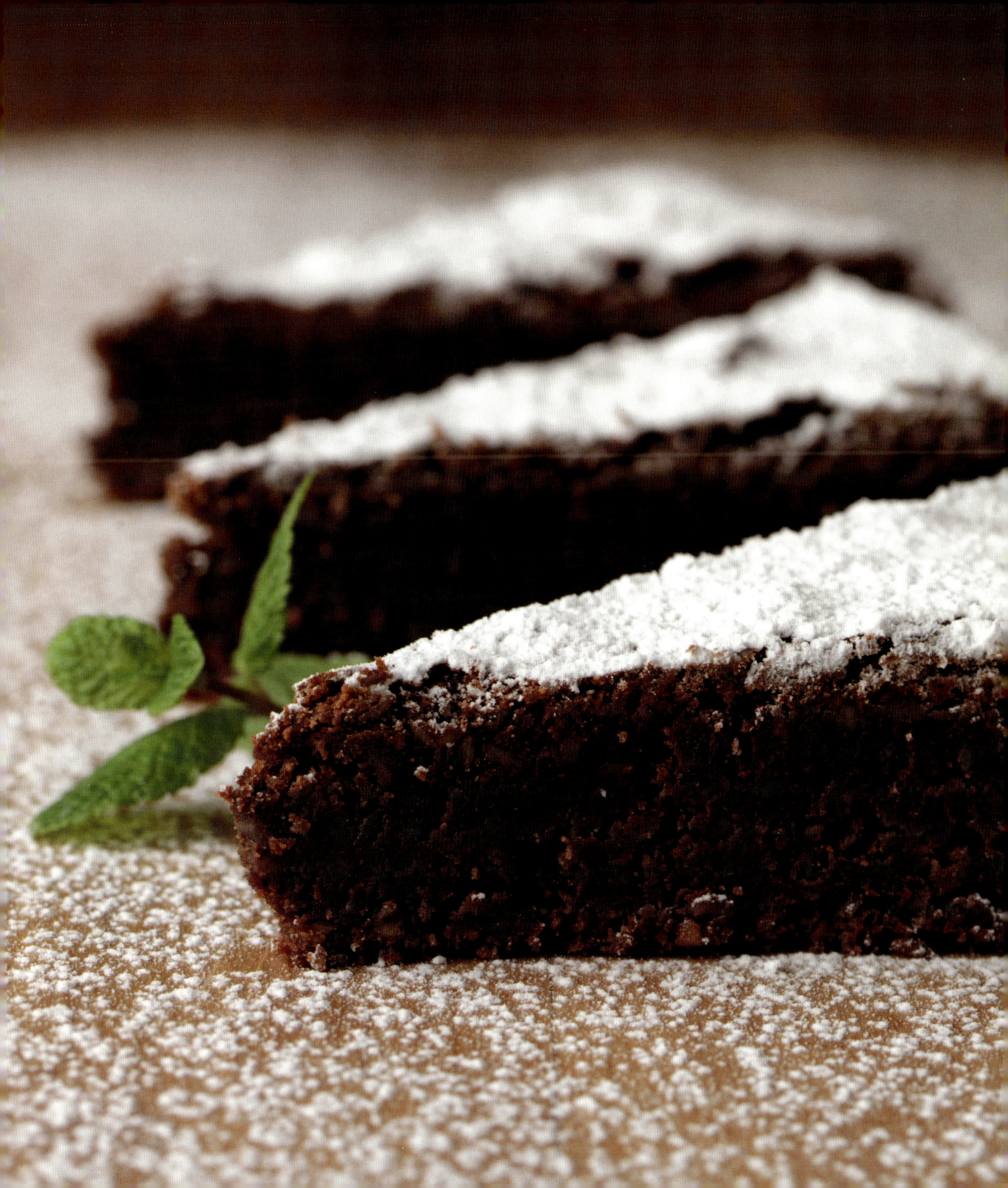

Ricotta and Pear Tart

This is a very old recipe, and there are dozens of variations of it, all of them calling for different types of ricotta. We use a traditional Amalfi Coast recipe, which calls for buffalo milk ricotta and small, sweet Mastantuono pears from the Sorrento Peninsula.

Serves 8

6 tablespoons unsalted butter
¼ cup confectioners' sugar, plus more for finishing
1 egg yolk
Grated lemon zest to taste
1 cup unbleached all-purpose flour, sifted
½ cup granulated sugar
11 ounces Mastantuono pears
3 medium eggs
1 teaspoon vanilla extract
1 pound buffalo milk ricotta
1 cup mascarpone
Gragnano cherry jam for serving

Suggested Wine Pairing

Brachetto Pian dei Sogni
Producer:
Forteto della Luja
Grape:
Brachetto
Region:
Piedmont

Preparation

- Beat the butter and the ¼ cup confectioners' sugar together until combined and somewhat softened. Place the egg yolk, lemon zest, and flour in a large bowl.
- Add the butter mixture to the bowl and pinch it with your fingertips to make a mixture with the consistency of wet sand. Transfer to a 10-inch round nonstick cake pan and flatten with the palm of your hand to form an even layer.
- Refrigerate for 30 minutes.
- Preheat the oven to 330°F.
- Combine ½ cup water and ¼ cup of the granulated sugar in a small pot and bring to a simmer, stirring to melt the sugar. Meanwhile, peel and core the pears, cut them into small dice, and cook in the sugar syrup for 10 minutes. Set aside to cool.
- Beat the whole eggs with the remaining ¼ cup sugar and the vanilla.
- Combine the ricotta and mascarpone and fold in the egg mixture. Use a spatula and work gently from bottom to top to deflate the mixture as little as possible.
- Remove the diced pears from the syrup with a slotted spoon and fold into the ricotta mixture.
- Transfer the ricotta mixture to the cake pan on top of the crust. Bake in the preheated oven until set, about 50 minutes.
- Let the cake cool completely and dust with confectioners' sugar.
- Serve with Gragnano cherry jam.

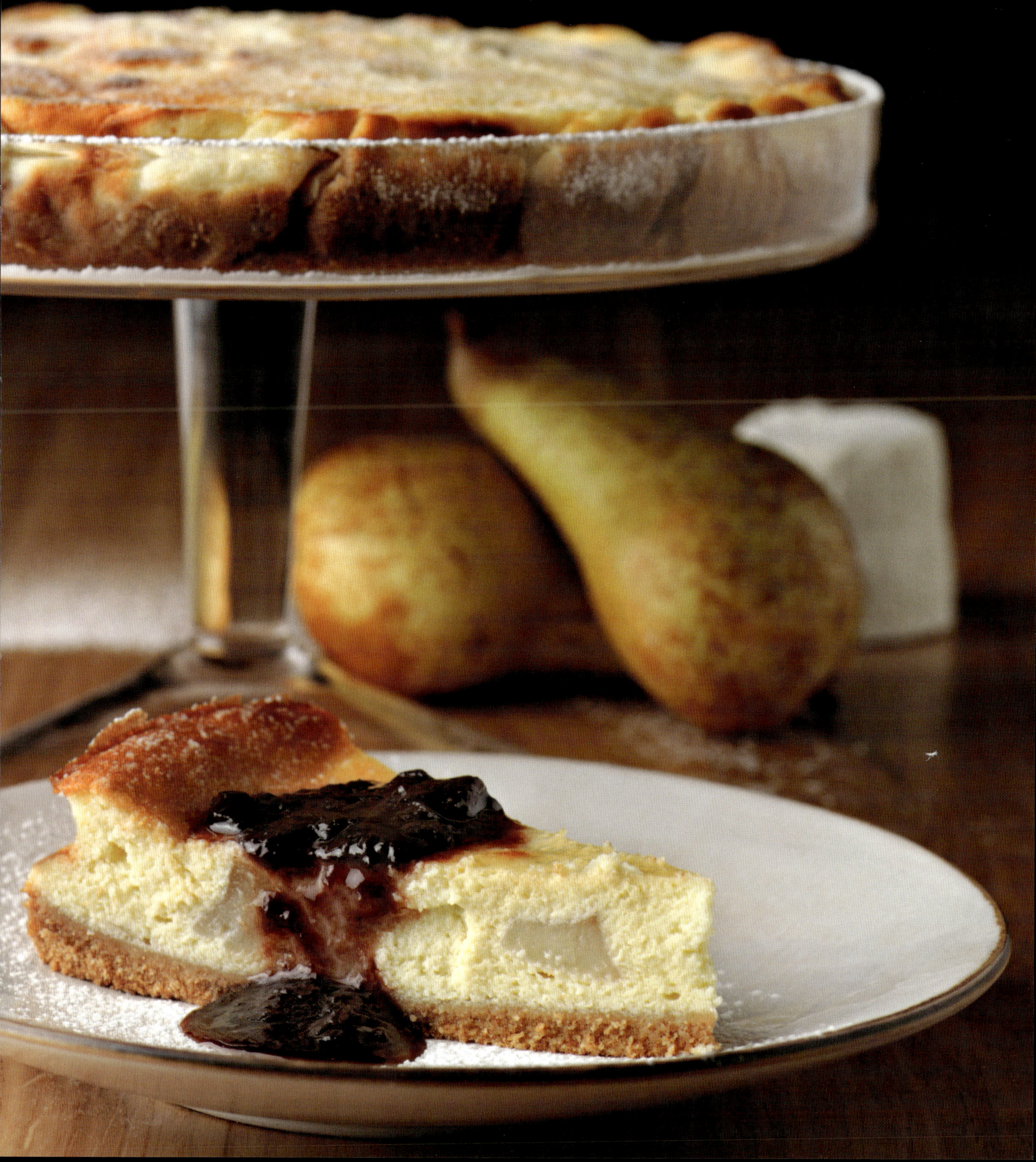

Tiramisù

The regions of Tuscany, Piedmont, and Veneto all lay claim to tiramisù. The official version of this dessert's history says that it was invented in the seventeenth century in Siena, when a group of pastry chefs collaborated to make a dessert to celebrate the grand duke of Tuscany, Cosimo de' Medici. Legend has it that the trifle invented for the duke became the favorite dessert of the aristocracy, who believed it was an aphrodisiac—hence the name tiramisù, which means "pick-me-up."

Serves 8

5 medium eggs, separated
½ cup sugar
2 tablespoons Passito di Noto wine
2¼ cups mascarpone
1 pinch salt
7 ounces Italian ladyfingers
1 cup espresso
Unsweetened cocoa powder to taste

Suggested Wine Pairing

Albana di Romagna Passito Scaccomatto
Producer:
Fattoria Zerbina
Grape:
Albana
Region:
Emilia Romagna

Preparation

- Beat the egg yolks with ¼ cup sugar in an electric mixer until foamy. Beat in the wine and the mascarpone until smooth.
- In a clean bowl, beat the egg whites with the salt until they form stiff peaks. Beat in the remaining ¼ cup sugar. Fold the egg whites into the egg yolk mixture using a spatula and working gently from the bottom of the bowl to the top to deflate the mixture as little as possible.
- Place about 1 tablespoon of the egg mixture in the bottom of each of eight individual serving dishes (or you can make the tiramisù in a large serving dish and spoon it out at the table). Dip the ladyfingers with the espresso, then divide them among the bowls, cutting them to fit if necessary.
- Top the ladyfingers in each bowl with another tablespoon of the egg mixture and smooth the top. Repeat with another layer of ladyfingers, dipped in espresso, and egg mixture. Again, smooth the tops.
- Refrigerate for a few hours and sprinkle with cocoa powder just before serving.

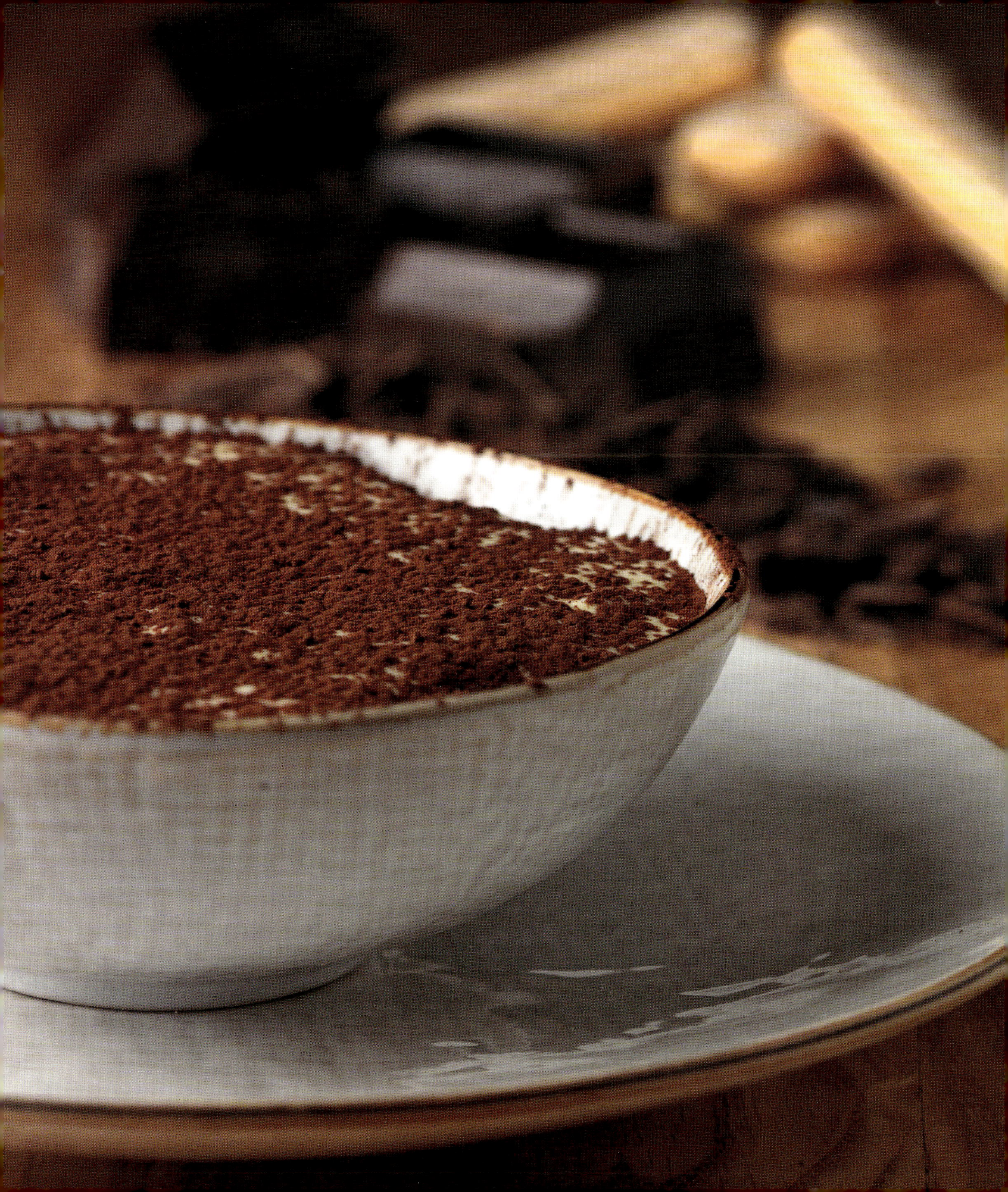

Crema with Bronte Pistachios

This dessert is similar to a crème brûlée, but we use a lightly salted pistachio paste to give it a savory slant that makes it special.

Serves 4

⅓ cup plus 2 tablespoons whole milk
1¾ cups whipping cream
1 vanilla bean
6 egg yolks
½ cup granulated sugar
2 tablespoons cornstarch
¼ cup lightly salted pistachio paste
1 tablespoon demerara sugar or brown sugar
3 tablespoons Bronte pistachios

Suggested Wine Pairing

Ben Ryé
Producer:
Donnafugata
Grape:
Zibibbo
Region:
Sicily

Preparation

- Place the milk, cream, and vanilla bean in a small saucepan and gently bring to boil.
- Meanwhile, whisk the egg yolks and the granulated sugar together.
- Add the cornstarch to the egg yolk mixture and whisk until creamy.
- Remove the milk mixture from the heat and allow to cool. Pass it through a sieve and remove the vanilla bean. Stir the milk mixture into the egg yolk mixture.
- Pour the mixture into a saucepan and gently bring to a boil, stirring constantly. Cook, stirring constantly, until thickened. Remove from the heat.
- Add the pistachio paste and blend well.
- Divide the mixture among four individual dishes or ramekins and let cool to room temperature.
- Refrigerate for 3 hours.
- Before serving, sprinkle on the demerara sugar and caramelize using a small blowtorch.
- Scatter pistachios on top.

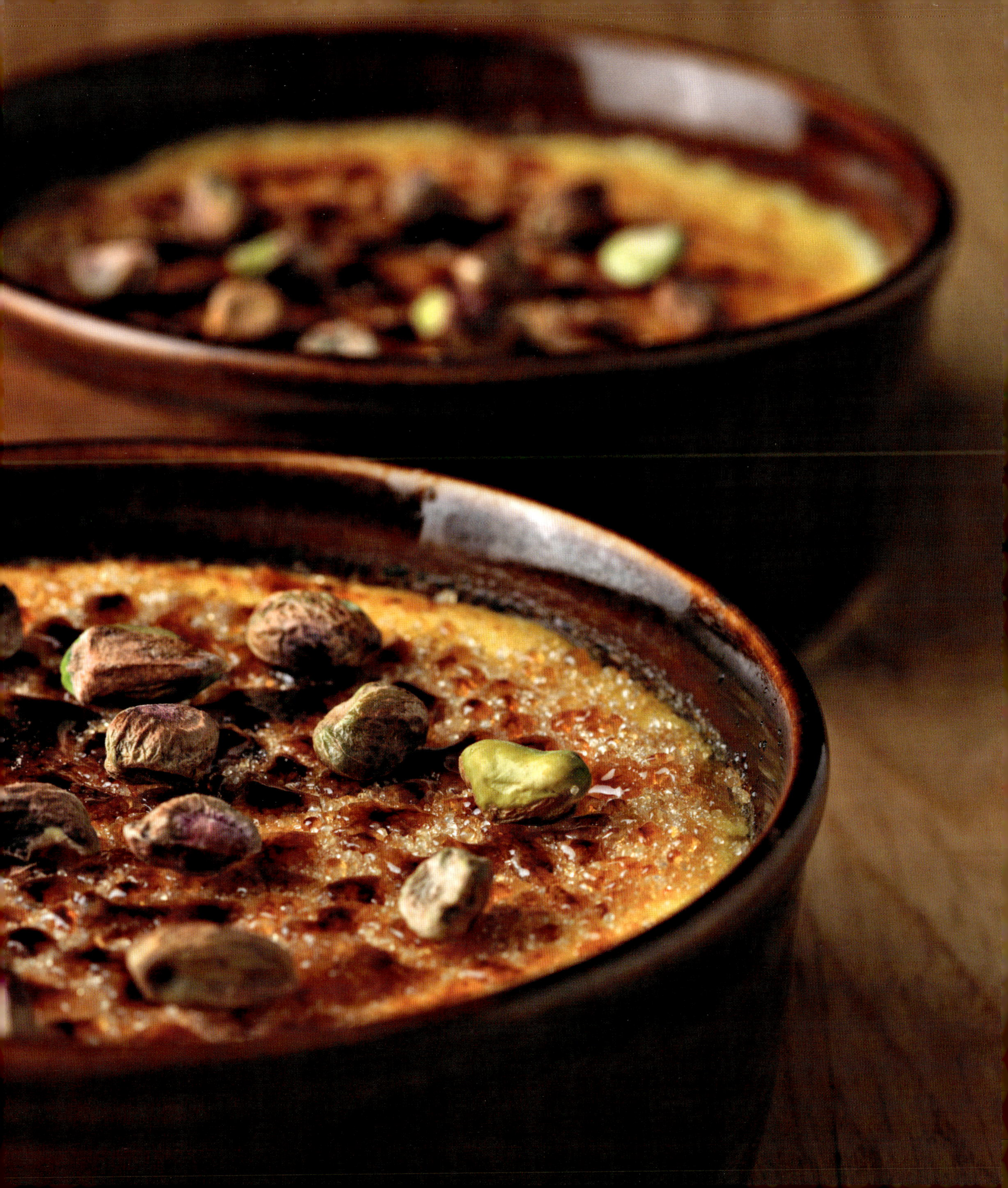

Monte Bianco with Candied Chestnuts

Piedmont and Lombardy have made this French dessert famous. It's a spoon sweet made with chestnuts, sugar, cocoa, and rum. Some, including us, like to incorporate meringue to make the dish a little lighter.

Serves 8

1 pound chestnuts
1¾ cups plus 2 tablespoons whole milk
½ cup granulated sugar
1 teaspoon vanilla extract
1½ tablespoons rum
1 tablespoon plus 1 teaspoon unsweetened cocoa powder
½ cup crumbled cooked meringue
2¼ cups whipping cream
2 tablespoons confectioners' sugar
¼ cup diced candied chestnuts

Suggested Wine Pairing

Moscato d'Asti
Producer:
Saracco
Grape:
Moscato
Region:
Piedmont

Preparation

- With a paring knife, cut an X into the base of each chestnut. Place the chestnuts in a pressure cooker, add water to cover, and cook at high pressure for 10 minutes. Remove from the heat and let the chestnuts cool in their cooking liquid. Peel and skin the chestnuts.

- Place the peeled chestnuts in a small saucepan with the milk, granulated sugar, and vanilla and cook over medium heat until most of the milk has evaporated, about 20 minutes.

- Let the chestnuts cool, then puree them with a potato ricer with medium to small holes.

- Mix the pureed chestnuts with the rum and 1 tablespoon cocoa powder. Refrigerate for a few hours.

- Scatter about two-thirds of the crumbled meringue on a serving platter. Fit the potato ricer with the disk with the largest holes and puree the chestnut mixture through the potato ricer again. It should form long strands. Arrange these strands on the platter over the crumbled meringues in the shape of a mountain. (You can let them drop directly onto the platter from the potato ricer, then gently adjust them if the shape isn't quite right when you're done.)

- Whip the cream with the confectioners' sugar to stiff peaks. Transfer the whipped cream to a pastry big fitted with a metal tip and pipe the cream all over the mountain.

- Garnish with the candied chestnuts and the remaining crumbled meringues. Dust with the remaining 1 teaspoon unsweetened cocoa powder.

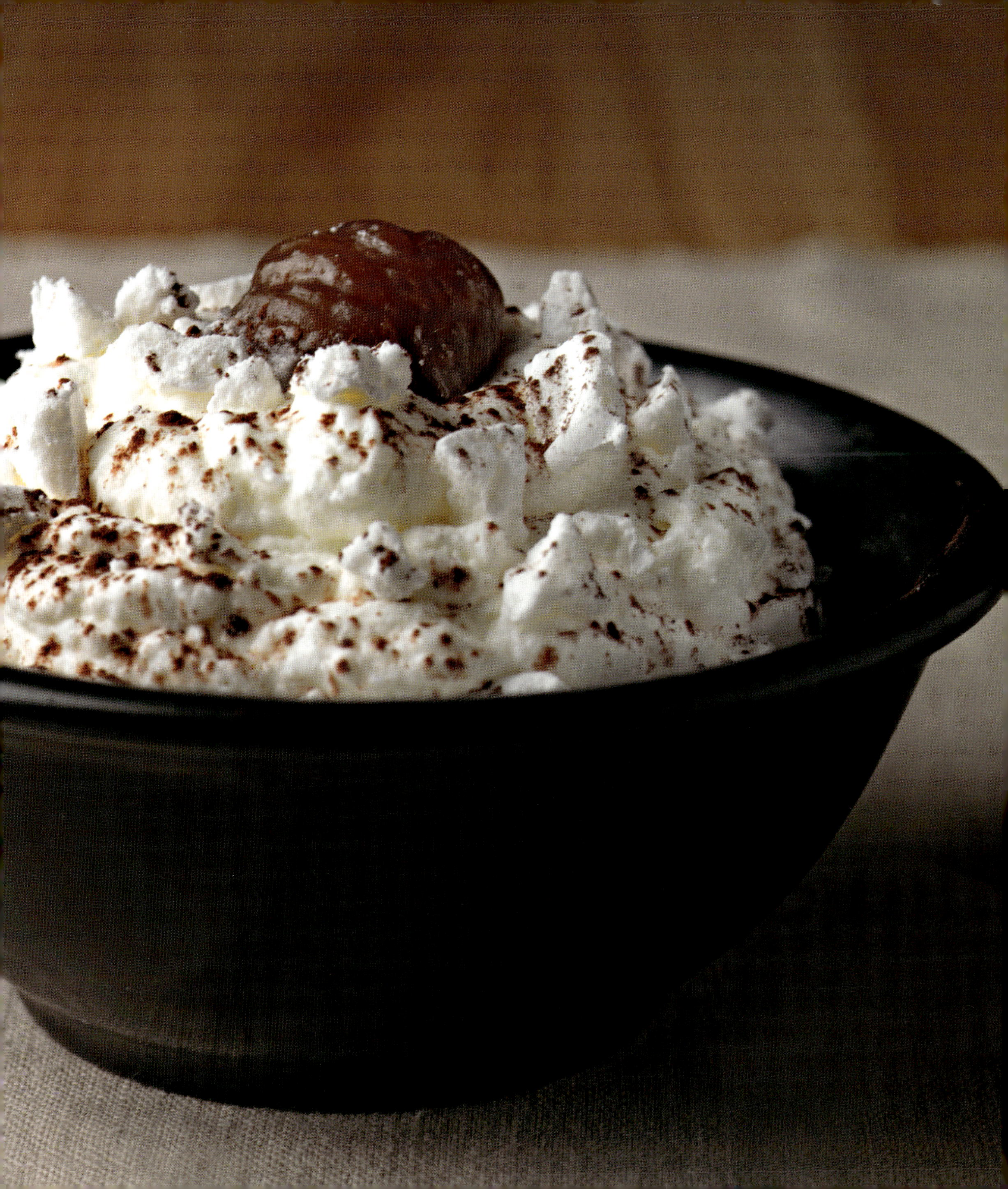

Zuccotto with Dark Chocolate

This Tuscan dessert was served in Florence as far back as the sixteenth century. It owes its name to the colorful skullcap worn by a high priest, known as a *zucchetto* and shaped like this dessert. The original zuccotto is a bombe made by lining a mold with slices of sponge cake brushed with alchermes and filling it with ricotta, almonds, and candied fruit. Our updated version uses an assortment of nuts and chocolate in place of the candied fruit and brandy in place of the alchermes.

Serves 6

1¾ cups whipping cream
¼ cup sugar
1¾ ounces dark chocolate (75% cacao), chopped
¼ cup almonds
¼ cup hazelnuts
¼ cup walnuts
7 ounces sponge cake
1½ tablespoons brandy
Unsweetened cocoa powder for serving
Chocolate shavings for serving

Suggested Wine Pairing

Fiano Passito Privilegio
Producer:
Feudi di San Gregorio
Grape:
Fiano
Region:
Campania

Preparation

- Whip the cream with the sugar and fold in the chocolate. Toast the nuts, set aside a few almonds for garnish, then grind the rest coarsely. Set aside to cool.

- Cut the sponge cake into thin slices and brush the slices with the brandy. Line a bombe mold with the cake slices, cutting them to fit if necessary and reserving slices of cake to cover the top of the mold.

- Fold the ground nuts into the whipped cream mixture, then fill the cavity with it. Cover the top of the mold with the remaining sponge cake.

- Freeze until very firm. When frozen, remove from the freezer and place a serving platter upside down on top of the mold. Turn the mold and the platter together and lift off the mold to unmold the zuccotto onto the platter.

- Sift on the cocoa powder and garnish with chocolate shavings and the reserved whole almonds.

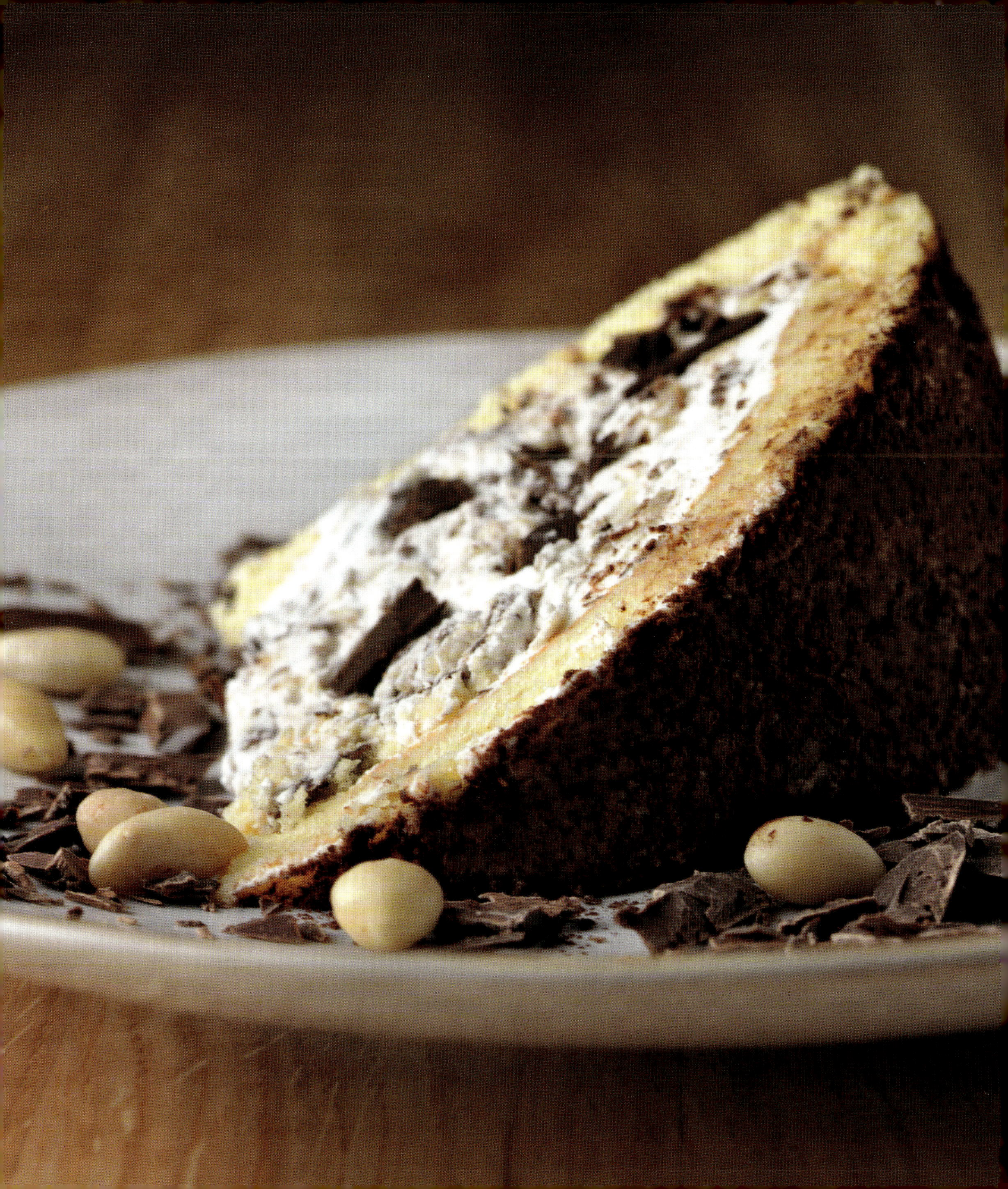

Limoncello Babà with Vanilla Custard

A babà is a little, yeast-risen cake from Naples, anywhere from 2 to 16 inches in diameter, that is served with custard and whipped cream and sometimes with fruit. We soak miniature babàs in limoncello, then serve them in a vanilla custard.

Serves 6

4 egg yolks
½ cup sugar
2 tablespoons cornstarch
1 teaspoon vanilla extract
2 cups plus 2 tablespoons whole milk
¾ cup plus 2 tablespoons limoncello
18 (1-ounce) babà cakes
Zest of ½ lemon, cut into thin strips

Suggested Wine Pairing

Limoncello di Capri
Description:
Lemon liqueur
Region:
Campania

Preparation

- For the custard, whisk the egg yolks with the sugar in a saucepan, then whisk in the cornstarch and the vanilla. Continue to whisk constantly while adding the cold milk in a thin stream.
- Place the saucepan over low heat and bring to a boil. As soon as the mixture begins to bubble, remove it from the heat. Let cool, whisking occasionally to avoid lumps.
- Place a rack over a sheet pan or platter. In a bowl, whisk the limoncello with ½ cup water. Soak the cakes in the liquid one at a time, removing them to the rack.
- Divide the vanilla custard among individual glass bowls and top each serving with three cakes.
- Garnish with lemon zest.

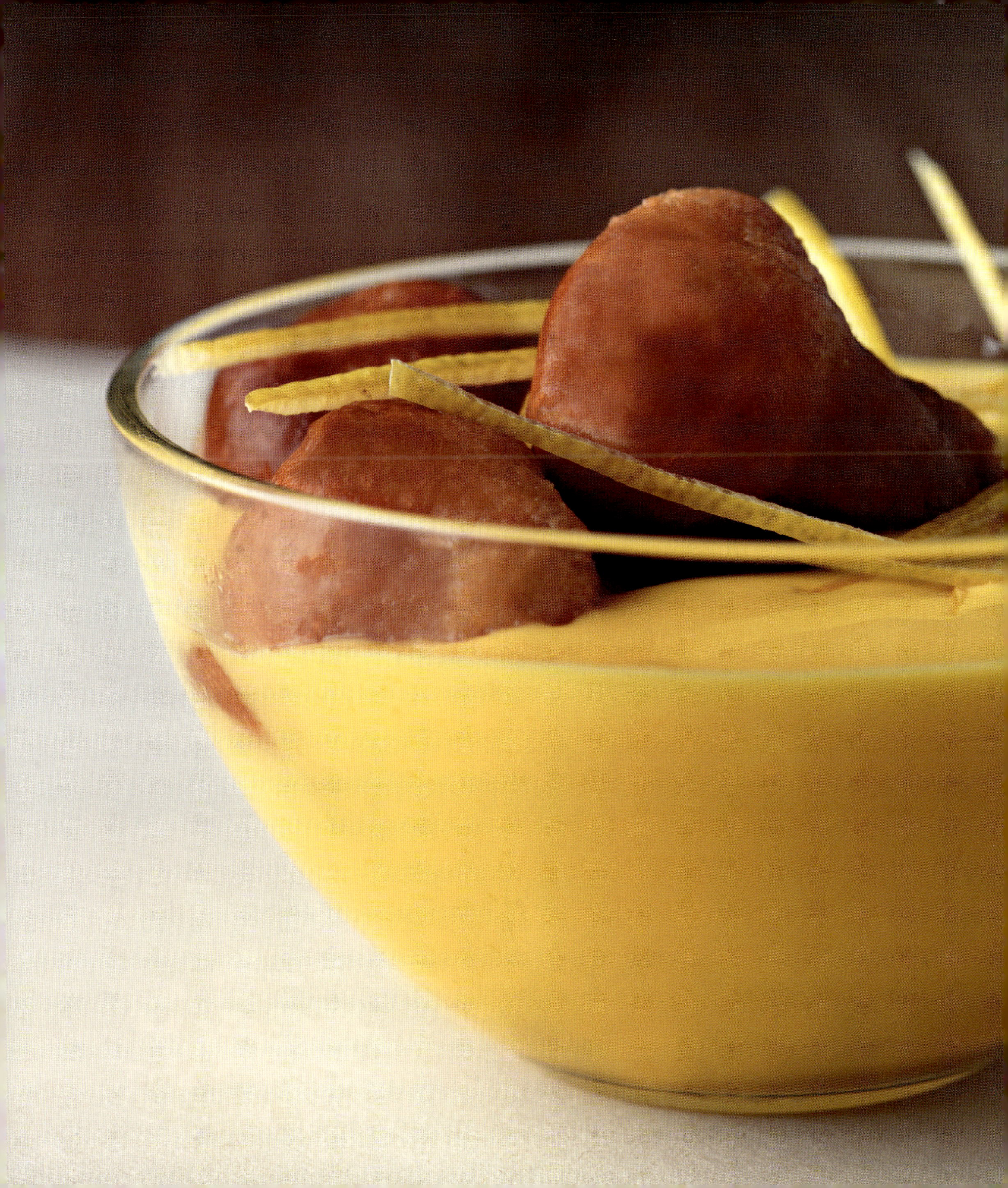

LONDON,
Draycott Avenue

Vini Italiani

Rossi:
- Inferno Valtellina Superiore
- Teroldego
- Barbera
- Nebbiolo
- Dolcetto
- Barolo
- Amarone
- Chianti
- Brunello di Montalcino
- Morellino di Scansano
- Vino Nobile di Montepulciano
- Rosso Conero
- Montepulciano d'Abruzzo
- Taurasi
- Carignano del Sulcis
- Nero di Troia
- Primitivo
- Gioia del Colle
- Cirò
- Cerasuolo di…

Bianchi:
- Ribolla Gialla
- Pinot Grigio
- Soave
- Lugana
- Gavi di Gavi
- Vernaccia di San Gimignano
- Verdicchio dei Castelli di Jesi
- Trebbiano d'Abruzzo
- Falanghina
- Gravina
- Greco di Tufo
- Vermentino di Gallura
- Romangia

©Luke Hayes

Nuestros Pequeños Hermanos

At the beginning of this book, I wrote that I believe food is of key importance if we are to establish a healthy relationship with nature, the seasons, and ourselves.

As hard as it may be for us to believe, each day millions of people around the world do not get enough food and go hungry.

So we decided to share our good fortune and get our staff and customers involved in several fundraising campaigns. Over the years, these have led to the construction of several "mobile bakeries" in Haiti, organized by the Francesca Rava NPH Foundation. Thousands of loaves of bread are made in those bakeries every day and handed out to those in need.

This fills us with great pride.

Silvio Ursini visiting the St. Damien orphanage in Haiti.

OPPOSITE:
With the construction of a third mobile bakery in Les Cayes, bread is provided daily to 300 students at the Saint Luc Street School in Saint Paul du Sud, one of the poorest parts of the city.

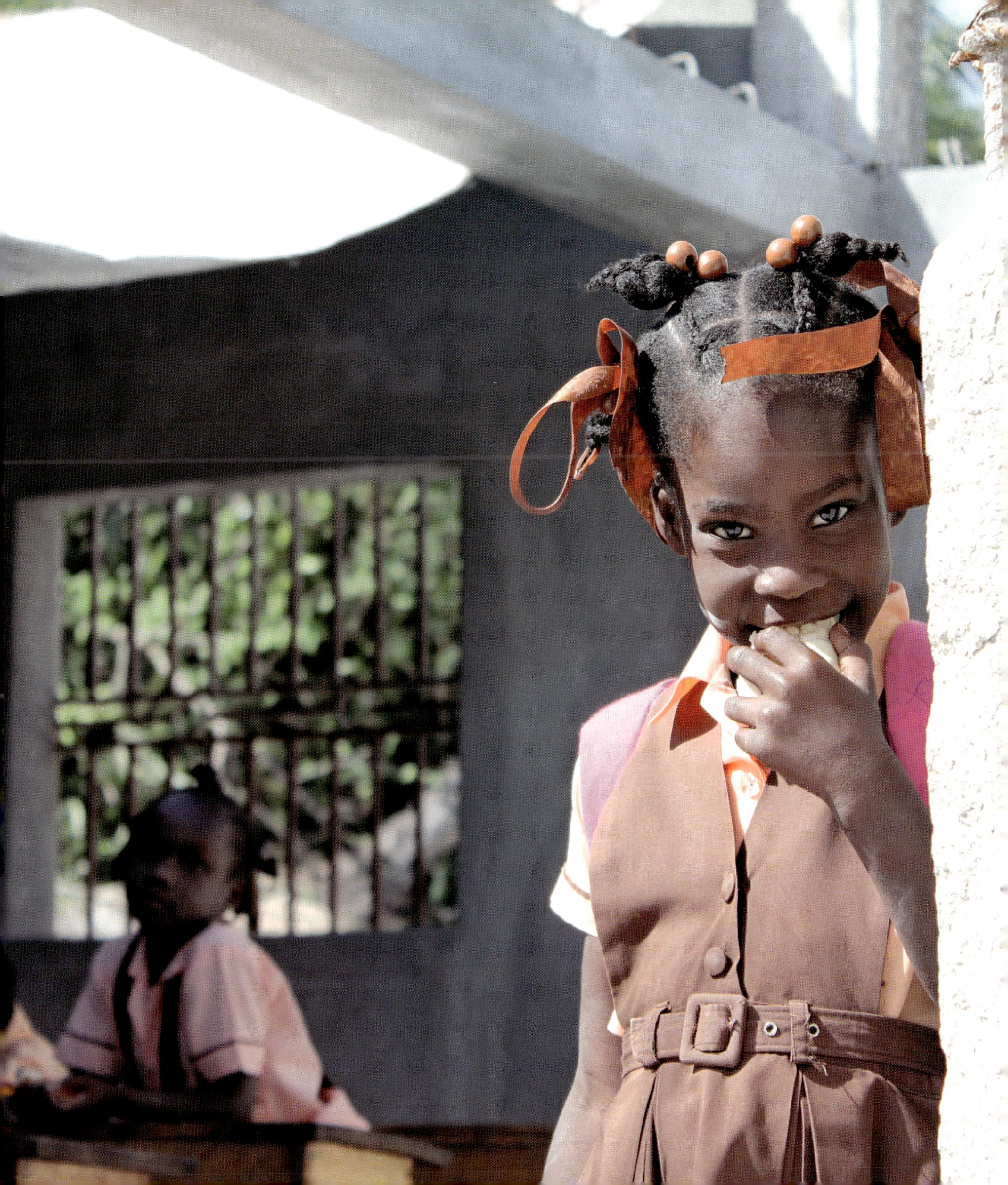

"*It only takes a quick scan of the menu to set your stomach rumbling and your eyes darting around for a waiter.*"

FINANCIAL TIMES

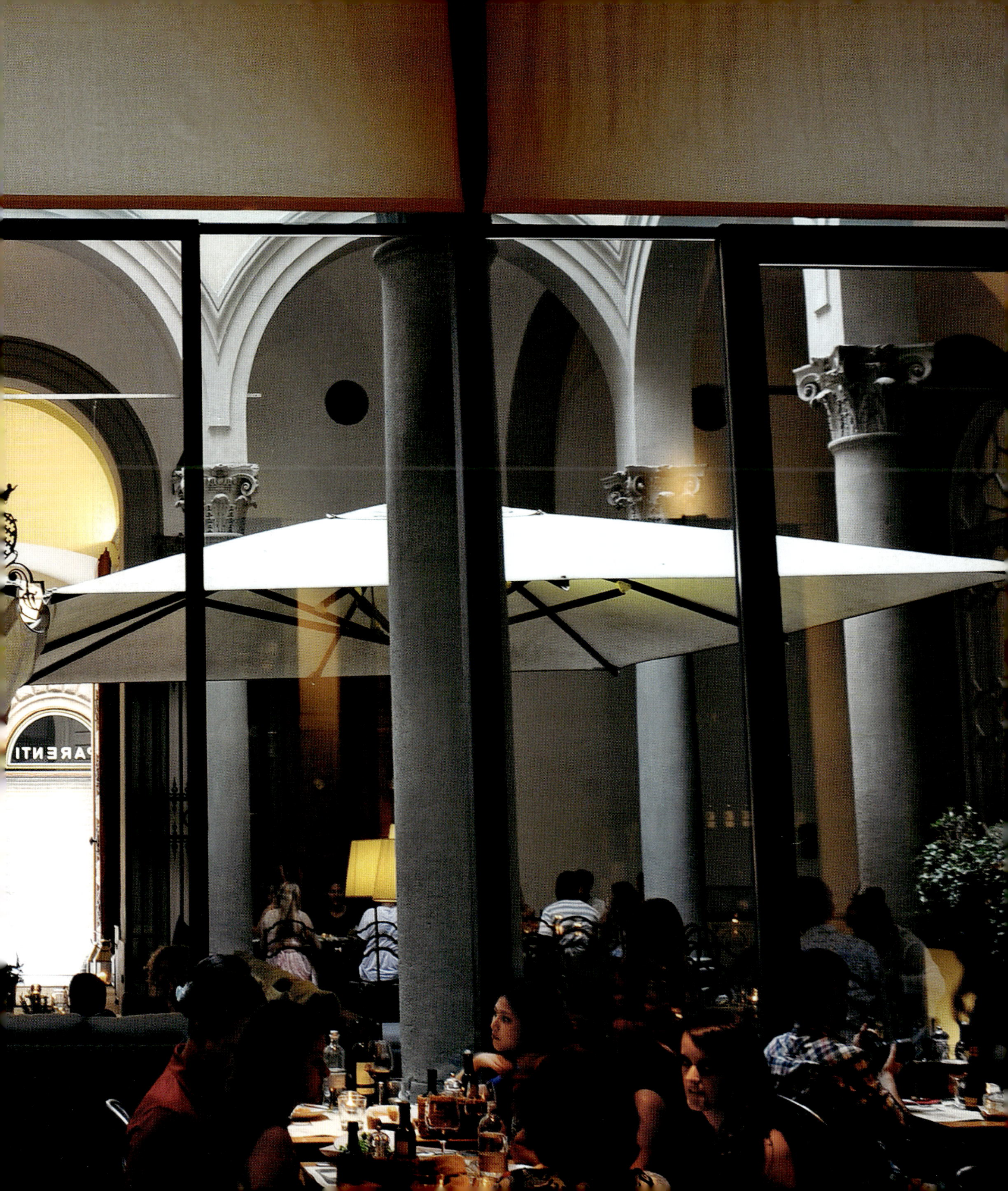

Index of Recipes

Mozzarella Bar
Some Obvious Pairings and Some Less Obvious Ones

Fresh Tomatoes with Basil Pesto, 36

La Motticella Peeled Tomatoes and Andria Mozzarella Braid, 38

Piennolo del Vesuvio Tomatoes, 42

Neapolitan Papaccella, 44

Castellammare Purple Artichokes, 46

Speck di Trota with Herbs, 48

Cetara Anchovies and Dried Tomatoes, 50

Bottarga di Cabras, 52

Capocollo di Martina Franca, 54

Culatello di Zibello, Aged 18 Months, 56

Prosciutto Crudo di Parma DOP, Aged 20 Months, 58

Prosciutto Nero dei Nebrodi, 60

Mortadella di Prato, 62

Bresaola di Fassona, 64

Soppressata di Gioi, 66

Ciauscolo di Visso, 68

Speck di Sauris, 70

Violino di Capra della Valchiavenna, 72

Antipasti

Caponata alla Siciliana, 78

Ciauscolo and N'duja Crostini, 80

Crostini with Porcini Mushrooms, Grilled Peppers, Olives, and Capers, 82

Eggplant Croquettes, 84

Mozzarella in Carrozza, 86

Potato and N'duja Croquettes, 88

Arancini, 90

Eggplant Parmigiana, 92

Escarole Pie, 94

Potato Pie, 96

Insalate

Prosciutto Cotto, Walnuts, and Parmigiano Reggiano, 102

Blu di Bufala, Baby Spinach, Apples, and Walnuts, 104

Grilled Squash, Buffalo Milk Caciocavallo, and Pumpkin Seeds, 108

Smoked Trout with Herbs, Avocado, Mâche, Arugula, and Grape Tomatoes, 110

Bresaola di Fassona, Stracchino, Spinach, and Grape Tomatoes, 112

Barley, Carrots, and String Beans, 114

Paste

Schiaffoni alla Sorrentina, 120

Trofie with Pesto, Potatoes, and String Beans, 124

Linguine with Yellowfin Tuna, 126

Scialatielli alla Nerano, 128

Tortiglioni with Sea Urchin, 130

Pasta all'Uovo, 132

Pappardelle with Sausage and Fennel, 134

Pumpkin Ravioli with Amaretto Cookies, 136

Ravioli with Ricotta and Eggplant, 138

Lasagne with String Beans and Pesto, 140

Lasagne with Chianina Ragù, 142

Cannelloni with Zucchini and Stracciatella, 146

Potato Gnocchi, 148

Gnocchi with Blu di Bufala and Spinach, 150

Gnocchi with N'duja and Tomatoes, 152

Orecchiette with Garden Peas and Sugar Snap Peas, 154

Orecchiette with Broccoli and Provolone, 156

Fregola with Tuna and Tomatoes, 158

Zuppe

Tomato Soup, 164

Squash with Bronte Pistachios, 166

Zucchini with Mint, 168

Lentil and Potato Soup, 172

Farro and Spinach Soup, 174

Zolfini Bean and Tuscan Kale Soup, 176

Pasta e Ceci, 178

Risotti

Risotto with Porcini Mushrooms, 184

Risotto with Shrimp and Asparagus, 186

Risotto with Zucchini and Bottarga, 188

Risotto with Black Truffle and Stracciatella, 190

Risotto with Luganega Sausage and Radicchio, 192

Pizze

Making Pizza Dough, 198

Shaping and Baking, 202

Organic Tomato and Stracciatella di Burrata, 204

Grilled Vegetables and Smoked Buffalo Milk Mozzarella, 206

Grilled Peppers and Tuna, 208

Soft Buffalo Milk Cheese, 210

Luganega Sausage and Friarelli, 212

N'duja and Stracciatella di Burrata, 216

Anchovies and Capers, 218

Bottarga and Grape Tomatoes, 220

Open Calzone with Prosciutto Crudo di Parma, 222

Prosciutto Cotto and Norcia Black Truffle, 226

Soppressata Calabrese and Ricotta, 228

Porcini Mushroom and Black Truffle, 230

Dolci

Ricotta with Honey and Pine Nuts, 236

Torta di Capri, 238

Ricotta and Pear Tart, 240

Tiramisù, 242

Crema with Bronte Pistachios, 244

Monte Bianco with Candied Chestnuts, 246

Zuccotto with Dark Chocolate, 248

Limoncello Babà with Vanilla Curd, 250

Acknowledgments

"I'd like to take this opportunity to thank everyone who helped with the writing of this book: Raimondo Boggia for the wine pairings, Cristina Cecchini Saulini, who edited the recipes, and Marianna Tognelli for the art direction.

I would also like to thank all those who inspired me, and the people I've met who have taught me the importance of approaching food, cooking, and service the right way: Carlo Petrini, Gualtiero Marchesi, Ferran Adrià, Alain Ducasse, Filippo La Mantia, Nancy Silverton (whom I also wish to thank for saying that she was inspired by Obicà when creating Osteria Mozza in Los Angeles), Herve Humler, Leonardo Inghilleri, and Attilio Marro.

My earliest partners: Andrea Corsetti, Davide Paolini, Paolo Scarlatti, Flavia Spena, and Francesco Trapani.

Our management team: Maite Azcona, Mattia Pierantoni Cerquozzi, Mia Fossati, Giuliana Tardivo, Giovanna Todini, Marianna Tognelli, and all the staff, directors, servers, and chefs who bring life to our restaurants.

Our team of lawyers, accountants, and legal experts: Luca Benigni, Domenico De Simone, Claudio Tesauro, and Francesca Turitto.

Our international partners: Takashi Ayashi and Michio Akimoto in Japan; Khaled Al Fahim, Khalil Kharkar, and Lamine Ounnas in Dubai; Raimondo Boggia and Vasco Noya di Lannoy in the United States.

Maria Claudia Clemente, Francesco Isidori, and all the architects at Studio Labics who created our interior design concept and developed it over time.

Marco Ausenda, Cecilia Curti, and Laura Nava at Rizzoli for their faith in this book.

And, lastly, my mother, Olga Nicodemi Ursini, for teaching me to love cooking. "

Silvio Ursini

Printed in August 2014
by Errestampa S.r.l.
Orio al Serio (Bergamo)